KNOWLEDGE PAINFULLY ACQUIRED

Neo-Confucian Studies

KNOWLEDGE PAINFULLY ACQUIRED

The *K'un-chih chi*
by Lo Ch'in-shun

Translated, Edited, and with an Introduction by
Irene Bloom

New York
Columbia University Press
1987

The author and publisher gratefully acknowledge the generous support toward publication given them by the National Endowment for
the Humanities.

Library of Congress Cataloging-in-Publication Data

Lo Ch'in-shun, 1465–1547.
   Knowledge painfully acquired.

   (Neo-Confucian studies)
   Translation of: K'un-chih chi.
   Bibliography: p.
   Includes index.
   1. Neo-Confucianism.   I. Bloom, Irene.   II. Title.
B127.N4L5913   1987   181'.09512   86-17203
ISBN 0-231-06408-X   ISBN 0-231-06409-8 (pbk.)

Columbia University Press
New York   Chichester, West Sussex
Copyright © 1987, 1995 Columbia University Press
All rights reserved

Printed in the United States of America
p 10 9 8 7 6 5 4 3 2 1

for Wing-tsit Chan,
teacher and friend

Neo-Confucian Studies

Acknowledgments

I have been privileged to have three teachers as extraordinary in their generosity of spirit as in their knowledge of Ming thought, and to each of them I owe a greater debt of gratitude than I can ever express.

Professor Wm. Theodore de Bary has guided my studies in Chinese thought from the beginning and, through his incomparable quality of mind, commitment to humane scholarship, and sympathetic appreciation for the importance of ideas and values in individual human lives as well as in the longer cultural span, has helped me toward a fuller understanding of the rich possibilities of studies in the humanities. Among Western scholars, he has been primarily responsible for recognizing that comparative studies of Neo-Confucianism in China and Japan represent an important, and perhaps indispensable, means of reaching a deeper understanding of the processes of intellectual and cultural change in East Asia in the early modern period. It was he who first suggested that a study of Lo Ch'in-shun could be of distinct interest to others concerned with comparative studies and who advised that a translation of the K'un-chih chi might be a useful contribution to future efforts in this area. The consummate educator and mentor, he has given the most profoundly encouraging help and counsel throughout the course of my work.

Professor Pei-yi Wu, remarkable both in his knowledge of Ming literature and intellectual history and in his psychological insight, has been a superlative teacher of classical Chinese and guide to the nuances of the most allusive and elusive texts. It is rare to find a scholar with such a gift for reading between the lines and gleaning something of a Ming writer's disposition or habit of mind, and I have appreciated the combination of erudition and sensitivity that Professor Wu brings to bear in this endeavor. He has been unsparing in his generosity with his time and constantly thoughtful in his friendly concern.

The unfailing kindness of Professor Wing-tsit Chan and his willingness to share gems from his seemingly inexhaustible knowledge of the Chinese philosophical tradition have been heartening as well as edifying. I have benefited not only from his instruction in the most varied aspects of Chinese thought and his extensive knowledge of the texts from which such knowledge must be mined, but from his admirable personal example. Professor Chan's translations of Neo-Confucian philosophical writings set a standard of excellence which none of his disciples can hope to attain. While I have hoped that this translation of the work of Lo Ch'in-shun might serve as a companion volume to Professor Chan's translation of Wang Yang-ming's *Instructions for Practical Living,* the idea of placing a book of translation on a shelf next to one of his would have been almost laughable were it not for the fact that his genuine desire to help in every possible way and his reassurance that apparently hopeless enigmas could be solved have made the effort thoroughly worthwhile and pleasurable. Consultations with Professor Chan over the course of the past ten years and letters from him at crucial junctures have provided keys to the most perplexing scholarly puzzles and have provided a kind of Sinological education in themselves. It is inconceivable to me that any scholar could be more ready to share with his students the benefit of his own work and experience, and it is out of respect for this gift of sharing, as well as deep affection for the giver, that I dedicate this book to him.

I have been fortunate in other resources of scholarship and friendship as well. Having been at Columbia at the time when Professor Fang Chao-ying and Mrs. Lienche Tu Fang were completing their work on the *Dictionary of Ming Biography,* it was my privilege to have them among my teachers. During that time, and long after their retirement as well, both Professor and Mrs. Fang were patient and kind in responding to questions about Ming history and in helping to resolve innumerable textual problems. Professor Philip Yampolsky, with his combination of dharma wisdom and prodigious knowledge of all manner of bibliographic resources, could not have been more informative and encouraging. Professors John T. Meskill, Paul Oskar Kristeller, Donald J. Munro, Conrad Schirokauer, and Edward T. Ch'ien read this study in draft form and made many valuable suggestions for correcting and improving it. I am deeply indebted to all of them. I should like to express my gratitude also to Professors Liu Ts'un-yan, Yü Ying-shih, Wang Yuquan, Ren Jiyu, Hok-lam Chan, Peter Bol, Herman Ooms, Burton Watson, Judith Berling, Richard Edwards, Terry Kelleher, and Ann-ping Chin for special kindness and for help with questions which fell within the areas of their expertise. I very much appreciated thoughtful communications from Mr. Philip J. Ivanhoe and Dr. Chu Hung-Lam. Mr.

Jack Jacoby and the staff of the C.V. Starr East Asian Library at Columbia University have been unfailingly helpful with tracking down books.

I should also like to thank Mr. David Diefendorf of Columbia University Press for being the most thoughtful, congenial, and expert of editors and Mr. William P. Germano, formerly editor-in-chief of the Press, and his assistant, Ms. Peggy Seip, for expending special effort on my behalf, always with courtesy, warmth, and good humor. Miss Jennifer Roberts has been both gracious and resourceful in her work on the book's design.

In the course of my work I have received support from the Danforth Foundation and a Whiting Fellowship at Columbia and through a translation grant from the National Endowment for the Humanities. The National Endowment for the Humanities has also provided a grant to Columbia University Press to assist in the publication of this book. I wish to express my appreciation to each of these institutional benefactors and at the same time to acknowledge that the ideas and conclusions found in this book do not necessarily reflect their views.

It is part of the ritual of scholarship for an author to absolve all those who have assisted in the project of any responsibility for whatever errors of fact or interpretation have slipped by undetected and to assume that responsibility personally. This, of course, I do also, and, as a translator of what must be reckoned a demanding text, I beg the indulgence not only of the reader but of the precise and exacting spirit of that most devoted of scholars, Lo Ch'in-shun.

Irene Bloom
Hastings-on-Hudson, New York
April 1986

Contents

Introduction

The *K'un-chih chi* (Knowledge Painfully Acquired) is a collection of reading notes and reflections on philosophy and history by Lo Ch'in-shun[1] (1465–1547), the most prominent adherent of the Ch'eng-Chu school[2] in the mid-Ming period. It is a mature work, first published in 1528 when Lo was in his sixties, and bears the signs of long years of study and contemplation by a man of intense seriousness and incisive intelligence. Readers who are predisposed to find in Ming orthodoxy an epigonic devotion to the writings of the Sung masters may be surprised to find that the work, far from being imitative or mimetic, is informed by a lively skepticism and a resolute insistence on cogency and consistency as against established authority as the basis for accepting any philosophical position.

An orthodox spirit reveals itself in an appreciation for the achievements of his predecessors in the Sung period (960–1279), though it is clear that Lo Ch'in-shun saw their work as unfinished, as indeed his own would be at the close of his life. Perceiving himself as heir to a tradition that was constantly evolving, he was convinced that the contributions of the Ch'eng brothers and Chu Hsi represented a constructive response to the challenge of Buddhism and Taoism as they had encountered it in their own time. Yet history was marked by both continuity and change, and Confucian philosophy could not be regarded as a closed system. A dialogic quality is as evident in his accounts of his predecessors as in his debates with his contemporaries.

Lo's contemporaries included some of the most creative thinkers that the Ming dynasty (1368–1644) produced—among them, Wang Yang-ming (Wang Shou-jen, 1472–1529), Chan Jo-shui (Chan Kan-ch'üan, 1466–1560), and Wang T'ing-hsiang (1474–1544)—and the affinities between his thought and theirs may to some readers be as striking as the differences.

[1] *Tzu* Yün-sheng; *hao* Cheng-an.

[2] The term is used here to designate the broad and evolving tendency of thought and scholarship which, despite considerable internal diversity, has clearly identifiable origins in the philosophy of Ch'eng Hao (1032–1085) and Ch'eng I (1033–1107) in the eleventh century and Chu Hsi (1130–1200) in the twelfth century.

Each of these mid-Ming thinkers found reason to differ with Chu Hsi, and, of the four, Lo Ch'in-shun's criticisms, which came from within the Ch'eng-Chu tradition itself, were in some respects the most profound. But though he remained convinced that Ch'eng I and Chu Hsi had not "finally achieved unity,"[3] and felt compelled to confront certain unresolved problems in their thought, Lo never doubted that he was working within the same tradition. To his mind the principal criterion of orthodoxy was not the acceptance of received doctrines, but an essential fidelity to the tradition and to the richness of human experience that it embodied. Virtually every page of the *K'un-chih chi* testifies to the author's conviction that the work of Confucian philosophy involved drawing on the strengths of the tradition while at the same time contributing actively to its life.

The Author

Like his three great contemporaries, whose careers often intersected with his, Lo led an active life of public service. A native of T'ai-ho *hsien* in Kiangsi, he was born on December 25, 1465.[4] Having placed third in the metropolitan examination of 1493, he was granted the rank of Hanlin compiler. By 1502 he had been promoted to the post of Director of Studies at the Imperial University in Nanking where he served together with Chang Mou (1436–1521),[5] the newly appointed Chancellor. In 1505 he requested an extended leave in order to be able to care for his father but

[3] *K'un-chih chi,* Part I, sec. 13.

[4] Except as otherwise noted, all of the biographical information that follows is drawn from Lo's chronological autobiography, "Cheng-an lü-li chi," in *K'un-chih chi hsü-pu,* 7:11b–28b. I am aware that the date of birth given here differs from the date assigned in the *Dictionary of Ming Biography,* 1:972–74.

[5] Actually, Lo Ch'in-shun served concurrently as Chancellor and Director of Studies prior to Chang Mou's arrival in Nanking, since Chang himself was observing mourning at the time of his appointment. Like Lo, Chang was associated with the Ch'eng-Chu school. See his biography in *Ming-shih* (History of the Ming Dynasty), 179:2099–2100 and an account of his thought in Huang Tsung-hsi, *Ming-ju hsüeh-an* (Philosophical Records of Ming Confucians), *ch.* 47.

was notified early in 1507 that his request had been officially denied.[6] Lo reluctantly complied with an order to return to office but insisted on submitting another petition to be allowed to reside with his father. This aroused the ire of the notorious eunuch Liu Chin (d. 1510), who had assumed power at this time, and in the fourth month of 1508 Lo received notice that he had been deprived of both rank and office. He returned home once again, this time as a commoner.

What amounted to a self-imposed withdrawal from official life during this difficult and precarious time seems to have spared Lo some of the bitterness experienced by Wang Yang-ming, who, by daring to memorialize against the high-handedness of Liu Chin,[7] brought on himself the punishment of flogging in court and banishment to remote Kuei-chou,[8] or Wang T'ing-hsiang, who was also punished and demoted at Liu Chin's instigation.[9] After remaining in retirement for nearly two years, Lo was restored to his previous post in 1510, following the execution of Liu Chin in that year.

From this point on he received a number of promotions in rapid succession, being appointed Vice Minister of the Court of Imperial Sacrifices in Nanking in 1512, Junior Vice Minister of Personnel in Nanking in 1515, and Senior Vice Minister in 1519. In 1521 he was appointed Senior

[6] It is indicated in Lo's autobiography that the rule was that permission to care for a parent for the duration of the parent's life was granted to an official only when he was the only son. Lo Ch'in-shun was the eldest of three sons of Lo Yung-chün (d. 1523). However, both of his brothers, Lo Ch'in-te (1472–1550) and Lo Ch'in-chung (1476–1529) were also officials at this time. The fact that the case was somewhat unusual may explain the slowness of the responsible officials in the Ministry of Rites in reaching a decision on it.

[7] Wang's memorial in defense of Tai Hsien (*chin-shih*, 1496) and others who had protested Liu Chin's usurpation of power is found in *Wang Wen-ch'eng kung ch'üan-shu* (Complete Works of Wang Yang-ming), *ch.* 9. See Wing-tsit Chan, trans., *Instructions for Practical Living and Other Neo-Confucian Writings by Wang Yang-ming* (hereafter abbreviated as Chan, *Instructions for Practical Living*), Introduction, p. xxiv.

[8] See Wang's chronological biography in *Wang Wen-ch'eng kung ch'üan-shu*, *ch.* 32. Chan, *Instructions for Practical Living*, Introduction, pp. xxiv–xxv.

[9] Wang T'ing-hsiang had apparently inspired the resentment of Liu Chin through his friendship with Ts'ui Hsien (*chin-shih*, 1505), Li Meng-yang (1472–1529), and Ho Ching-ming (1489–1522). He was punished by being sent as a judge to Po-chou in South Chih-li. See his biography in *Ming-shih*, 194:2270–71 and an account of him in Huang Tsung-hsi, *Ming-ju hsüeh-an*, *ch.* 50.

Vice Minister of Personnel in Peking, and in 1522 he became Minister of Personnel in Nanking. Following the death of his father in 1523, Lo began the observance of mourning. When at the end of the mourning period he was recalled to office, first as Minister of Rites and subsequently as Minister of Personnel, he twice declined, a decision which his biography in the *Ming-shih* (History of the Ming Dynasty) attributes to an unwillingness to be associated with Chang Ts'ung (1475–1539) and Kuei O (d. 1531), whose influence in the government dated from this time.[10]

After his request for retirement was finally granted in 1527, Lo spent the remaining twenty years of his life at home in quiet study and reflection. The results of his studies were recorded in the *K'un-chih chi,* which first appeared in an edition of two sections, or *chüan,* in 1528, when Lo was sixty-three. A third and fourth *chüan* were added as supplements (*K'un-chih chi hsü*) in 1531 and 1533. A fifth *chüan* was included in 1538 under the title *K'un-chih chi fu-lu* (Addendum to the *K'un-chih chi*), and a sixth *chüan* was added as another addendum in 1546, the year before his death. His death came on May 13, 1547, when he was eighty-two. Lo was given the title of Grand Guardian of the Heir Apparent (T'ai-tzu t'ai-pao) and the posthumous name Wen-chuang, and in 1724 his tablet was placed in the Confucian temple.

All accounts of Lo's life attest to his intense seriousness and scrupulous sense of personal integrity, qualities that seem to have guided his intellectual life as well as his official career. Huang Tsung-hsi (1610–1695) in his biographical account of Lo in the *Ming-ju hsüeh-an* (Philosophical Records of Ming Confucians) conveys a sense of his austere dedication to scholarly pursuits:

> When he dwelled at home he arose each day at dawn, dressed himself correctly, and went up to the Hall for the Study of Antiquity (Hsüeh-ku lou), followed by his disciples. After receiving their greetings and obeisances, he sat in a dignified posture and engaged in study. Even when he dwelled alone, he was not careless in his demeanor. He was frugal in his diet, had no pavilions or garden houses, and employed no music when he entertained.[11]

Frequently cited by biographers, including Kao P'an-lung (1562–1626) of the Tung-lin school of the late Ming, is a tribute paid by Lin Hsi-

[10] *Ming-shih,* 282:3169.

[11] *Ming-ju hsüeh-an,* 47:1a.

yüan,[12] who wrote, "From his initial service in the Hanlin to his service as a minister, his conduct both in and out of office was like pure gold and precious jade. One could find no flaws."[13]

Lo's own description of his life and work are characterized by candor and humility. The fact that the *K'un-chih chi* was first published when he was in his sixties and that toward the end of his life he undertook to refine and elaborate the views set forth in the original work[14] suggests both a sense of personal reserve and a conviction that intellectual and spiritual growth are achieved at the cost of diligence and painstaking effort. The title of his work is itself suggestive: it recalls the passage in the *Mean* (20:9) which counsels, "Some are born with knowledge (*huo sheng erh chih chih*); some come to know through study (*huo hsüeh erh chih chih*); and some know only through painstaking effort (*huo k'un erh chih chih*)."[15] Evidently this experience of *k'un* or painstaking effort conditioned all of Lo's inquiries. As Wang Yang-ming's philosophical endeavors came to maturity through the "hundred deaths and thousand sufferings"[16] of his personal life, so it

---

[12] A *chin-shih* of 1517, Lin was the author of a preface to the Chia-ching 14 (1535) edition of the *K'un-chih chi*.

[13] Quoted in "Lo Wen-chuang kung chuan" (Biography of Lo Ch'in-shun) in *Kao Tzu i-shu* (Written Legacy of Master Kao P'an-lung), 10A:6b.

[14] In *K'un-chih chi fu-lu*, 6:7a–17b. This section was completed in 1546.

[15] A similar passage is found in *Analects*, 16:9. Wing-tsit Chan observes that traditional commentaries on these passages suggest several different, though not necessarily mutually exclusive, interpretations of *k'un* as the motive for study and the experience of learning. Cheng Hsüan's (127–200) commentary on the *Mean* indicates that he understood *k'un* as distress; he explained that one feels inadequate in matters of propriety and then studies to learn. K'ung Ying-ta (574–648) in his subcommentary said that one has trouble in handling affairs and then studies to learn, not limiting his concern to propriety alone. Chu Hsi's commentary in the *Chung-yung chang-chü* (Commentary on the Words and Phrases of the *Mean*) indicates that both the "knowing" referred to in this passage and the "earnest practice" referred to in the following line are to be understood to involve "penetration of the Way" (*ta-tao*). In both cases courage (*yung*) is implied. Here he apparently has in mind the sustained exertion involved in the study of the Way and the practice of humanity (*jen*). Here and in his commentary on *Analects* 16:9 in the *Lun-yü chi-chu* (Collected Commentaries on the *Analects*), Chu indicates that the differences in human endowment (*ch'i-p'in* or *ch'i-chih*) dictate differences in the degree of effort required, but maintains that ultimately the attainment will be the same for all.

[16] *Wang Wen-ch'eng kung ch'üan-shu*, (SPTK ed.), preface, 15a. Quoted in Chan, *Instructions for Practical Living*, Introduction, p. xxxvi.

would seem that Lo's efforts were rewarded only after long and difficult years
of uncertainty and self-doubt.[17]

The Text

Before turning to the philosophical views elaborated in the *K'un-
chih chi*, it is appropriate to comment briefly on the nature of the text and
what we may expect to learn from it. Not surprisingly, the work does not
offer a systematic or sustained discussion of particular problems or themes;[18]
rather, it is a loosely organized collection of notes and reflections recorded
over the course of many years.[19] In his reading notes Lo sets forth his critical reactions to the books he has read, sometimes attending to general
themes and problems and occasionally commenting on nuances of vocabu-
lary and syntax. Frequently he quotes in extenso from his sources, almost
always with absolute fidelity.[20] The tone is lively and argumentative
throughout, and yet there is also a mellowness, an autumnal quality to the
work.

It is no doubt appropriate that Wang Yang-ming should be best
known for his *Ch'uan-hsi lu* (Instructions for Practical Living), a collection
of highly personal and often intimate conversations between Wang and his
disciples and letters written to them and others on a variety of subjects, but
focusing on individual problems of self-cultivation. The importance of the
master-disciple relationship and the shared experience of life that it involved is apparent throughout, and the work is characterized by all of the

---

[17] See especially *K'un-chih chi*, Part II, sec. 41.

[18] The critique of Buddhism in *K'un-chih chi hsü*, ch. 3, may be considered somewhat exceptional in this regard.

[19] Lo indicated in his preface to the original work that it had occupied him for
more than twenty years, which suggests that it was begun during the period when he was
employed in the Imperial University in Nanking.

[20] This is in contrast with the practice of Wang Yang-ming who was apparently
inclined to take liberties in quoting other writers, paraphrasing or abbreviating where this was
possible without distorting the essential meaning of a text. See Chan, *Instructions for Practical
Living*, translator's note, p. xiv.

poignancy and intensity associated with active personal interchange between a teacher of great moral authority and disciples deeply influenced by his personal example. The *K'un-chih chi* is by contrast a work of the study, clearly composed in solitude. The tone is reflective; the choice of language is precise; issues are sharply defined. Lo is revealed here as a scholar of formidable erudition, given to meticulous accuracy in his textual research and rigorous development of his philosophical views. Yet, as the text also reveals, Lo was not merely rehearsing or recasting the views of his predecessors. For all of his immersion in the Neo-Confucian tradition, his concern with precision and consistency, and his attention to nuances of language and interpretation, Lo emerges in this work as a creative thinker who sets forth certain metaphysical, epistemological, and psychological positions which are both new and recognizably modern.

These positions would seem to have been carefully thought out by 1528 when the first two *chüan* of the *K'un-chih chi* were completed. As has been noted above, Lo reworked and refined them in later years, but he made no substantive changes, nor can his relative emphases be said to have shifted discernibly. Research on the *Ch'uan-hsi lu* indicates that it can provide considerable evidence of Wang Yang-ming's philosophical development and that, in fact, Wang's perspective did change noticeably in his later years.[21] But the *K'un-chih chi* is not a comparable document. Inasmuch as it contains only Lo's mature thought, we cannot approach it with the expectation of finding similar evidence concerning the course of his intellectual development.

Yamashita Ryuji has concluded after careful and perceptive scrutiny of both the *Ch'uan-hsi lu* and the *K'un-chih chi* that there is reason to believe that Lo, when commenting on the writings of his contemporaries, put down his thoughts on a given work soon after he encountered it.[22] In this sense the *K'un-chih chi* represents Lo's direct responses to current issues and doctrines. As Professor Yamashita observes, it may be possible to get some clues about the evolution of Wang Yang-ming's thought by taking

---

[21] In his *Yōmeigaku no kenkyū* (Studies on the Wang Yang-ming School), 2:108–115, Yamashita Ryūji explores the implications of the change between the earlier and later periods of Wang Yang-ming's thought, the latter having been characterized by the development of the doctrine of extending innate good knowing (*chih liang-chih*).

[22] *Yōmeigaku no kenkyū*, 2:111.

note of where in the *K'un-chih chi* a particular formulation of Wang's was criticized by Lo. But since there is no clear evidence that Lo was directly influenced by Wang in his own formulations,[23] knowledge of this possibility helps us more in interpreting the *Ch'uan-hsi lu* than in adding to our knowledge of the *K'un-chih chi*. Lo's temperament was no doubt more reserved, his habit of mind more deliberate, and his students and potential recorders fewer. We are left in the end with only what in Neo-Confucian terms might be described as his "mature views" or "final conclusions."

Some insight into the background of the *K'un-chih chi* and the intellectual preparation of its author may be found in a brief autobiographical reflection found in the course of a passage (*K'un-chih chi*, Part II, sec. 41) in which Lo criticizes the personal style and teaching methods of Lu Hsiang-shan (Lu Chiu-yüan, 1139–1193). Lo explains that he himself had in his earlier years been drawn to Ch'an Buddhism. He describes a meditative experience which at the time he had taken for enlightenment, but which in later years he recognized more truly as a "vision" *(kuang-ching)*, elusive and unreliable. Then some time after the experience of the "vision," while he was employed at the Imperial University in Nanking, he began a program of extensive reading in classical texts in the course of which he arrived at very different conclusions about the nature of reality and of knowledge. As he put it, "I spent several decades engaged in the most earnest effort. Only when I approached the age of sixty did I finally attain

---

[23] *Ibid.*, especially pp. 108–112. Professor Yamashita's argument is tightly reasoned and based on his own careful study of the texts of the *Ch'uan-hsi lu* and the *K'un-chih chi* as well as on the work of Imai Usaburō in "Zenshu hon *Denshūroku* kō," in *Shibun* (1945), 27:7–9. The subject is too complex to allow for brief summation, but part of the argument (p. 112) is as follows: "In the first two *chüan* of the *K'un-chih chi* he [Lo Ch'in-shun] reacts to the early period of Wang Yang-ming's thought in the *Ch'uan-hsi lu*, Part 1, and the words *liang-chih* (innate good knowing) are not mentioned even once. Consequently we can see that at the time of the writing of the *K'un-chih chi*, Lo Ch'in-shun did not know of the later thought of Wang Yang-ming, i.e., he did not know of the absolutism of *liang-chih* and the distinctive thought that made principle and material force two aspects of *liang-chih* . . . However one reconstructs it, his reading of the Letter in Reply to Lu Yüan-ching [which contains Wang's famous statement that 'principle is the order according to which material force operates; material force is the functioning of principle'] seems to have been after 1526. The fact that in his second letter to Wang Yang-ming [written in 1528] he finally brought up his doubts concerning the theory of *liang-chih* enables us to conclude that Lo's reading of the original text of the *Ch'uan-hsi lu*, Part 2, must have been around 1528. For this reason I believe that we see no influence at all in the first two *chüan* of the *K'un-chih chi* [completed in 1528 on the basis of work begun around 1505]."

insight into the reality of the mind and the nature and truly acquire the basis for self-confidence."

Lo's interest in and exposure to Ch'an Buddhism are hardly unusual for a Neo-Confucian thinker. A great many, including Chu Hsi himself, had experiences that were in some ways similar. More remarkable are the clarity with which he later delivered his judgment about the ultimate limitations of meditative discipline and the almost touching devotion with which he committed himself to intellectual cultivation. Chu Hsi had favored a form of cultivation in which appropriate attention was given to both textual study and quiet-sitting (*ching-tso*). In many of Chu Hsi's writings and conversations on this subject there is the implication that extensive learning and intensive cultivation must be balanced if one is to know the world in all its phenomenal diversity and also to appreciate one's involvement in it as a moral agent capable of "forming one body" with Heaven, earth, and all things. Lo, who was concerned about a disparity between a "vision" of the oneness of all being and a more sustained intellectual apprehension of an objective reality of oneness in nature itself, put virtually all his stress on intellectual cultivation. He too appears to have practiced quiet-sitting on occasion as a means of personal cultivation.[24] Like many Neo-Confucians, he remained convinced that intellectual endeavor culminates and is perfected in spiritual awareness. But, for him, intellectual achievement was the basis for a necessary objectivity that should allow one to attain an accurate perspective on the self and the natural world as a whole. His own intellectual achievement came to fulfillment out of long, silent years of study and effort, though as evidence concerning the course that he followed during those years is lacking, there is no way that his progress can be traced, no way that we can watch him at work.[25]

What can be inferred about his line of approach on the basis of the available textual evidence is that, once the essentials of his philosophy had been worked out in the course of his deliberations on the classics and

---

[24] There is one reference which would suggest this in a poem on his study entitled, "Hsüeh-ku lou ko" (Song on the Hall for the Study of Antiquity) in *Lien-Lo feng-ya* (Poems from the Schools of Lien-hsi and Lo-yang) (*Cheng-i-t'ang ch'üan-shu* ed.), 9:4a–b. The line reads, "Now and then I practice quiet-sitting to preserve my mind and nourish my nature."

[25] Lo's chronological autobiography, "Cheng-an lü-li chi," (in *K'un-chih chi hsü-pu*, 7:11b–28b)) provides a great deal of useful information, but it is not of the sort that permits a real reconstruction of his intellectual progress.

Neo-Confucian writings of the Sung, Yüan, and early Ming periods, Lo
went back and reexamined certain aspects of Buddhist philosophy that had
long interested and troubled him. References to Buddhism and particularly
to Buddhist concepts of mind are found throughout the *K'un-chih chi,* and
a reading of the text suggests that Lo's theory of knowledge was worked out
against the background of his understanding of Buddhist epistemology. A
recurrent argument found in the text is that the Buddhist concept of mind
encourages a form of mental cultivation and discipline so highly subjective
as to vitiate any possibility of a genuine perception of non-duality as this
had come to be understood in Neo-Confucian terms—that is, as a unity
which exists at some level in Nature but which also must be recreated through
human moral effort. Several passages in the text are devoted to the content
of Buddhist sutras and Buddhist commentary literature and to the matter of
translation of Buddhist texts.[26] One passage (Part II, sec. 71) suggests that
Lo found Chu Hsi's understanding of terms and concepts in the *Diamond
Sutra* to be inaccurate.[27]

   While evidence for this is not conclusive, it seems highly prob-
able that Lo's concentrated attention to Buddhist texts occupied a large part
of his time in the 1520s and 1530s. Like other Neo-Confucian thinkers, he
had had youthful experience of Buddhism, and particularly of Buddhist
meditative practice. Unlike most of them, he was to return to philosophical
Buddhism and devote his most intensive effort to it in his later years after
his own philosophy had been fully elaborated. At this point his own political career was over, and he was at the height of his productive capacity as
a scholar. This may afford at least a partial explanation for the fact that in
his critique of Buddhism he was less concerned with the problem of activity
versus quiescence, which had so engaged the attention of Chu Hsi during
the period when he was a disciple of Li T'ung (1093–1163),[28] than with
the nature of knowledge and of material reality, two fundamental themes of
the *K'un-chih chi.*

[26] See especially *K'un-chih chi,* Part II, secs. 70–74.

[27] *K'un-chih chi,* Part II, sec. 71.

[28] See Tomoeda Ryūtarō, *Shushi no shisō keisei* (The Formation of Chu Hsi's Thought),
pp. 51–61. Also, Tomoeda Ryūtarō, "The Characteristics of Chu Hsi's Thought," in *Acta
Asiatica* (October 1971), 21:53–55.

Ming Editions of the *K'un-chih chi*

A number of factors, including general recognition of the exceptional popularity and influence of the thought of Wang Yang-ming during the middle and later years of the sixteenth century, have tended to obscure the fact that the *K'un-chih chi* also circulated widely and exerted considerable influence during the Ming period. Abe Yoshio, whose research on the textual history of the *K'un-chih chi* was most thorough, examined or found reference to at least eight Ming editions in addition to three Ch'ing editions and several Korean and Japanese editions of the work.[29] It was with an edition of c. Chia-ching 27 (1548) that the work was expanded to eight *chüan*, including the two *chüan* of the original work, its two supplementary (*hsü*) *chüan*, the addenda (*fu-lu*) in two *chüan*, continuation (*K'un-chih chi hsü-pu*) in one *chüan*, and an outer chapter (*K'un-chih chi wai-pien*) in one *chüan*. In the edition of T'ien-ch'i 3 (1622) the *K'un-chih chi* in eight *chüan* was combined with the essays, poetry, and occasional writings of Lo Ch'in-shun in the *Lo Cheng-an ts'un-kao* (Literary Remains of Lo Ch'in-shun) to form the *Lo Wen-chuang ho-chi* (Collected Works of Lo Ch'in-shun).

The Translation

The work translated here represents the text of the *K'un-chih chi* as it was published in its original form in 1528. Considerable new material is found in the various supplements to the work, particularly in the highly literate and philosophically mature critique of Buddhism mentioned above. But the consensus in recent scholarship has been that all of the essentials of Lo's philosophy are contained in the original work.[30] A number of excerpts from the first supplementary *chüan* are included in the present

[29] Abe Yoshio, *Nihon Shushigaku to Chōsen* (The Chu Hsi School in Japan and its Relation to Korea), pp. 514–16.

[30] Yamashita Ryūji, *Yōmeigaku no kenkyū*, 2:114.

translation, as are the two letters written by Lo to Wang Yang-ming in 1520 and 1528 and included in the addendum of 1538 (*K'un-chih chi fu-lu, ch.* 5). The latter are of considerable philosophical interest and importance, and, placed alongside Wang's letter of 1521 to Lo, found in Part 2 of the *Ch'uan-hsi lu,*[31] they help us to reconstruct a remarkable debate of the 1520s that was to have echoes and reverberations for many years thereafter.

The text on which the translation is based is a T'ien-ch'i 3 (1622) edition of the *K'un-chih chi* in the Library of Congress, Washington, D.C. Wherever possible, all allusions or quotations in the text have been identified in the translation to enable the reader to examine the original context. In a few cases it has not been possible to provide such annotation either because a work cited or quoted is rare, or, so far as can be determined, no longer extant, or because the source could not be definitely identified. Citations of the *K'un-chih chi* itself are first to the *chüan* and then to the individual sections or entries into which the text was divided by Lo Ch'in-shun.

Chinese philosophical terms have been translated as consistently as possible into English. In nearly all cases I have followed the standard translations established by Wing-tsit Chan, with a few deviations dictated by the particular requirements of this text. For example, the word *chih* is translated here as "will," while the word *i* is translated as "intention," or "intentions," as in the idea of "making the intentions sincere" (*ch'eng-i*) in the *Great Learning*. It has sometimes been necessary to sacrifice consistency, as, for example, in the case of the word *t'ien*, which in some instances is translated as "nature" and in others as "heaven." Obviously, classical Chinese does not harbor such a distinction, and the need to make a choice in translation is in itself an unfortunate sign of distancing from the text itself and from a world of thought far more integrated and whole than our own. Romanized Chinese words have been included sparingly, and usually parenthetically, in the interests of readability. However, in a few places I have lapsed from the more consistent and rigorous practice followed by Professor Chan in translating all philosophical terms and have for the sake of simplicity or clarity used the by now familiar terms *li* and *ch'i* in place of the translations "principle" and "material force" or *liang-chih* in place of "innate, good knowing." Chinese words are rendered according to the Wade-

---

[31]Chan, *Instructions for Practical Living*, pp. 157–65.

Giles system of romanization except in the case of names differently romanized by their bearers. All Chinese or Sanskrit words which appear in *Webster's Third New International Dictionary* are treated here as having been incorporated into English.

The *K'un-chih chi* and Ming Intellectual Debates

The *K'un-chih chi* is a text which had a career in Korea and Japan as well as in China. Part of the interest it holds stems from its potential to add to our understanding not only of Ming China but of Ch'ing China, Yi Korea, and Tokugawa Japan, and of the broader possibilities of Neo-Confucian thought. But it was in the first instance a document of the Ming period by an author who looked back on the Sung and Yüan periods but, obviously, could not anticipate the future and foresee what influence his ideas might have or what place he himself would later be accorded in the Neo-Confucian tradition. And while there are points at which it is evident that he was deeply concerned about the judgments that would be handed down by posterity on himself and his contemporaries, Lo, like virtually all Confucians of his time, wrote primarily for his contemporaries.

At times he speaks of meetings with men like Wang Yang-ming at which they attempted to thrash out philosophical differences through discussion, the practice of *chiang-hsüeh*. At others, he expresses regret that such direct encounters were impossible to arrange, no doubt because the most philosophically active of his contemporaries were occupied for much of their lives with high official posts. In writing the *K'un-chih chi* Lo was evidently reflecting on their ideas and values as they bore on the evolving Confucian tradition and on the intellectual and political realities of the day. Even those reflections which appear most theoretical or speculative can be seen to have been motivated by a lively sense of engagement and a highly practical intent.

One of Lo's highest priorities in this work is to expose what he took to be the errors of Buddhism and to demonstrate the "disastrous legacy" it had created for Confucians. Though it is widely acknowledged in modern scholarship that Buddhism had entered a prolonged decline following the Sung period, its influence on Chinese intellectual and spiritual life continued to be very significant throughout the Ming. Lo felt it to be a threat not so much in its institutional form as in its allure for those who, while not ostensibly Buddhist, were nonetheless caught in the trap of subjectivism which Buddhist thought and practice somewhat paradoxically entailed. Even apart from his sustained critique of Buddhism in the supplement to the *K'un-chih chi,* much of the original work is given over to arguments against those ideas which Lo considered most deceptive and dangerous based on his view of their subtle infiltration, amounting almost to subversion, of Confucian intellectual life.

As already suggested, Lo's critique of Buddhism did not hinge on the notion that Buddhism was quietistic in practice, apathetic in politics, or "selfish" in its focus on the escape from suffering. Such arguments had often been made by the Sung Neo-Confucians for whom political reform and personal commitment to public life had been compelling issues. But the Ming context was different, and, for Lo, the deeper and more enduring problem was the clear danger that the Confucian value system was being undermined from within through an impairment of the longstanding commitment to intellectual understanding of the objective world. Some Confucians became fascinated with Buddhist modes of thought and practice and drifted toward Buddhism. An even more insidious problem lay in the abandonment by others of vital Confucian philosophical ground in consequence of their emphasis on personal integration at the expense of intellectual cultivation. For many, moral wholeness or adequacy, an inner sense of being in control of one's own being, had become the paramount concern, while investigating the things of the objective world was thought to carry with it the risk of "fragmentation." Far more dangerous than the Buddhists, who were overt about their beliefs, were the crypto-Buddhists who made such serious concessions to Buddhism in their approach to knowledge and their understanding of the nature of reality. Lo's criticisms of Lu Hsiang-shan and Yang Chien (1141–1226) in the Sung and of Ch'en Hsien-chang (1428–1500) and Wang Yang-ming in his own time afford a clear indication of why he was concerned.

The *K'un-chih chi* opens with an extended reflection on the problem of the mind (*hsin*) and the nature (*hsing*) and a critique of the Buddhist notion of "clarifying the mind and perceiving the nature." Lo argues that, while the Buddhists preserve a verbal distinction between the mind and the nature, this only partially conceals their proclivity for dwelling solely on the mind. Ontologically, the Buddhists are committed to viewing all reality as mental. Epistemologically, they are prone to an extreme subjectivism, a confirmed disposition to attend only to the "pure intelligence and consciousness" of the mind while overlooking the "perfect subtlety and absolute unity" of the nature. The mind, however, is a subjective function; the nature is an objective reality. They must not be confused (*K'un-chih chi*, Part I, sec. 5). Later in the work and in Lo's letters to Wang Yang-ming it becomes evident that he thought that Buddhist absorption in the mind and corresponding lack of insight into the nature have much to do with the fundamental error made by those Confucians who question Ch'eng I's statement that the nature is principle and contend instead that the mind is principle. The ontological error—the identification of the subjective functioning of the mind with the objective reality of the principle—has the most serious and unfortunate epistemological corollaries. Inwardly, it leads to distraction from the discipline required for the human moral sense to be fulfilled. Outwardly, it leads to constriction of one's sphere of concern, of one's perception of the setting in which human life is carried on. Essentially, the charge against both Lu Hsiang-shan and Wang Yang-ming is that their conception of ethical cultivation, while apparently deep, is yet confined and limited. As they are drawn away from the traditional Confucian doctrines of "the investigation of things" and "the probing of principle," they allow both the world of experience and the scope of learning to be dangerously narrowed.

But Lo's concerns are not confined to what he takes to be the errors of Lu and Wang and their followers. Much of Part I of the *K'un-chih chi* is devoted to undisguised criticisms of certain of the theories of Ch'eng I and Chu Hsi, while a number of passages in Part II are given over to even more pointed criticisms of views put forward by their successors in the early Ming. Identifying himself as a follower of the Ch'eng-Chu tradition, Lo explains that, as one who honors and trusts his predecessors, he is duty-bound to confront certain unresolved problems in their thought. In discussing the ideas of Ch'eng I and Chu Hsi he reiterates at a number of points that he has yet to see that they "finally achieved unity" (*ting yü i*) or "recovered the ultimate unity" (*kuei yü chih i*). The discovery that their understanding of fundamental metaphysical categories, concepts of human nature, psychological attitudes, and views of personal cultivation betray signs

of dualism poses a difficult series of intellectual problems for Lo. He understands such lapses to involve philosophical inconsistencies; painstakingly
working through these inconsistencies, he hopes to approach a consistent
and unified understanding of a Nature which reveals in the order of its
operations the ultimate consistency and unity of principle.

When Lo observes that Ch'eng I and Chu Hsi had not "finally
achieved unity," he has in mind above all the fundamental ontological dualism
which attached to the prevailing Sung view of *li* and *ch'i*, or principle and
material force. An argument of considerable philosophical subtlety is developed in the course of many pages of the *K'un-chih chi* concerning this dualism of *li* and *ch'i*. Resorting to the "Discussion of the Trigrams" ("Shuo-
kua") and the "Appended Remarks" ("Hsi-tz'u chuan") in the *Book of Changes*
(I-ching), Lo constructs an elaborate case to demonstrate that such a dualism is without classical precedent. Refraining, whether out of discretion or
conviction, from observing that such a dualism might also have arisen under Buddhist influence, he concentrates instead on formulating a view of *li*
and *ch'i* which will be in conformity with the ideas of Confucius and thus
deserve the claim of classical authority as well as philosophical cogency.

The burden of the argument is that all reality, both physical
and phenomenal, is *ch'i*, which is "originally one, but follows an endless
cycle of movement and tranquillity, going and coming, rising and falling."[32] The regularity, the reliability, the spontaneous order which can be
observed in this endless process of recurrence is *li*. Lo explicitly rejects Chu
Hsi's view that *li* represents a causal or determinative power distinct from
ch'i, as expressed in Chu's statement that "*li* attaches to *ch'i* and thus operates" *(li fu yü ch'i i hsing)*. *Li* is simply the pattern to be observed in the
natural process rather than its origin or final cause. With *ch'i* being the
fundamental reality of the universe, *li* is a designation *(ming)* for the "unregulated regularity" or spontaneous order to be discovered in *ch'i*. It is not,
in itself, a "thing" *(wu)*. It cannot be understood as either ontologically
prior to *ch'i* or superior to it or as allied with *ch'i* but nonetheless metaphysically distinct from it. As energy, *ch'i* is originally one; as order or
regularity, *li* is also one in the sense that it recurs in all the processes of
nature.

There was still another respect in which Ch'eng I and Chu Hsi

_____

[32] *K'un-chih chi*, Part I, sec. 11.

had failed to "recover the ultimate unity," and that was in their view of human nature. Following the lead of Chang Tsai (1020–1077), they had come to accept a distinction between man's original nature *(pen-hsing)* or heavenly nature *(t'ien-ming chih hsing)*, or the nature of heaven-and-earth *(t'ien-ti chih hsing)*, and his physical nature or, more literally, "nature of the *ch'i* constitution"[33] *(ch'i-chih chih hsing)*. The original nature, which was associated with the Principle of Nature and the Mind of Tao, was pure and perfectly good; the physical nature, which was bound up with the individual's endowment of *ch'i*, was to one or another degree tainted and impure by dint of its materiality. The original nature was universal; the physical nature was particular. The object of personal cultivation, in this view, was to refine away the impurity of the physical nature so that the full goodness of the original nature could be more fully expressed.

While this conception of human nature does not, strictly speaking, depend on a metaphysical dualism of *li* and *ch'i* (and indeed there are differences of opinion as to whether the thought of Chang Tsai, with whom it originated, was actually monistic or dualistic), it forms a natural counterpart to such a dualism. There is invariably the suggestion that *li* and *ch'i* commingle in a living being, and the potential for goodness is understood to derive from the *li*-component and the potential for evil from the *ch'i*-component of human personality. In line with his monism of *ch'i*, Lo Ch'in-shun rejects the notion of two natures, insisting once again that it is without either classical precedent or philosophical justification. The nature is one.

While taking the position that the nature is one, and thus denying the dualism that characterized Ch'eng I's view, Lo still accepts Ch'eng I's assertion that the nature is principle. At the outset it had not been easy for him to see how a monism of *ch'i* and the concept of a single human nature could be reconciled with the idea that "the nature is principle." He observes that Ch'eng I himself had said that it was wrong to regard the nature and material force as two, but that "he had not been able to see them as one." Having, by his own account, devoted years to this problem, Lo finally came to realize that "the subtle truth of the nature and endowment is summarized in the phrase, 'principle is one; its particularizations are

---

[33] Following one of the translations adopted by Ira E. Kasoff in *The Thought of Chang Tsai (1020–1077)*, pp. 72–76.

diverse' " (*li-i fen-shu*). This pregnant formula, generally thought to have originated with Ch'eng I, is reinterpreted by Lo to account for the fact of unity within phenomenal diversity, which had been and remained a central problem in Neo-Confucian ontology.

He does not say, as some of his predecessors seem to have been saying, that principle is one in the sense that it is identical everywhere and in everything but yet different in that it is confirmed or compromised according to the purity or impurity of the various physical natures or endowments of *ch'i* with which it is associated. Rather, principle is one in the sense that it is universally expressed in all things at the inception of their life and then also variously expressed as they assume discrete forms and follow particular patterns of life. The very fact of diversity or particularity *is* in itself natural principle, which "is always present within diverse particularizations" (Part I, sec. 14).

For Lo to maintain the view that "the nature is principle" without deviating from his monism of *ch'i* has often been seen as a problem, and the success or failure of this move has remained a matter of considerable controversy. In his biography of Lo in the *Ming-ju hsüeh-an* (Philosophical Records of Ming Confucians), Huang Tsung-hsi criticizes Lo on the ground that his view of the mind and the nature is at odds with his understanding of *li* and *ch'i*. Huang argues that, while Lo refuses to accept a dualism of *li* and *ch'i* in the sense of *li* being ontologically prior to *ch'i*, he nonetheless clings to the view that the nature is prior to the mind.[34] For

---

[34] *Ming-ju hsüeh-an*, ch. 47. Huang Tsung-hsi's criticism of Lo (in part a parody of *K'un-chih chi*, Part I, sec. 11) was as follows: "Lo's theory of the mind and the nature and his theory of *li* and *ch'i* are mutually contradictory. That which in Heaven is *ch'i*, in man is the mind. And that which in Heaven is *li*, in man is the nature. What is true of *li* and *ch'i* will also be true of the mind and the nature, for there is definitely no question of a difference between them. By virtue of receiving *ch'i* from Heaven, man is born. He has only one mind, but through endless cycles of movement and tranquillity, the emotions of pleasure, sorrow, anger, and joy follow one another in endless succession. When he ought to feel pity and compassion, he naturally feels pity and compassion, and when he ought to know shame, he naturally knows shame, and when he ought to feel respect, he naturally feels respect, and when he ought to have the sense of right and wrong, he naturally has the sense of right and wrong. And amid all of this prolific variety and phenomenal diversity there is a detailed order and elaborate coherence which cannot ultimately be obscured. That is what is called the nature. It is not a separate entity that exists prior to the mind or that attaches to the mind.

According to Lo, man's Heaven-endowed nature originates when life is first engendered, but consciousness arises after one is born. In his view consciousness is mind and not

Huang, Lo's monism breaks down at a crucial point. Many scholars of a range of persuasions have followed Huang here, and his argument is still quoted by many contemporary scholars, including Marxists, who take Lo's position on human nature as evidence of a lapse from an otherwise admirable consistency. What is clear, however, is that the relation of *li* and *ch'i* and the mind and the nature was a central concern for Lo and, having addressed it with sustained concentration over the course of several decades, he himself was satisfied that he had arrived at a satisfactory understanding of it. If there is any inconsistency here, it could hardly be a matter of inadvertence on his part.

Actually, there may be no inconsistency if one adopts the following line of interpretation: Lo's concept of the nature was unlike the prevailing Sung views but remarkably like the view of the nature found in the earliest strata of Chinese thought. That is, the nature is understood as a natural developmental tendency or pattern.[35] Lo thought of the nature as an objective reality accessible to but not identical with the human mind. The nature is prior to the mind in the sense that life itself precedes consciousness. It is to be understood as the object of the mind's inquiry and reflection, which properly lead not merely to self-consciousness but to awareness of the nature of things in general. Lo focuses not so much on the nature as a disposition to moral goodness as on the nature as a reality which can be known. Moral goodness is understood to follow from an objective awareness of the principle which unites oneself and others. Such awareness is equivalent to insight into one's place in the totality of things, one's role in the processes of life as a whole.

Such a revised view of the nature is in keeping with Lo's revised

nature. If this is the case, then the nature is substance and the mind is function. The nature originates before a person is born and is tranquil. The mind moves when it is aroused by external things and is active. The nature is the principle of Heaven and earth and the myriad things. It is common to all. The mind is what one personally possesses. It is particular to oneself. Clearly, this is first to set up the nature as prior [to the mind] and to regard it as master of the mind. This is no different from the theory that principle can engender material force. Isn't this in marked contradiction to his theory of *li* and *ch'i*? How could it possibly be that *li* and *ch'i* are *li* and *ch'i* and the mind and the nature are the mind and the nature, and that the two separate Heaven and man so that they are not wholly interrelated?"

[35] See A. C. Graham, "The Background of the Mencian Theory of Human Nature," in *Ch'ing-hua hsüeh-pao* (Tsing Hua Journal of Chinese Studies), (December 1967), NS VI, nos. 1–2, pp. 215–71, esp. pp. 216–24.

view of principle. Not only does he reject a dualism of *li* and *ch'i* but, equally significantly, he interprets *li* in a new way. As the spontaneous order, the unregulated regularity to be perceived in natural and human events, *li* is the reliability, coherence, and unity that characterize those events. It is not a separate entity, a causal agent that mingles with or attaches to *ch'i* and ensures its order; it is that order itself. Just as principle is the pattern that is created with and by life itself, human nature is the pattern or order that is observed in human behavior and development. It is not to be identified with the mind or consciousness per se; rather, it is the appropriate object of the mind's reflection.[36]

One of the corollaries of Lo's denial of the notion of two natures, an original nature and a physical nature, was his rejection of the idea, basic to the psychological thought of most of the Sung Neo-Confucians, that there was a fundamental antagonism between the Principle of Nature (*t'ien-li*) and the human desires (*jen-yü*). Selfish desires had often been thought to arise from the physical nature, to be counter to the original nature, and to demand either eradication or fairly rigorous curtailment. Human desires, in Lo's view, are, like the emotions, signs and expressions of human nature. They are natural and in conformity with principle. What requires control and regulation is the extremity of "selfishness" per se, the lack of awareness that one is fundamentally like others and has the same dispositions and needs. For the sake of oneself as well as others, one's desires need to be moderated, yet they must not be repressed. Throughout the *K'un-chih chi* Lo develops an essentially naturalistic psychology, with frequent resort to Mencius and to the "Record of Music" in the *Book of Rites* to lend support to his contention that the ancients recognized the human emotional and appetitive nature as fundamental and worthy of cultivation.

The epistemological corollary of Lo's monism of *ch'i* and his revised attitude toward human nature may be seen in his assertion of the

---

[36] Yamanoi Yū, writing in Onozawa Seiichi, Fukunaga Mitsuji, and Yamanoi Yū, eds., *Ki no shisō*, points (p. 368) to the special problem that those advocating a philosophy of *ch'i* had with the established theory of the nature as good. In Professor Yamanoi's judgment (p. 368), Wang T'ing-hsiang dealt most resolutely with this problem by taking the unusual step of abandoning the Mencian doctrine of the goodness of human nature and stating (in *Ya-shu*, Book 1) that "there are both good and bad in the nature." I would suggest that Lo Ch'in-shun was making a similar move, though more subtly, by following Ch'eng Hao on the issue of the relation of good and evil in the nature but recasting the entire problem in terms of the formula *li-i fen-shu* (*K'un-chih chi*, Part I, sec. 65).

importance and validity of sense knowledge and sense experience. Sense knowledge had been deprecated by some Sung Neo-Confucians, including Chang Tsai and Ch'eng I, who assigned a higher value to knowledge attained through the moral nature, a mode of apprehension more akin to the experience of enlightenment than to ordinary sense perception. Lo does not accept the notion that there are modes of knowing independent of and qualitatively superior to "the knowledge of seeing and hearing" (*chien-wen chih shih*). Seeing and hearing represent the primary modes of apprehending the world. For him, the only genuine epistemological issue is the care and discernment with which these senses are employed.

At the same time that the primacy of sense knowledge is asserted by Lo, the central doctrine of the Ch'eng-Chu school—the "investigation of things" and the "plumbing of principle"—is strongly reaffirmed. Though at one point he suggests that the most satisfactory definition of the *ko* in *ko-wu* is that of Chu Hsi's friend and collaborator, Lü Tsu-ch'ien (1137–1181)—that is, "penetrating the 'three primal powers' with no separation" (*t'ung ch'e san-chi erh wu-chien*)[37]—he takes this to be an extension and an enlargement of the view held by the Ch'eng brothers. In fact, the whole enterprise of *ko-wu* assumes even greater significance in light of Lo's emphasis on sense experience, his uncompromising commitment to objectivity, and his resolute opposition to the radical reinterpretation of *ko-wu* by Wang Yang-ming. Wang, in defining *ko* as "correcting," rather than as "investigating" or "penetrating," was seeking to make *ko-wu* entirely a moral affair which was, in effect, to limit the sphere of significant human experience. Against this strategy, Lo offers not only a defense of intellectuality in the Ch'eng-Chu tradition but a vision of the broad sphere within which human endeavor is to be carried on.

We are reminded at many points in the *K'un-chih chi* that "returning to unity" or "recovering the ultimate unity" is the guiding theme of the author's endeavors and that the object of "returning to unity" is to be construed historically as well as metaphysically, epistemologically, and morally. So far as Lo is concerned, the various dualisms that figured so significantly in Sung Neo-Confucianism involve an inadequate understanding of the nature of reality and of knowledge. The categories of *li* and *ch'i*, of the original nature and the physical nature, and of Heavenly principle

---

[37]*K'un-chih chi*, Part I, sec. 10.

and human desire, as deployed by most of the Sung masters, involve an artificial division of reality, while the categories of "knowledge attained through the moral nature" and "the knowledge of seeing and hearing" represent an arbitrary distinction between modes of knowing. As part of the ongoing Confucian project, such distinctions, which may be seen as dividing the Sung Neo-Confucians from Confucius and Mencius and their forebears in the classical past, need to be resolved.

The reason that Lo's interpretation of the formula *li-i fen-shu* is so important is that his monism does not seek to erase the awareness of phenomenal diversity but actually to heighten it. Living things are not one in the sense that distinctions among them are illusory and unreal figments of a deluded imagination. Nor are they one only when understood in terms of a morally untainted and pure component of principle to be discovered within a relatively pure or impure vehicle of *ch'i*. All things are one in the sense that they are endowed with an energy which is seen as continuous; given discrete physical forms, this energy finds distinct expressions. The reason that the mind and the nature must still be distinguished is that there is necessarily a difference between the conscious mind and the objects of consciousness. Consciousness has many objects and modes, but the consciousness of principle involves awareness of what it is that is common or shared among all living things and consistently and reliably true in their life processes. This is the ultimate object of knowledge; because of its complexity such knowledge is painfully acquired.

Interpreting the *K'un-chih chi*

From even this brief account of the main themes of the *K'un-chih chi* the reader may have anticipated certain interpretive problems. One of these is the question of how "orthodoxy" in the Ming is to be understood and whether there is not some contradiction in identifying Lo as both a devoted follower of the Ch'eng-Chu tradition and an innovative critic of Chu Hsi. Unless one is prepared to accept that "orthodoxy" was not a body of fixed doctrines handed down from generation to generation as a "correct faith," requiring strict devotion from the adherent, it may be difficult to appreciate Lo's professions to be at once a dedicated follower and a constructive critic. Once one accepts them at face value, it becomes necessary to look to something other than specific doctrines to discover the heart of orthodoxy. Perhaps it is better understood to lie in the concept of a tradition, which implies both stability and a capacity for growth, rather than in the fixity associated with "received doctrines." It seems also to involve a personal dimension: throughout this text Lo Ch'in-shun reveals himself to be much concerned with the dispositions, purposes, and motives of his predecessors. It is as if he is carrying on not their doctrines but their work.

There is also the question of whether and how Lo's intellectual method, which was inherited from his Sung predecessors, was related to his philosophy of ch'i, which was quite unprecedented. Most interpreters have emphasized either the inheritance or the departure from his forebears in the earlier Ch'eng-Chu school, rarely both.

Writing in the early 1940s, Jung Chao-tsu characterized Lo as a "latter-day stalwart of the Chu Hsi school."[38] In a more recent reassessment of the continuities between Sung and Ming Neo-Confucianism and the textual scholarship of the Ch'ing period, Yü Ying-shih concurred in that opinion.[39] Professor Yü's thesis, which is an important one, will be described more fully in what follows. Not surprisingly, Marxist scholars, writing since 1949, have tended to take a different approach entirely. In *Chung-kuo wei-wu-chu-i ssu-hsiang chien-shih* (A Brief History of Chinese Materialist Thought), Zhang Dainian identified Lo Ch'in-shun and Wang T'ing-hsiang as "the two most important materialist philosophers of the Ming period." In Zhang's view Lo's purposes were iconoclastic, and his principal achievement lay in controverting both the "objective idealism" (*k'e-kuan wei-hsin-chu-i*) of the Ch'eng-Chu school and the "subjective idealism" (*chu-kuan wei-hsin-chu-i*) of the Lu-Wang school.[40] Professor Zhang was writing in 1957; subsequent studies by Chinese Marxist scholars have adopted a generally similar perspective.

[38] Jung Chao-tsu, *Ming-tai ssu-hsiang shih* (A History of Ming Thought), p. 196.

[39] Yü Ying-shih, "Ts'ung Sung Ming ju-hsüeh ti fa-chan lun Ch'ing-tai ssu-hsiang shih," (Ch'ing Thought as Seen Through the Development of Sung and Ming Confucianism) (hereafter abbreviated as Yü, "Sung Ming ju-hsüeh"), in *Chung-kuo hsüeh-jen* (September 1970), 2:27.

[40] Zhang Dainian, *Chung-kuo wei-wu-chu-i ssu-hsiang chien-shih* (A Brief History of Chinese Materialist Thought), p. 101.

The most thorough study of Lo Ch'in-shun's philosophy was undertaken by Yamashita Ryūji in a 1961 article, "Ra Kinjun to ki no tetsugaku" (Lo Ch'in-shun and the Philosophy of *Ch'i*).[41] In that work Professor Yamashita proposed to study the philosophy of *ch'i* developed in the *K'un-chih chi* in the attempt to resolve certain basic questions in Ming intellectual history, the most important of which was how Lo related to the Ch'eng-Chu tradition, or, more pointedly, whether he was pro-Chu Hsi or anti-Chu Hsi.[42] His conclusion, which will be examined in greater detail below, was that Lo's thought represented not a defense of Chu Hsi's philosophy, but, like that of Wang Yang-ming, a reaction against it.[43] The question of Lo Ch'in-shun's role in the Chu Hsi tradition was likewise one that concerned Abe Yoshio in his study of the Chu Hsi school in Japan and its relation to Korea. As one primarily concerned with Lo's influence in Japan, Professor Abe too tended to emphasize Lo's break with the traditional Ch'eng-Chu philosophy.[44]

To some extent such differences of opinion may turn on variant interpretations of identical evidence. This is particularly the case when the views of Marxist and non-Marxist scholars are compared. However, if the more recent Marxist interpretations are set aside for separate consideration, one finds little evidence that the other scholars cited here are in substantial disagreement. Though their conclusions may appear to be in conflict, it emerges upon scrutiny of their arguments that they are adducing different evidence in the course of confronting different problems.

When in his *Ming-tai ssu-hsiang shih* Jung Chao-tsu described Lo as having defended the Chu Hsi school, he had in mind primarily the matter of intellectual method or style, or what in Chinese is often expressed in the term *hsüeh-shu*. Jung observed that at the point when Wang Yang-ming was approaching the height of his influence, and the theory of innate, good knowing (*liang-chih*) was being advanced with telling effect, Lo Ch'in-shun

---

[41] Yamashita Ryūji, "Ra Kinjun to ki no tetsugaku," in *Nagoya Daigaku Bungakubu kenkyū ronshū* 27, Tetsugaku 9 (1961), pp. 1–54. The article in substantially the same form was later incorporated into vol. 2 of the author's *Yōmeigaku no kenkyū*. The citations which follow are to the latter version.

[42] Yamashita Ryūji, *Yōmeigaku no kenkyū*, 2:61.

[43] *Ibid.*, p. 125.

[44] Abe Yoshio, *Nihon Shushigaku to Chōsen*, especially pp. 502–14.

was noteworthy for having upheld an older style of learning that hearkened back to the Sung. Among the contemporaries of Wang Yang-ming, it was Lo who "received the inheritance of Ch'eng and Chu and stressed the 'plumbing of principle' (ch'iung-li), the 'investigation of things' (ko-wu), and 'inquiry and study' (tao wen-hsüeh)."[45] He thus attempted to further the cause of "extensive learning" (po-hsüeh) against the more intuitive approach to knowledge advocated by Wang and his followers.

When Yü Ying-shih arrived at a similar conclusion, it was in the course of an analysis that represented one of the fundamental tensions between the Ch'eng-Chu school and the Wang Yang-ming school as one of "intellectualism" versus "anti-intellectualism." Professor Yü saw the opposition between Lo Ch'in-shun and Wang Yang-ming as a conflict between Confucian intellectualism, with its roots in the Ch'eng-Chu tradition, and anti-intellectualism, with its source in the philosophy of Lu Hsiang-shan. In his view, Chu Hsi and Lu Hsiang-shan, though divided over the issue of whether primacy should be accorded to "inquiry and study" or to "honoring the virtuous nature (tsun te-hsing), were not nearly so far apart on this score as were their Ming successors, Lo Ch'in-shun and Wang Yang-ming, by whom the arguments on either side were carried to their divergent epistemological conclusions.[46]

Professor Yü suggested that, among the reasons the opposition had not been sharper in the earlier period was that, in the Sung period, Taoism and Buddhism (especially Ch'an Buddhism) were still flourishing. Since Sung Confucians were necessarily concerned with dealing with these "outside enemies," serious internal disagreements did not develop.[47] In the Ming, however, the emergence of Wang Yang-ming's philosophy at first intensified the tendency to anti-intellectualism because Wang attached such high value to intuitive knowledge, regarding extensive learning as a secondary concern and even a diversion from the task of attaining sagehood. According to Professor Yü, the fundamental issue dividing Wang and Lo was the attitude toward book-learning and the transmission of knowledge, the most obvious difference between them being illustrated in the perspective of each on the classics. But when the controversy between Wang and Lo

---

[45] Jung Chao-tsu, *Ming-tai ssu-hsiang shih*, p. 196.

[46] Yü, "Sung Ming ju-hsüeh," pp. 22–32.

[47] *Ibid.*, p. 23.

reached a point at which resort to classical authority became necessary in order to resolve fundamental disagreements by determining which ideas were actually in conformity with the basic intentions of the sages and worthies of the past, fresh impulse was given to intellectualism in both schools, and, finally, to the revival of textual scholarship in the late Ming and early Ch'ing periods.[48]

Both Jung Chao-tsu and Yü Ying-shih suggested an affinity between Lo Ch'in-shun and Ch'en Chien (1497–1567),[49] who in his *Hsüeh-p'u t'ung-pien* (General Critique of Obscurations of Learning) had also urged the value of intellectual inquiry and study of the classics, and, like Lo, though with far greater vehemence, criticized the anti-intellectualism of Lu Hsiang-shan and Wang Yang-ming.[50] Neither Jung nor Yü was directly concerned with the fact that Lo was among the first Chinese thinkers to have explicitly rejected the Sung dualism of *li* and *ch'i* and developed a monistic philosophy of *ch'i*. Yü remarked that this issue represented one point of disagreement between Lo and Chu Hsi, but given the subject of his own inquiry, he saw it as a difference that was less than crucial. As an historian of thought, and one concerned to discover an inner logic in the development of ideas, Yü's interest was in the issue of intellectual method or style. More specifically, he wished to explore the approach to book-learning and study of the classics as a link between the style of learning favored by the more intellectually oriented Ch'eng-Chu school of the Sung and Ming periods and the development of textual scholarship and evidential research in the Ch'ing period.[51]

When, on the other hand, Yamashita Ryūji reached the conclusion that Lo Ch'in-shun had reacted against the philosophy of Chu Hsi and departed significantly from it, he did so on the basis of an analysis of

---

[48] *Ibid.*, pp. 30–32.

[49] Ch'en Chien was known both as a defender of the Ch'eng-Chu school and an historian of the Ming period. His *Huang-Ming t'ung-chi* (General Account of the Great Ming Dynasty) in 27 *chüan* is an annalistic history of the Ming from its beginning to the end of the Cheng-te reign (1521). Though banned by imperial decree in 1571, the work had several supplements and a wide circulation in late Ming and Ch'ing China as well as in Korea.

[50] Jung, *Ming-tai ssu-hsiang shih*, pp. 196–205. Yü, "Sung Ming ju-hsüeh," p. 27.

[51] Yü, "Sung Ming ju-hsüeh," pp. 30–31.

Lo's philosophy of *ch'i* and the implications of this philosophy for Ming thought. While he did not minimize the importance of intellectual method or style, and, in fact, delved into this problem in some depth, his assumption was that it was a basic difference in ontological perspective that determined the intellectual or scholarly method that Lo advocated. As the title of Professor Yamashita's original study suggests, his focus was on the problem of *li* and *ch'i*, as one of the primary substantive issues in Lo's thought, and on Lo's reaffirmation of the human desires and feelings as a corollary of his monism of *ch'i*.

Yamashita gave credit to Yamanoi Yū, who in a 1951 article, "Min Shin jidai ni okeru 'ki' no tetsugaku" (The Philosophy of *Ch'i* in the Ming and Ch'ing Periods),[52] placed Lo Ch'in-shun at the beginning of an intellectual trend which he recognized as having extended from the mid-Ming period through the Ch'ing period and culminated in the thought of the great eighteenth-century philosopher Tai Chen (1724–1777). In Professor Yamanoi's judgment, the philosophy of *ch'i* to which a significant number of Ming and Ch'ing thinkers subscribed represented a decisive break with the dualistic tradition of the Ch'eng-Chu school of the Sung. Yamashita, while differing with Yamanoi in a number of respects, supported this general conclusion.

On the basis of his own research on the subject, Professor Yamashita concluded that Lo Ch'in-shun and Wang Yang-ming, working contemporaneously, both developed new philosophies that represented a reaction against the prevailing Chu Hsi school of the Ming period, which under the influence of Hu Chu-jen (1434–1484), had become strongly oriented toward a philosophy of *li* or principle. Yamashita assembled textual evidence to show that the philosophy of *ch'i* could be considered original with Lo Ch'in-shun but went on to demonstrate that, after Lo, it developed most completely among thinkers who were influenced by the theory of *liang-chih* of the Wang Yang-ming school. Having observed that the philosophy of Wang Yang-ming was not only not opposed to the philosophy of *ch'i* but conducive to it, Yamashita concluded that a profound change was underway in Chinese thought in the first half of the sixteenth century. However,

---

[52] Yamanoi Yū, "Min Shin jidai ni okeru 'ki' no tetsugaku," in *Tetsugaku zasshi* (1951), vol. 66, no. 711.

contrary to Marxist interpreters, he took the position that the terms "idealism" and "materialism" were inapplicable to the philosophical realities of
the Ming period and that a different conceptual framework was required to
understand the important shift that was underway at this time.[53]

It will be readily apparent that, whereas Yü Ying-shih's perspective on the problem of intellectualism and anti-intellectualism led him to
the conclusion that Lo Ch'in-shun and Wang Yang-ming were considerably
further apart than Chu Hsi and Lu Hsiang-shan before them, Yamashita's
focus on the problem of li and ch'i and the development by both Lo and
Wang of a philosophy of ch'i led him to quite a different conclusion. As
seen by Yamashita, Lo and Wang, responding to some of the same needs
and challenges, were engaged in a similar effort and were much closer to
one another than either was to his Sung forebears. These views are, of
course, not strictly incompatible, since the particular problem under consideration in each case is not the same. However, the difference of perspective
is more than coincidental and may from an historiographical standpoint be
quite instructive.

This difference in perspective becomes the more apparent when
we examine the work of Abe Yoshio, who, while differing with Yamashita
Ryūji at certain points, defined the essential philosophical issues in similar
terms. Professor Abe observed that, quite early in its history, the Chu Hsi
school in Japan was divided between two distinct tendencies of thought.
The first, identified with the philosophy of ch'i, was associated with such
thinkers as Hayashi Razan (1583–1657), Kaibara Ekken (1630–1714), and
Kinoshita Jun'an (1621–1698) as well as the thinkers of the Ancient Learning (Kogaku) school, Yamaga Sokō (1622–1685) and Itō Jinsai (1627–1705).
The second, identified with the philosophy of li, was associated with Yamazaki Ansai (1618–1682) and his followers in the Kimon school and Ōtsuka Taiya (1677–1750) and his followers in the Kumamoto school. For
Professor Abe, the understanding of what principle was and what relation
it had to material force represented the essential difference between these
two tendencies or schools of thought in the Tokugawa period. He saw the
strongly intellectual and empirical orientation of the school of ch'i as a
direct consequence of its perception of ch'i as the underlying reality of the

[53]Yamashita Ryūji, Yōmeigaku no kenkyū, 2:115–25.

universe, and the ethical and religious orientation of the school of *li* as a consequence of its conviction that behind the individual concrete things of the world lay the more fundamental and enduring reality of principle.[54]

Like Yamashita, Abe recognized Lo Ch'in-shun as the first openly to have raised doubts about Chu Hsi's *li-hsüeh*,[55] and he represented Lo's philosophy of *ch'i* as a clear and portentous departure from Chu Hsi's philosophy of *li*. With Wang Yang-ming also having rejected the philosophy of *li* for his own philosophy of *ch'i*,[56] and this philosophy of *ch'i* having become dominant in the later Wang Yang-ming school, the philosophy of *li* gradually declined in China in the late fifteenth and early sixteenth centuries. It had what Professor Abe described as its final flourishing in the Tung-lin school of the late Ming.[57]

Abe showed that the active impulse for the philosophy of *li* in early Tokugawa Japan came not from China directly, where by the late sixteenth century it was already in decline, but from Korea, through the mediation of the great sixteenth-century thinker Yi T'oegye (1501–1570). However, the initial development of the philosophy of *ch'i* he attributed in large part to the influence of Lo Ch'in-shun's *K'un-chih chi*, which reached Japan, again by way of Korea, following the military campaigns of the Bunroku (1592–1595) and Keichō (1596–1610) periods. A Korean edition of the *K'un-chih chi* was hand copied by Hayashi Razan. Professor Abe's research suggests that it was also a Korean edition which became the source for the first Japanese woodblock edition, printed in 1658 and apparently read within a few years thereafter by Ando Seian (1622–1701), Kaibara Ekken, and Itō Jinsai, among others.[58] Professor Abe has observed that the implications of Lo's monism of *ch'i* and his concern for objective investiga-

---

[54] Abe Yoshio, *Nihon Shushigaku to Chōsen*, p. 493. See also Professor Abe's article, "Development of Neo-Confucianism in Japan, Korea and China: A Comparative Study," in *Acta Asiatica* (1970), especially 19:17–31.

[55] Abe, *Nihon Shushigaku to Chōsen*, pp. 493–94.

[56] In Professor Abe's view (*Nihon Shushigaku to Chōsen*, p. 494), "Yang-ming's statement that 'the mind is *li*' could also have been rendered 'the mind is *ch'i*.' Yang-ming's position was not *li-hsüeh* but *ch'i-hsüeh*, a philosophy of *ch'i*."

[57] Abe, *Nihon Shushigaku to Chōsen*, p. 494.

[58] *Ibid.*, pp. 494–97.

tion were considerable for a scholar like Ekken, who in turn went on to
extend the scope of "investigation" to the world of nature as well as military
science, law, and philology.[59]

Abe's conclusions concerning the significance of Lo's thought,
which no doubt reflected his own interest in the subsequent influence of
some of the important Japanese Confucians who read the *K'un-chih chi,*
were as follows:

> Lo Ch'in-shun pointedly criticized and broadly modified Chu Hsi's philosophy
> of *li* and *ch'i* and the mind and the nature, established a philosophy which
> can aptly be described as a monism of *ch'i,* and restyled the Sung philosophy
> which negated the desires into one which affirmed the desires. He sharply
> attacked the idealism of both the Lu-Wang school and Ch'an Buddhism and
> further developed the rationalist and objectivist aspect of the Chu Hsi school.
> Through this he opened the road which led to the rationalist thought of the
> modern world.[60]

Even so brief and selective a survey of the scholarly literature
would seem to indicate that when non-Marxist Chinese historians have
chosen to probe Ming intellectual history from the perspective of the Ch'ing
period, the aspect of the Ming intellectual debate that has assumed the
clearest importance has been the issue of priorities in intellectual and personal cultivation, and particularly the role of textual scholarship. This is
evident in the work of Yü Ying-shih, which, as he indicated, was prompted
by the recognition that there was a greater degree of continuity between
Ming and Ch'ing styles of learning than had been allowed in the older
tradition of scholarship associated with Liang Ch'i-ch'ao (1873–1929) and
Hu Shih (1891–1962). Whereas both Liang and Hu presented the movement culminating in the evidential research of the Ch'ing period as a reaction against the speculative quality of Ming thought,[61] Professor Yü, in
the interests of historical accuracy, selected for scrutiny precisely those aspects of Ming thought which can be shown to have prefigured or prepared

---

[59] Abe Yoshio, "Influence of Lo Ch'in-shun's *K'un-chih chi* in the Early Edo Period
and the State of Practical Learning among the Students of Kinoshita Jun'an and Yamazaki
Ansai," pp. 3–4.

[60] Abe, *Nihon Shushigaku to Chōsen,* p. 503.

[61] Liang Ch'i-ch'ao, *Ch'ing-tai hsüeh-shu kai-lun,* p. 20. See Immanuel C. Y. Hsü,
trans., *Intellectual Trends in the Ch'ing Period,* p. 45. Hu Shih, "The Scientific Spirit and
Method in Chinese Philosophy," in Charles A. Moore, ed., *The Chinese Mind,* p. 128.

the way for Ch'ing developments. Sensitive to the historiographical problems that arose because the continuities between Sung and Ming thought and Ch'ing scholarship had been so consistently neglected, Professor Yü brought to bear a more careful and probing approach in order to get at the "inner logic" of intellectual developments. In general, it seems fair to say that outworn and inaccurate assumptions about the quality of Ming intellectual life were revised and corrected through his work, while a similar retrospective context was preserved.

Nor need one go far to discover why it should be that problems in Ming intellectual history have often been approached with the particular concerns of the Ch'ing period in mind. From the vantage point of the intellectual historian concerned with the problem of modernization, the signs of modernity in seventeenth-century China have frequently been sought in the origins of Han learning *(Han-hsüeh),* with its orientation toward textual problems, its insistence on a particular kind of scholarly rigor, and its impatience with the apparent remoteness of "abstract" philosophy. The dedication of Ku Yen-wu (1613–1682) and his successors to classical study involved above all a commitment to intellectual or scholarly method. (The fact that Ku's expressed admiration for Lo Ch'in-shun took the form of an appreciation of the latter's scholarly integrity and his absolute insistence on scrupulous accuracy in the use of texts rather than of any more innovative philosophical role may itself be suggestive.)[62]

Many of the major Ch'ing thinkers, including Wang Fu-chih (1619–1692) in the seventeenth century and Tai Chen in the eighteenth century, also espoused a philosophy of *ch'i,*[63] and it may well be argued that the philosophy of *ch'i* was a necessary concomitant of, if not a precondition for, the new style of evidential research in the Ch'ing. But whereas the

[62] Ku commented appreciatively on Lo's scholarship and quoted in extenso from Lo's letter of 1520 to Wang Yang-ming in his own essay, "Chu Tzu wan-nien ting-lun" (Chu Hsi's Final Conclusions Arrived at Late in Life), a critique of Wang's essay of the same title. In *Jih-chih lu* (Record of Daily Knowledge), 6:116–21.

[63] On Wang Fu-chih, see Ian McMorran, "Wang Fu-chih and the Neo-Confucian Tradition," in Wm. Theodore de Bary, ed., *The Unfolding of Neo-Confucianism,* pp. 413–67. See also Chung-ying Cheng, "Reason, Substance, and Human Desires in Seventeenth-Century Neo-Confucianism," in *The Unfolding of Neo-Confucianism,* especially pp. 473–85. On Tai Chen, see Chung-ying Cheng, *Tai Chen's Inquiry Into Goodness,* Introduction, especially pp. 17–22.

philosophy of *ch'i* was no doubt one of the underlying themes of Ch'ing thought, and clearly a concern of several of the most prominent Ch'ing thinkers, it appears not to have been the active focus of interest and debate throughout most of the period.[64] The explicit focus of debate was rather on problems of method or style, as indicated by the scholarly concerns of Ku Yen-wu and his successors as well as by the resistance registered by such thinkers as Yen Yüan (1635–1704) and Li Kung (1659–1733), whose rejection of academic formalism involved a reaction against the intellectualism of both the Sung learning and the newer Han learning, particularly as expressed in the textual orientation which they shared in common.[65]

Important as the problem of intellectual method or style was as a focus of concern in China from the mid-seventeenth century onward, a very different set of problems confronted the Japanese of the same period. One of the notable philosophical developments in Japan at this time, associated, as the work of Abe Yoshio demonstrated, with such figures as Hayashi Razan, Andō Seian, and Kaibara Ekken, was toward a philosophy increasingly oriented toward empirical observation of the natural world. This was a trend which ran directly counter to the philosophical tendencies associated with the Buddhism of the Kamakura and Muromachi periods. As we have seen, all three of those mentioned, along with Itō Jinsai and his son, Itō Tōgai (1670–1736), are known to have read the *K'un-chih chi,* and in the case of Razan and Ekken particularly, the influence of the *K'un-chih chi* is clear.[66] Since the *K'un-chih chi* was one of a number of Ming works that fell on fertile soil in Japan, it is understandable that Japanese historians might regard the philosophy of Lo Ch'in-shun as one of the influences which contributed to a new current in modern thought. Even in a scholarly framework in which the intellectual developments of the Tokugawa period are not the explicit focus of discussion, awareness of such conceptual possibilities may have had a significant role in determining the kinds of questions

---

[64] It is interesting to note that Liang Ch'i-ch'ao in his *Ch'ing-tai hsüeh-shu kai-lun* never discussed the philosophy of *ch'i* either as a Ming development or as a trend in Ch'ing thought. This is not even mentioned in his account of the philosophy of Tai Chen. See Immanuel C. Y. Hsü, trans., *Intellectual Trends of the Ch'ing Period,* pp. 54–62.

[65] This is especially apparent in Yen's *Ts'un-hsüeh pien.* See Mansfield Freeman, trans., *Preservation of Learning.*

[66] Abe, *Nihon Shushigaku to Chōsen,* pp. 520–24.

that have been posed and the way in which issues in intellectual history have been defined.

What is suggested here is that the retrospective context characteristic of non-Marxist Chinese scholarship has often been such as to encourage the study of Ming philosophical developments from the standpoint of Ch'ing thought and to emphasize those issues which continued to be important in the Ch'ing context. Recent Japanese scholarship has been informed by an alternative sense of the conceptual possibilities of those same Ming developments. This sense appears to have derived from the interest of Japanese interpreters in the way those same philosophical currents came to be played out in Tokugawa Japan. This difference in perspective is pointed out not in an attempt to simplify the historiographical problem but rather to illustrate its ample complexity and to suggest how fruitful, or even essential, a comparative approach may be. Because it was influential not only in China but in Japan and Korea, a text like the *K'un-chih chi* presents a promising field for scholars concerned with the problem of the role of ideas in history. A study of its influence offers the intriguing possibility of exploring the potential of ideas as against their actual evolution in a given historical context.

One final interpretive strand, noted earlier but not yet followed up, is that of Marxist analyses which concentrate on understanding the various Neo-Confucian philosophies of *ch'i* as representing a kind of indigenous materialist ancestry. This in turn raises the equally challenging problem of the placement of a sixteenth-century philosophy of *ch'i* in the family of ontologies known in the West as "materialism" and of its bearing, if any, on Marxian "dialectical materialism" in its modern Chinese variant. Here it may be noted that, on either side of a noticeable gap corresponding to the years of the Cultural Revolution, a number of interesting histories of Chinese philosophy have been published by scholars in the People's Republic of China. These histories are characterized by a generally similar overall framework with considerable variation in the more detailed philosophical analysis.

The broad trend in the treatment of Neo-Confucianism in these Marxist histories of Chinese thought has been to depict its history as a sustained clash between idealism (*wei-hsin-chu-i*) and materialism (*wei-wu-chu-i*). Idealism has been understood to have two forms: the subjective idealism of the Buddhists and the school of Lu Hsiang-shan and Wang Yang-ming and the objective idealism of the Ch'eng-Chu School. Contraposed against both of these strains of idealist thought is the materialism of (among others) Chang Tsai, Wang An-shih, Ch'en Liang, Lo Ch'in-shun, Wang T'ing-hsiang, and Wang Fu-chih. Chinese materialist thought has been seen, dialectically, to have progressed through a series of viewpoints on reality which represent ever closer approximations to truth.

Lo Ch'in-shun, according to the history edited by Ren Jiyu, was,

> with Wang T'ing-hsiang, one of the progressive elements in the landlord class of the mid-Ming and was involved in contradictions with the big bureaucratic class of the time. His philosophy was essentially opposed to the subjective idealism of Wang Yang-ming, and he was even more thoroughgoing than previous materialists in his criticisms of the idealistic philosophy of the Buddhists. At the same time that he opposed the subjective idealism of Lu and Wang and the Buddhists, he advanced a powerful critique of the objective idealism of Ch'eng and Chu. The learning of Lo Ch'in-shun opened the way for the theories of the later materialist, Wang Fu-chih.[67]

This materialism, which has generally been regarded as "naive materialism" (*p'u-su wei-wu-chu-i*) as distinguished from dialectical materialism (*pien-cheng wei-wu-chu-i*), was considered by Professor Ren and his associates to have approached dialectical materialism at certain points, while at others it faltered under an ideological load from which it suffered owing to Lo's compulsion to uphold feudal morality.

Lo is regarded by Marxist scholars to have contributed significantly to the development of materialism through his ontological monism of *ch'i*, his view of *ch'i* as the source and basis of all phenomenal reality, his concept of the relation between *li* and *ch'i* and between *tao* and concrete things (*ch'i*), and especially his recasting of the formula of "the unity of principle; the diversity of its particularizations" (*li-i fen-shu*). Both Professor Ren's group and the scholars of Chinese philosophy of the Department of Philosophy, Beijing University, saw the original doctrine of *li-i fen-shu* as the objective idealist proposition put forward by the Ch'eng-Chu school of the Sung to counter the subjective idealism of Hua-yen and Ch'an Buddhism. The intent of Ch'eng and Chu, as they understood it, was to establish that all things were manifestations of *li*, or of the Great Ultimate, *t'ai-*

---

[67]Ren Jiyu, ed., *Chung-kuo che-hsüeh shih* (A History of Chinese Philosophy), 3:313.

chi, and that only in sharing in *t'ai-chi* did all things assume their own form. In contrast to the Ch'eng-Chu school, which regarded *li* as the primary reality, Lo recognized *ch'i* as the primary reality. And whereas Ch'eng and Chu had tried to explain the ultimate unity of all being through the lofty and transcendent spiritual reality of *t'ai-chi,* Lo had been able to show that this concept of *li* was empty. *Li* were only the *li* of *ch'i,* and the universal significance of laws could only be revealed in their capacity to unify discrete phenomena.

In his interpretation of *li-i fen-shu* in *K'un-chih chi,* Part I, sec. 14, Lo had, in the judgment of Professor Ren's group, "already come into contact with the dialectical relationship between the particular and the general."[68] The philosophers of Beijing University did not credit Lo with having achieved quite this much, but they agreed that he "revised the theory of *li-i fen-shu,* making it an essential component of his materialist system." This he accomplished "by first bringing the supremely lofty and transcendent concept of principle *(t'ai-chi)* of Ch'eng and Chu into the status of immanence and restoring it once again to the material world, making it only the *li* of *ch'i,* while still explaining this in terms of the proposition *li-i fen-shu.*"[69] Sun Shu-p'ing was more guarded, observing that one understanding of the "diverse particularizations" of principle is that "each thing has its own distinct law, but that they also have general laws which apply to all in common." This, he held, is correct. "But the general laws which apply to all in common do not originate in the 'oneness of principle,' but in the unity of the material *(wu-chih ti t'ung-i).* The unity of the world lies in its materiality, and not in the fact that it is unified by a world-transcending 'principle.' "[70] Having evidently believed that Lo Ch'in-shun was ambivalent on this point, Professor Sun considered it necessary to express this important reservation.

There has been agreement among the Chinese Marxist scholars that, while having developed a coherent ontological monism of *ch'i,* Lo

[68] *Ibid.,* p. 314.

[69] Beijing Ta-hsüeh, Che-hsüeh hsi, Chung-kuo che-hsüeh shih chiao-yen shih (Beijing University, Department of Philosophy, Research Center on the History of Chinese Philosophy) comp., *Chung-kuo che-hsüeh shih,* (A History of Chinese Philosophy), 2:130–31. (This work is hereafter abbreviated as Beijing University, *Chung-kuo che-hsüeh shih.*)

[70] Sun Shu-p'ing, *Chung-kuo che-hsüeh shih-kao* (Essays in the History of Chinese Philosophy), 2:238.

relinquished his hold on consistency in defending the idea of an innate human nature (hsien-t'ien hsing) and an innate morality (hsien-t'ien tao-te). By "innate human nature" they refer to the view, shared by all Neo-Confucians, that there is a constant human nature (prior to and independent of what in Marxist terms is called "class nature" or "social nature") which explains certain constant tendencies in human behavior. By "innate morality" they refer to a common Neo-Confucian belief, which can be traced back to Mencius, that there is a human disposition to goodness which is an observable part of this nature. Lo Ch'in-shun's denial of a valid distinction between the "nature endowed by heaven" (t'ien-ming chih hsing) and a physical nature (ch'i-chih chih hsing) has been endorsed, as has his refusal to accept a distinction between the Principle of Nature (t'ien-li) and human desires (jen-yü). These moves have been seen by the Chinese Marxist scholars as having been in conformity with a monism of ch'i and have been acknowledged as having anticipated the views of Wang Fu-chih and Tai Chen. However, the fact that Lo continued to subscribe to Ch'eng I's view that "human nature is principle" (hsing chi li) has been interpreted as a retreat into objective idealism in the manner of both Ch'eng I and Chu Hsi.

Ren Jiyu and his group found in Lo's various statements concerning human nature a theory based on the following points:

> First, feudal ethical morality is the heavenly nature (t'ien-hsing) of man, and it is also the principle of nature (t'ien-li). Second, "the nature" is the vital principle of man and the ultimate source of life. Third, "the nature" is the original substance, while the activity of consciousness is a function or manifestation of the nature. Fourth, human nature is innate, as are the moral laws which human nature possesses, whereas knowledge and consciousness are acquired.[71]

On the basis of this conception, Lo opposed Wang Yang-ming's theory of innate good knowing (liang-chih) not on the ground that it involved an invalid notion of innate morality—which would have been the appropriate line of criticism had he been consistent in his materialism—but on the ground that Wang confused the nature and consciousness, substance and function. Lo was prevented from faulting Wang's subjective idealism on the basis of a rigorous materialism because:

---

[71] Ren Jiyu, ed., Chung-kuo che-hsüeh shih, pp. 323–24.

Given his class standpoint, he did not and could not hold a different ethical view from the one put forward by the like of Ch'eng and Chu. Thus his view of human nature was consonant with that of Ch'eng and Chu, and this is the point of internal contradiction in Lo's philosophical system.[72]

The philosophers of Beijing University went further here, taking the position that in his view of human nature, Lo Ch'in-shun "not only returned to the *tao-hsüeh* of the Sung but to Confucius and Mencius. In harkening back to the idea of "humaneness being man's mind" and "the Principle of Nature being endowed by heaven in human beings," Lo was "at one with his predecessors in taking feudal moral principles to be the Principle of Nature and the feudal order to be an order established by nature. His criticism of *hsin-hsüeh* (the learning of the mind) involved nothing more than opposing subjective idealism on the basis of objective idealism."[73]

Here is yet another quite distinct scholarly perspective on Lo Ch'in-shun and the *K'un-chih chi*. Yü Ying-shih's concern with the problem of subjectivity and objectivity as it bears on scholarly method and intellectual style finds no echo here, though "subjective" and "objective" remain the operative terms. The similarities between Lo and Wang Yang-ming discussed by Yamashita Ryūji, notably their sharing in a philosophy of *ch'i*, also do not figure into the analysis. Lo is seen as having broken with the Ch'eng-Chu school in his materialist ontology but having been drawn back into objective idealism and into the vortex of feudal morality owing to his view of human nature. In this perspective, which is both dialectical and teleological, the movement is from an historical stage when only "naive materialism" could pertain, and when contradictions abounded, toward a stage in the Chinese future when dialectical materialism would assume its proper role. Once again it is clear that the retrospective context which these scholars established at the outset conditions not only their judgments of Lo's philosophy but their perception of which aspects of his thought are most significant. And again, there figures in the background of the Marxist discussions yet another conception of modernity.

---

[72] *Ibid.*, p. 324.

[73] Beijing University, *Chung-kuo che-hsüeh shih*, pp. 239–40.

The Possibilities of Neo-Confucian Thought

The *K'un-chih chi* has been seen by some of its interpreters as
having contained the seeds of an empiricism, by others as having pointed
the way toward materialism. However these possibilities are evaluated, it
should be evident that, if they did, in fact, exist within "orthodoxy" itself,
Neo-Confucianism cannot be broadly characterized as either remote from
or inimical to the trends of modernity. The notion that Neo-Confucian
"orthodoxy" was destined by its supposed rigidity, preoccupation with the
past, or narrowly ethical orientation, to be resistant to any very profound
philosophical change or development is one of remarkable tenacity but the
most doubtful validity.

Viewed from a modern Western perspective, the empiricism of
the *K'un-chih chi* may be viewed as a rather tentative enterprise. The signs
of it are found in Lo's insistence that the "investigation of things" must in
the first instance be directed toward actual events and things in the objective world, that knowing things in their concrete particularity must precede
grasping their unifying principle, and that sense experience must be recognized as the primary mode of attaining knowledge of the world. There is
little evidence of any sustained interest on Lo's part in the development of
a critical method. Though his emphasis in *K'un-chih chi*, Part I, sec. 7 and
Part 3, sec. 1 on the importance of verification of knowledge might be
construed as implying an awareness of the limiting conditions of generalize-
ability, there is at most the hint of an interest in critical method per se.
Lo's actual concern was apparently more with the need for an encompassing
view which would omit from consideration nothing in the human or natural
sphere so that their relatedness could ultimately be comprehended.

However, it must also be remembered that the *K'un-chih chi* was
written a century before Francis Bacon's *Novum Organum* appeared in the
West. Perhaps more noteworthy than the fact that its empiricism is not
fully elaborated is the fact that a Chinese work of the early sixteenth century should have gone as far as it did in this direction. On the one hand,
Lo was, in his epistemology, making a critical break with the Sung Neo-
Confucians, or, at least, with those who had reservations about the significance of sense experience. On the other, he professed to be, and no doubt
was, returning to a taproot which went very deep in the Chinese intellec-

tual tradition. In all likelihood it was the sense of returning to something fundamental in the Chinese tradition that finally gave him such assurance and conviction after many years of questioning and uncertainty.

In recent years the longstanding Western view of Chinese culture as static or stagnant—what Joseph Needham has dismissed as "a typical occidental misconception"[74]—has been substantially modified. But, despite some cogent argument to the contrary, the notion has persisted among historians in the West, and, more recently among Chinese historians as well, that an element strikingly apparent in Western thought but absent from Chinese thought is the idea of progress. This supposed deficiency is commonly thought to be the result of the stifling effects of Ch'eng-Chu Neo-Confucianism. If the classics represented for Confucians a secure repository of all significant wisdom, such that new knowledge was superfluous, the notion of progress—which in some sense represents the background for all empirical inquiry—would be implausible. Likewise, if Ch'eng-Chu Neo-Confucianism were so narrowly moral in its vision and didactic in its temper that the task of "investigating things" could not be construed in extra-moral terms, the minimum conditions for scientific inquiry could never be satisfied. Such a line of thought is not without its problems, however, for it tends to misrepresent both Chinese and Western realities.

First, it has been long since remarked by J. B. Bury that the idea of progress was a rather late idea even in the West, probably emerging only around the time of Francis Bacon in the seventeenth century.[75] Second, according to Anthony Quinton, the idea of progress was, with Bacon, quite specifically associated with another idea, then quite new—that knowledge was cumulative. Another aspect of Bacon's view, and apparently a crucial element in his motivation, was the idea that knowledge had a particular sort of moral and practical utility. As Quinton observed in his study of Bacon's thought,

> Bacon is the most confident, explicit, and influential of the first exponents of the idea of progress. J. B. Bury, the historian of that idea, could find only slight and soon obliterated traces of the belief in progress before Bacon: a momentary scintillation in Democritus that was not perceived by his Epicurean successors, a rather stronger hint in Bacon's medieval namesake, Roger.

[74] Joseph Needham, "Time and Eastern Man," in *The Grand Titration*, p. 284.

[75] J. B. Bury, *The Idea of Progress: An Inquiry into Its Origin and Growth*.

Bacon's progressivism is the outcome of two strains in his thought. The first of these is his more or less unprecedented notion of knowledge as cumulative. The second is his insistence that knowledge is for practical use, specifically for "the relief of man's estate."[76]

Joseph Needham has argued that the notion of knowledge as cumulative was a persistent idea in China over the course of many centuries. "In fact it would seem that the idea of cumulative disinterested co-operative enterprise in amassing scientific information was much more customary in medieval China than anywhere in the pre-Renaissance West."[77] Likewise Needham has contended that the "theme of empiricism was extremely strong in the Chinese tradition" and that the "investigation of things" (*ko-wu*) "was the watchword of Chinese naturalists and scientific thinkers all through the ages."[78]

It was also, of course, carried over from the *Great Learning* and kept at the heart of Ch'eng-Chu philosophy. If it is valid to interpret Ch'eng-Chu "orthodoxy" as having been concerned not with "received doctrines" but with a living tradition, and as having centered around the idea of "investigating things," it must also be clear that the understanding of knowledge as cumulative was basic to it. Certainly it was the sense of knowledge as cumulative that inspired Lo's conception of orthodoxy, motivated his scholarship, and sustained him in his *k'un*, or painful exertions in knowing. Likewise, if it is accepted that a moral concern for "the relief of man's estate" was an important element in the thought of Bacon and his successors, it may be questioned whether a comparable concern, which is apparent both in Lo's own reflections on law, government administration, society, and the economy, and in the medical and botanical studies of his successors in Tokugawa Japan, should in itself have prejudiced the empirical character of their inquiries.

In one important respect—his emphasis on the centrality of sense experience—Lo stands in a position in China not unlike that of Bacon in the early modern West, though an important qualification would be that Lo regarded himself as returning to an earlier tradition rather than as strik-

[76] Anthony Quinton, *Francis Bacon*, pp. 29–30.

[77] Joseph Needham, "Time and Eastern Man," in *The Grand Titration*, pp. 280–81.

[78] *Ibid.*, p. 282.

ing out in a new direction. In another respect—the concern with critical method—the differences between them seem more striking than the similarities. Of all Bacon's contributions, perhaps the most forward-looking was his development in the *Novum Organum* of the method of "eliminative induction," as expressed in his famous remark: *major est vis instantiae negativae* ("in establishing any true axiom the negative example is the more powerful"). There is, as has already been suggested, no real parallel to this in the *K'un-chih chi*.

More fundamental, however, may be the fact that unlike William of Ockham in the fourteenth century or Francis Bacon in the seventeenth century, neither Lo Ch'in-shun nor his Neo-Confucian successors were prompted to make a distinction between the study of nature and the study of the supernatural or divine. Neither did they advance the view that certain questions come solely within the domain of faith and others entirely within the province of reason. As Anthony Quinton has remarked of the history of Western empiricism, Bacon's classification of the sciences around this distinction in the *Advancement of Learning* and the *De Augmentis* marked a "clearly proclaimed diversion of interest from the divine to the natural" and represented a crucial move toward "a new conception of true, basic, paradigmatic knowledge."[79] But a distinction between the divine and the natural or between faith and reason has scarcely any analogue in the history of Chinese thought and certainly had no purchase in the early sixteenth century. For Ming Neo-Confucians, no matter what their position in the debates over ontological and epistemological issues, the human world and the world of nature remained fully integrated and coherent. Their primary concern was ultimately the moral one of preserving and perfecting within the human sphere the same order and harmony that they believed existed reliably in the universe as a whole.

It could conceivably be argued that the Neo-Confucians, who in this sense experienced fewer tensions, at least of the intellectual and spiritual sort (and none whatever between the claims of faith and the dictates of reason), did not share the motive that impelled their Western counterparts to delimit the sphere of their inquiries. Thus they may have been working within so vast and unstructured an intellectual framework that it was less likely that it should have occurred to them that empirical studies

[79] Anthony Quinton, *Francis Bacon*, p. 30.

of nature might require a distinct critical method. This latter view came, of course, to be more and more commonly held in the West as a concomitant, if not as a fundamental motif, of its increasing secularization. Still, if it was a limitation of Ch'eng-Chu Neo-Confucianism that its sixteenth- and seventeenth-century adherents felt no need to advance their empirical studies by strictly defining both their scope and their method, this fact speaks more for the openness of their world view than for any dogmatic narrowing of it.

The question of materialism and the *K'un-chih chi* is somewhat more problematical in that, unlike "empiricism," "materialism" is subject to such a wide variety of interpretations. Most non-Marxist historians of Neo-Confucian thought have preferred to avoid the language of "materialism" and "idealism" in describing the intellectual debates of the Sung and Ming periods, believing that the major issues in Neo-Confucian thought are not susceptible to cogent analysis in these terms. Chinese Marxist historians have seen "naive materialism" as a prelude to dialectical materialism, though, as the term "naive materialism" suggests, they have recognized significant differences between the earlier and later forms. Yamanoi Yū in a contribution to *Ki no shisō* (The Thought of *Ch'i*), does maintain that the philosophy of *ch'i* which began to evolve with Lo Ch'in-shun and Wang T'ing-hsiang in the mid-sixteenth century was materialism *(yuibutsuron)*, though he makes a strong case that Wang Yang-ming's thought cannot correspondingly be described as idealism.[80]

Whether the term "materialism" is to be used to describe the philosophy of *ch'i* found in the *K'un-chih chi* depends, obviously, on the definition of the term. In a recent study of issues in contemporary materialist philosophy, Mario Bunge has offered the following, broad definition of materialism:

> Materialism is a family of ontologies, or extremely general doctrines about the world. What all the members of that family have in common is the thesis that everything that exists really is material—or, stated negatively, that immaterial objects such as ideas have no existence independent of material things such as brains. Aside from this common core materialist ontologies may differ

[80]Onozawa Seiichi, Fukunaga Mitsuji, and Yamanoi Yū, eds., *Ki no shisō*, pp. 367–68.

widely. It is only by adding further requirements that a definite materialist ontology will be individuated or built.[81]

Bunge differentiated six distinct stages in the evolution of materialist thought. The first is ancient materialism, a thoroughly mechanistic view centering around Greek and Indian atomism and associated in the West with Democritus, Epicurus, and Lucretius.[82] The second is the revival of atomism during the seventeenth century in the work of Gassendi and Hobbes. The third is eighteenth-century materialism, a more varied phenomenon, represented by Helvétius, d'Holbach, Diderot, La Mettrie, and Canabis. The fourth is nineteenth-century "scientific materialism," a concomitant of the developments in biology and chemistry linked to the names of scientists such as Vogt, Moleschott, Czolbe, Tyndall, Huxley, and Darwin. The fifth is the "dialectical materialism" formulated by Marx, Engels, and Lenin. The sixth is a congeries of materialisms found in the work of an otherwise heterogeneous group of contemporary philosophers which includes O. Neurath, W. V. O. Quine, J. J. C. Smart, Samuel Alexander, and Roy Wood Sellars.[83]

If, given the latitude of such a definition, and pending the further requirements which it allows, a Neo-Confucian philosophy of ch'i is recognized as a form of materialism, it will certainly be found to be different from any of the forms mentioned above, not least from dialectical materialism. In addition to the differences brought out by Chinese Marxist scholars in their presentations of "naive materialism" and their assessments of it in relation to dialectical materialism, an historical perspective makes clear that Neo-Confucian philosophies of ch'i represented another legacy and responded to altogether different problems and questions.

Marx's central insight about the primacy of the structure of practical human social relations as the sole locus for the adequate explanation of human consciousness was, as one scholar has observed, essentially a legacy of the Enlightenment:

It was an insight developed in dialogue with idealist philosophers and theologians who seemed to be suggesting that consciousness was the motor of

[81] Mario Bunge, *Scientific Materialism*, p. 17.

[82] One might go on to specify the Cārvāka tradition in India.

[83] Mario Bunge, *Scientific Materialism*, pp. ix–x.

social and natural reality. In his time Marx had to fight for the contrary view against people who thought of practical affairs as in some ways secondary or vulgar. The concept of the primacy of practical, social conditions in society and its determinacy in explaining human thinking and action, was for Marx what Paul Tillich called a *Kampfbegriff*, a polemical concept born in argument, debate, and controversy.[84]

As a *Kampfbegriff*, formulated above all as a response to Hegelian idealism, Marx's materialism was defined in opposition to Hegel's theistic religious view which regarded the world as created by an extra-mundane deity, as subject to miraculous intervention by God or Absolute Spirit, and as mind-dependent. Against such a view, Marx contraposed his atheism, his idea of an eternally existing world governed by natural law, and his belief in the primacy of being or nature as opposed to thought or spirit. Reacting to Hegel's idea of thinking as an activity of the soul, Marx contended that thinking was inseparable from matter. Against the Hegelian notion of innate knowledge, and indeed against any notion of a priori knowledge, Marx insisted on sense perception as the basis of science.[85]

Although Chinese Marxist scholars have been inclined to see Neo-Confucian materialism as a corresponding reaction against the "idealism" of the Buddhists and the subjective and objective "idealism" of Neo-Confucians who had fallen to one degree or another under Buddhist influence, it is quite clear that Neo-Confucian thinkers did not confront a conceptual world divided up after the manner of the nineteenth-century West. Without any remotely comparable theism, atheism would hardly have been a meaningful position. And, though the ontological status of "natural laws"— or principles—might be debated, there was no reason for Neo-Confucians to debate the notion of a universe governed by natural laws, something that in their rationalism they had always taken for granted. Hegel's idea of the world as mind-dependent, while bearing some superficial resemblance to Buddhist views of mind, was actually based on a conception of a profound dichotomy between mental and physical reality (or between thinking and

---

[84]Richard Kilminster, "Theory and Practice in Marx and Marxism," in G. H. R. Parkinson, ed., *Marx and Marxisms*, pp. 161–62.

[85]For a cogent analysis of Marx's relation to Hegel, see Allen Wood, *Karl Marx*, especially chs. 13–14.

matter) that neither Buddhists nor adherents of Wang Yang-ming's style of "learning of the mind" would have recognized.

Nor would a dichotomy of being or nature as against thought or spirit have been any more intelligible to Wang Yang-ming than to Lo Ch'in-shun. On the contrary, Wang's view was that the mind was principle, that *liang-chih*, or innate good knowing, was the Principle of Nature, and that the extension of *liang-chih* was the activity which created the goodness and wholeness of the world. That thought should have been contrasted with being would have been thoroughly at odds with Wang's view that the actual human mind (never set apart from either the physical body or a distinct soul) *is* both material force and principle. Lo's view was that the mind cannot be identified with but rather apprehends the principles or patterns that operate independently in the world of nature. The mind's knowing these principles as objective reality enables the individual to be conscious of the wholeness of nature and to follow the course of goodness.

Thus Lo's view that the nature is principle, and that the human mind is the conscious agent whereby principle can be known, was opposed to Wang's, not over the issue of which is ontologically prior—nature or consciousness—but over the issue of whether or not all significant knowledge is innate. If the mind *is* principle, then all knowing involves the projection outward of a potentially perfect goodness which already exists within the individual person and needs only to be fully expressed in his actions. If the mind *knows* principles which exist as a pattern of operation in the world of external reality, then the individual must interact with the world of things over time, investigating their relationships and processes of development in a variety of ways, before principle can be reliably apprehended.

Wang's reservations about Chu Hsi's philosophical system stemmed from a sense that its scope was too daunting and Chu's method of "investigating things" too likely to lead to "fragmentation." One had, Wang thought, to focus on the interior dimensions of personal cultivation and on the most immediate demands of moral action in order to achieve a necessary integration and focus in one's life. Lo's contention was that, in pursuing this line, Wang was not taking account of reality as a whole, of the entire setting in which human endeavors were carried on, but rather limiting himself to a particular, and quite limited, conception of morality. But if this was what was at the heart of the argument between Wang and Lo, the intellectual debate of the early sixteenth century cannot be adequately characterized as a struggle between idealism and materialism. Wang too had adopted a philosophy of *ch'i* in the sense that the ontological support for the potency of *liang-chih* and the "clear intelligence" of the human mind was, for him, the fact that "all things share the same material force" or that "all things are permeated with one material force."[86] Given this disposition, Wang, like Lo, could hardly have been more actively concerned with the immediacies of practical affairs and practical social conditions. Even allowing for idealisms, as for materialisms, Wang was not an "idealist" in the sense that this term is commonly used in Western philosophical parlance.

Both Wang and Lo were attempting to resolve certain philosophical problems which they thought had existed for Buddhists and for most Sung Neo-Confucians. Both eliminated such dualisms as they perceived attaching to the categories of *li* and *ch'i*, the mind and the nature, and the original nature and the physical nature. Both attempted to see more clearly than their Sung predecessors had done the relation between knowledge and morality or between truth and goodness. This they did in distinctly different ways, Wang by making the individual's capacity for innate good knowing a truth of human existence, and Lo by making the endeavor to know the true nature of things the condition for moral goodness.

Lo Ch'in-shun's materialism may be seen in his focus on the ultimate reality of *ch'i* and on the importance of knowing things in their concrete particularity. Whether or not one finds any premonition of a dialectical perspective in his typically Neo-Confucian conception of the natural process as bound up with the mutual interaction between yin and yang and their cyclical pattern of action and response, his view is certainly not a teleological one. Nor is it one in which conflicts of historical forces have any place, or in which the relation between knowledge and morality becomes in any sense problematical, as some have seen it to be in orthodox Marxism.[87]

The world of thought of the sixteenth-century Neo-Confucians

[86] Yamanoi Yū documents this point persuasively in Onozawa Seiichi, Fukunaga Mitsuji, and Yamanoi Yū, eds., *Ki no shisō*, p. 367.

[87] Extremely interesting analyses of the problem of the place of morality in Marxism have been undertaken by Allen Wood in *Karl Marx*, Part Three ("Marxism and Morality") and by Steven Lukes in "Marxism, Morality, and Justice" in G. H. R. Parkinson, ed., *Marx and Marxisms*, pp. 177–206.

was still whole, and failure to perceive the unity of all nature or the continuity of knowledge and morality was seen by a would-be monist like Lo Ch'in-shun as a form of misrepresentation, a kind of conceptual injury to the oneness of things, which, through his philosophy of *ch'i,* he was at pains to repair. Given that this philosophy, both in its empiricism and its materialism, remained not only consistent with but conducive to a genuine spirituality, it is even possible that we may find in it something of value for our own efforts to relieve the pains of modernity through reinterpreting—or recognizing—the relation between knowledge and morality.

K'un-chih chi, Part I

1. The teaching of Confucius was entirely devoted to the matter of preserving the mind and nourishing the nature. Though he never clarified this, it was clarified by Mencius.[1] Mind is the spiritual intelligence of man. The nature is his vital principle. The place where principle resides is called the mind. That which the mind possesses is called the nature. The two must not be confused and considered as one.

It says in the "Counsels of the Great Yü": "The human mind (jen-hsin) is insecure; the mind of Tao (Tao-hsin) is subtle."[2] It says in the Analects, ". . . I could follow what my mind desired without transgressing the bounds of decorum."[3] It also says, "For three months there would be nothing in his mind contrary to humaneness."[4] Mencius said, "The nature of the superior man is that which humaneness, rightness, decorum, and wisdom have planted in his mind."[5]

This is the distinction between the mind and the nature. The two are always inseparable, yet they should not be confused. If one refines his understanding again and again, he will perceive them as they really are. If one mistakes the mind for the nature, it will truly be a case of an infinitesimal mistake in the beginning leading to an infinite error at the end.[6]

2. The "Appended Remarks" ("Hsi-tz'u") says, "Neither far nor near, neither dark nor deep exist, and thus one knows the things of the future. Were

---

[1] Mencius, 7A:1:1–2: "By fully developing one's mind, one knows one's nature. Knowing his nature, he knows heaven (or nature). Preserving one's mind (ts'un ch'i hsin) and nourishing one's nature (yung ch'i hsing) are the way to serve heaven.

[2] Book of History, "Counsels of the Great Yü." Cf. translation by James Legge, Shoo King, The Chinese Classics, 3:61.

[3] Analects, 2:4:6, describing the mental state of Confucius at seventy.

[4] Analects, 6:5, referring to Yen Hui (521–490 B.C.) or Yen Yüan, the disciple for whom Confucius reserved his deepest respect and affection.

[5] Mencius, 7A:21:4.

[6] Alludes to the I-wei t'ung-kua yen (Apocryphal Treatise on the Book of Changes: On Understanding the Verification of the Divination), A:5b.

it not for the most perfect (chih-ching) of all things in the world, how could this be done?"[7] "Through penetrating the transformations, the patterns of heaven and earth are completed, and as they become ever more inclusive, the images of the world are fixed. Were it not for the most changing (chih-pien) of all things in the world, how could this be done?"[8] "When it is quiescent, it does not move; when it is stimulated, it penetrates all phenomena in the world. Were it not for the most spiritual (chih-shen) of all things in the world, how could this be done?"[9] "The changes are the means by which the sage reaches the depths and studies the subtle activating forces [of all things]."[10]

The fact that the way of the changes should be thus is the Way of nature (or heaven, t'ien). Could it be otherwise in man? Thus the thing that is "most perfect" is the nature, the thing that is "most changing" is the feelings, and the thing that is "most spiritual" is the mind. What is important in preserving the mind is to "reach its depths" and "study its subtle activating forces," so that one does not neglect the rectitude of the nature and feelings. If one merely has some insight into what is "most spiritual" and immediately supposes the Way to lie in this, without being able to reach its depths or study its subtle activating forces, can he reasonably expect to "penetrate every will in the world" and "complete all the work of the world"?[11]

[7] Book of Changes, "Appended Remarks," 7:14a.

[8] Ibid., 7:14b.

[9] Ibid.

[10] Ibid., 7:15a.

[11] Ibid. The passage in the "Appended Remarks" to which Lo refers speaks of the use of the changes by the sage to "reach the depths and study the subtle, activating forces of all things." "Only through what is deep can one penetrate every will in the world. Only through the subtle, activating forces can one complete all the work of the world." The commentary in the Chou I cheng-i explains: "The sage uses the Way of the changes to reach the depths. The power (or virtue, te) of the sage is deep, and therefore he is able to penetrate every will in the world. This refers to the passage in the preceding text of the classic [i.e., the "Appended Remarks"] which says, 'he carries out his consultation in words and receives the command like an echo,' and thus he can know the things of the future. This is to penetrate every will in the world. There are still only subtle, activating forces, and therefore he can complete all the work of the world. The sage uses the Way of the changes to study the subtle, activating forces, and therefore he is able to know the subtle, activating forces of all affairs."

3. The mind of Tao[12] is quiescent and does not move.[13] Its substance, which is most perfect,[14] cannot be seen. Therefore it is subtle.[15] The human mind,[16] when it is stimulated, penetrates.[17] Its function, which is most changing,[18] cannot be fathomed. Therefore it is insecure.[19]

4. The mind of Tao is the nature. The human mind is the feelings. The mind is one, but one speaks of it as two because of the distinction of activity and tranquillity and the difference of substance and function. When tranquillity controls activity, it is auspicious. When activity results in confusion about returning, it is inauspicious.[20] It is only by means of what is perfect that one probes its subtle activating forces (chi), and it is only through what is unitary[21] that one preserves his sincerity. "Sincerely following the golden mean"[22] is the same as "following the desires of one's mind without transgressing the bounds of decorum,"[23] and this is what the spirit of the sage is able to accomplish.

5. The "clarifying the mind and perceiving the nature" of the Buddhists and the "fully developing the mind and knowing the nature" of Confucians seem similar but are in reality different. For pure intelligence and

[12] Here allusions to the "Counsels of the Great Yü" in the Book of History and to the "Appended Remarks" in the Book of Changes are juxtaposed. "The mind of Tao" alludes to the statement in the "Counsels of the Great Yü" that "the mind of Tao is subtle."

[13] Book of Changes, "Appended Remarks," 7:14b.

[14] Ibid., 7:14a.

[15] Book of History, "Counsels of the Great Yü."

[16] Ibid.

[17] Book of Changes, "Appended Remarks," 7:14b.

[18] Ibid.

[19] Book of History, "Counsels of the Great Yü."

[20] Book of Changes, fu hexagram, 3:12b.

[21] Or undivided (i). Alludes to the Book of History, "Counsels of the Great Yü."

[22] Ibid.

[23] Analects, 2:4:6.

consciousness[24] are the wonder of the mind, while perfect subtlety and absolute unity are the reality of the nature. Generally speaking, the Buddhists have insight into the mind but lack insight into the nature.

Thus in Buddhist teaching the first desideratum is that a person separate himself entirely from forms and seek what they call emptiness. Emptiness is vacuity. Next they want him to integrate both forms and emptiness so as to arrive at what they call enlightenment. Enlightenment is consciousness. When one has become enlightened concerning the nature, emptiness and forms are thoroughly comprehended and the functioning of the spirit is limitless. Spirit is intelligence.[25]

When one investigates thoroughly all that the Buddhists have to say about the nature, there is essentially nothing apart from these three points. Yet these three [the cultivation of emptiness, comprehension of emptiness and forms, and the functioning of spirit] all have to do with the subtle functioning of the mind. What have they to do with the nature? Were the Buddhists to get a firm hold on what they have attained through their insight, and had they the capacity to direct their inquiries to a higher plane,[26] they in turn might know "the moral sense which is bestowed by the Lord."[27] But considering theirs to be the supreme and mysterious Way, they are unaware that there are truths they cannot discover in an entire lifetime. Thus they presume to advance their theories, thereby misleading later generations so that they abandon human relationships and destroy the principle of nature. Can the pernicious influence of this disastrous legacy be expressed in words?

[24] This reference to *hsü-ling chih-chüeh* echoes Chu Hsi's preface to the *Chung-yung chang-chü* (Commentary on the Words and Phrases of the Mean) in *Ssu-shu chang-chü chi-chu* (Collected Commentaries on Words and Phrases of the Four Books), p. 1.

[25] The term *ling* is rich with possible meanings. It may mean intelligence or intelligent and also spirit, spirituality, or spiritual. As "spirit," it may suggest a concept of the soul. Depending on the context, it may also evoke a sense of the marvelous or the supernatural.

[26] The phrase *hsiang-shang*, translated here as "direct their inquiries to a higher plane," is one used by Ch'eng I in *I-shu* (Written Legacy), 1:4a. It is in this sense that Lo uses it. It is worth noting, however, that this is also a Ch'an expression meaning "to seek enlightenment," in which sense it is used, for example, in the *Pi-yen lu* (Blue Cliff Records) (T 2003), *ch.* 1. It is possible that there is a trace of irony in the use of the phrase here.

[27] *Book of History*, "The Announcement of T'ang." See Legge, *Shoo King*, p. 185.

To attack heterodox doctrines and expose heretical views is the traditional role of the Confucian school.[28] There are those who outwardly part company with the Buddhists yet secretly ally themselves with them. On the surface they denounce Buddhism, while in their hearts they follow it. Dazzling and deluding large numbers of men, they style themselves followers of Confucius. But who can believe them?

6. Filling the universe are the myriad things, and man is just one among the myriad things. "The Way of heaven works through change and transformation so that each thing receives its proper nature and destiny."[29] Man is like other living things, and I am like other men. Could there be any difference in respect to our principle? But after physical form is complete, the particularizations of principle are necessarily diverse. Because of the diversity of particularizarions, each has his own body. Because of the unity of principle, "everything is complete in me."[30]

The human mind has pure spirituality as its substance. Originally it is all-encompassing. It is only that it is blinded by the selfishness of egotism and thus it is clear about what is near at hand and vague about what is distant. It perceives what is small but neglects what is great. The fact that one is neglectful and vague always stems from not being sincere. Thus if knowledge is not yet complete, how can one expect the thoughts to be sincere?[31] Therefore the program of the *Great Learning* necessarily begins with the investigation of things as a means of curing blindness. Its instructions concerning the investigation of things resemble the nine items enumerated by Master Ch'eng,[32] any one of which may serve to elucidate

[28] Literally, "the house laws of the lineage of Confucius."

[29] *Book of Changes*, *ch'ien* hexagram, 1:4a.

[30] *Mencius*, 7A:4.

[31] Lo refers to the order set down in the *Great Learning* for the process of cultivation. This is to begin with the investigation of things, which in turn leads to knowledge becoming complete and the thoughts or intentions being made sincere.

[32] For Ch'eng I's "nine items," see Wing-tsit Chan, trans., *Instructions for Practical Living*, p. 162, n. 11. These are actually set forth by Chu Hsi in his *Ta-hsüeh huo-wen* (Questions and Answers on the *Great Learning*), based on sayings of Ch'eng I. As given by Professor Chan, they are: "Namely (1) to read books, discuss doctrines, and elucidate principles, to deliberate on people and events of the past and the present and distinguish their right and

all the rest. "It may be compared to the fact that, while there are thousands of tracks and paths by which one can enter the capital, one can enter if he has found just one way."[33] His idea was that by drawing analogies the rest can be understood inferentially, and in this he was extremely profound. Scholars of today often regard their inability fully to investigate the things of the world as a cause for doubting this. Have they ever spent a single day in earnest effort? They are merely deluding themselves, nothing more.

In such examples as the sigh [of Confucius] by the stream in the *Analects*,[34] "the hawks flying and the fish leaping" in the *Mean*,[35] and the discrimination by Mencius between the nature of a dog, an ox, and a man,[36] there is nothing that is not a "thing." If through careful reflection I can grasp this, is there anything in what is "complete in me" that I cannot fully comprehend?

Again, in the *Mean* it says, "How great is the Way of the sage. Like overflowing water it sends forth and nourishes all things and rises up to the height of heaven. All complete is its greatness! It embraces the three hundred [rules of ceremony] and the three thousand [rules of demeanor]. It waits for the proper man and then it is carried out."[37] Now of the "three hundred" [rules of ceremony] and the three thousand [rules of demeanor], there is none that does not pertain to human affairs, and the Way of the

---

wrong, to handle affairs and to settle them in the proper way, and to investigate a thing one day and another the next day; (2) to investigate the principles in all things, from one's own person to the ten thousand things; (3) not to investigate extensively all the principles in the world nor to investigate intensively the principles of only one thing but to investigate more and more and thus to accumulate; (4) to investigate either the easy or the difficult according to one's capacity; (5) to realize that every thing has its principle and should be investigated; (6) to know that the investigation of the principle of filial piety means to practice it; (7) to realize that every blade of grass and every tree has its principle and should be investigated; (8) to know where the highest good is to be found; and (9) to examine principle in one's own person."

[33] Quoting Ch'eng I in *I-shu*, 15:11a.

[34] Alludes to *Analects*, 9:16, which in Legge's translation (*The Chinese Classics*, 1:222) reads: "The Master standing by a stream, said, 'It passes on just like this, not ceasing day or night!' "

[35] Alludes to the *Mean*, 12:3, which in turn quotes Ode 239.

[36] Alludes to *Mencius*, 6A:3:3, where Mencius asks Kao Tzu: "Is the nature of a dog like the nature of an ox, and the nature of an ox like the nature of man?"

[37] *Mean*, 27:1–4.

sage surely lies in this. When it comes to "sending forth and nourishing all things," this is naturally the function and accomplishment of the creative transformations of the universe. Why is it that this is mentioned in connection with the Way of the sage? And how is he going to carry it out? If one carefully reflects on this and grasps it, heaven and man, things and the self, inner and outer, beginning and end, darkness and light, the lessons of birth and death, and the conditions of positive and negative spiritual forces[38] should form an all-pervading unity[39] with nothing left behind. Thus, when we speak of the myriad things, is there any that is after all external to our own nature?[40]

7. "In the investigation of things, there is nothing better than to seek within oneself. One's attainment is very personal."[41] This is a saying of Master Ch'eng. When answering a disciple's question he expressed the view that, "To seek in our own nature and feelings is indeed to be concerned with our own person. But every blade of grass and every tree possesses principle and should be examined."[42]

At that time Ch'an was flourishing. Students were often deeply immersed in theories of "clarifying the mind and perceiving the nature," and no longer directed their thoughts to the principles of heaven and earth and the myriad things. Being commonly reduced to onesidedness and solely preoccupied with the self, they were ultimately unable to enter the Way of Yao and Shun. The Ch'eng brothers were deeply distressed over this, and so they expounded the text of the *Great Learning* and explained the concept of the investigation of things. Their intent was that students should achieve corresponding illumination of things and the self, perfect interfusion of inner and outer, and complete integration of subject and object. This was the

---

[38] "The circumstances of dark and light," "the lessons of birth and death," and "the conditions of positive and negative spiritual forces," are allusions to the "Appended Remarks" in the *Book of Changes*, 7:5b–6a.

[39] *Analects*, 4:15:1.

[40] In *Chu Tzu yü-lei* (Classified Conversations of Master Chu Hsi), 4:5b, Chu states that, "In the universe there is no single thing that is external to our nature." Conrad Schirokauer notes also Hu Hung's statement in *Hu Tzu chih-yen* (Master Hu's Understanding Words), 1:6b: "There is no thing outside the nature and no nature outside things."

[41] Quoting Ch'eng I in *I-shu*, 17:1b.

[42] *I-shu*, 18:9a. Translation adapted from Wing-tsit Chan in *A Source Book in Chinese Philosophy*, p. 563.

profound way in which they saved them from error and guided them into the great Mean. Those who are aware of "the great pains that the skillful artisan takes"[43] are truly very few.

Principle as it operates in the world is such that out of unity there proceed the myriad things without the intervention of any artificial contrivance. And when the many reconverge into the one, what possibility could there be for the interference of any selfish manipulation? Thus to "seek within oneself" one must begin with one's own nature and feelings. One then goes on to extend to other things what one has perceived in oneself, and if it is found to be inconsistent, it is not ultimate principle. Seeking it in external things, there is no difference in respect to birds and beasts or plants and trees. If one has perceived something there, but refers back to one's own mind and finds any incongruity, it is not ultimate principle. Only with luminous clarity of insight into the mystery of the unity of all being does one realize that, while there is no difference of subject and object, the differences in its particularizations, being in themselves immensely prolific, cannot be confused. This is the consummate task of investigating things and extending knowledge. But how can it be accomplished without genuine and unremitting effort over a long period of time?

8. "The circumstances of dark and light," "the lessons of birth and death," and "the conditions of positive and negative spiritual forces"[44] have always been intelligible when things are investigated and knowledge is extended.

The Buddhists consider mountains, rivers, and the vast earth to be an illusion, birth and death to be a process of transmigration, and heaven and hell to be retribution. Given such evidence that they are not perspicuous in their knowledge, what is one to conclude about their "perceiving the nature"? At present there are those who employ the theory of "investigating this thing" and "extending this knowledge" in order secretly to purvey their theory of "clarifying the mind."[45] What kind of understanding is this? It is the fortune of the Buddhists and the misfortune of our school of the sage.

---

[43] Quoting a poem of Tu Fu, "T'i Li tsun-shih Sung-shu chang-tzu ko," in *Fen-men chi-chu Tu Kung-pu shih* (SPTK *chi pu*, 4 vols.) (Taipei: T'a-t'ung shu-chü, 1974), 4:16:19a–b (1151–52).

[44] *Book of Changes*, "Appended Remarks," 7:5b–6a.

[45] An implied criticism of Lu Hsiang-shan's idea of the investigation of things and the extension of knowledge in *Hsiang-shan ch'üan-chi* (Complete Works of Lu Chiu-yüan), 19:9a. See also below, *K'un-chih chi*, Part II, sec. 41.

9. Principle is truly extremely easy and extremely simple, and yet grasping the principles of the world in what is easy and simple is a matter of perfecting one's ability.[46] The tasks of the student are broad learning, careful inquiry, sober reflection, clear discrimination, and earnest practice.[47] Not one of these can be dispensed with. By proceeding on the basis of these five one may arrive at what is easy and simple. But if one dislikes the complexity involved in scholarship and yearns for a shortcut to the realm of ease and simplicity, this can hardly be called the ease and simplicity of principle. Fondness for the sublime and the desire for speed[48] are among the common failings of scholars. It happens that those who encourage such habits strike the fancy of others and accommodate their desires, so that people heedlessly follow them. It is no wonder that this is so, but how fearful it is to contemplate the harm they are causing to the Way.

10. The word *ko* is sometimes defined in the commentaries of antiquity as "to reach," as in such expressions as "[The display of these qualities filled the four extremities of the empire] and reached [heaven] above and [earth] below."[49] Sometimes it is defined as "to correct," as in such expressions as "correcting my bad heart."[50] The Ch'eng brothers always defined the *ko* in *ko-wu* as "reach." They simply assigned the meaning of the word in accordance with the context, insofar as it was appropriate. Lü Tung-lai[51] explained it as a "rule," as in "the rule governing the natural span of life,"[52]

---

[46] Alludes to the language of the "Appended Remarks" of the *Book of Changes*, which in the translation of Wilhelm/Baynes, *Changes*, pp. 286–87, reads: "The Creative knows through the easy. The Receptive can do things through the simple. What is easy, is easy to know; what is simple, is easy to follow . . . By means of the easy and the simple we grasp the laws of the whole world. When the laws of the whole world are grasped, therein lies perfection."

[47] *Mean*, 20:19.

[48] Cf. the caution to Tzu-hsia against "hurrying things" in *Analects*, 13:17.

[49] *Book of History*, "The Canon of Yao." Legge, *Shoo King, The Chinese Classics*, 3:15.

[50] *Book of History*, "The Charge to Ch'iung." Legge, *Shoo King, The Chinese Classics*, 3:585.

[51] Lü Tsu-ch'ien (1137–1181) was a leader of the Eastern Chekiang school of the twelfth century, a specialist in historical texts, and a close friend of Chu Hsi's.

[52] *Tseng-hsiu Tung-lai Shu-shuo* (Lü Tsu-ch'ien's Revised and Expanded Explanations of the *Book of History*) (in *Chin-hua ts'ung-shu*), 26:8b. Lü here alludes to the *Book of History*, "Prince Shih."

and also as "penetrating the 'three primal powers'[53] with no separation."[54] I would note that "penetrating with no separation" also has the meaning of "reaching," though by comparison with the word "reach," its import is much more clear, profound, and far-reaching. If, for example, one explained the phrase "reached [heaven] above and [earth] below," by saying, "penetrated above and below with no separation," who would say that this was incorrect? The *ko* in *ko-wu* has precisely the meaning of "penetrating everywhere with no separation." For when my endeavor approaches completion, it will involve penetration with no separation. Then things are myself and I am things, altogether unified without any differentiation. At this point the word "identify" *(ho)* becomes superfluous.[55]

11. When Confucius, in compiling the *Book of Changes (I-ching)*, began with the words "probing principle to the utmost" *(ch'iung-li)*,[56] what, in fact, did he mean by "principle" *(li)*? That which penetrates heaven and earth and connects past and present is nothing other than material force *(ch'i)*, which is unitary. This material force, while originally one, revolves through endless cycles of movement and tranquillity, going and coming, opening and closing, rising and falling. Having become increasingly obscure, it then becomes manifest; having become manifest, it once again reverts to obscurity. It produces the warmth and coolness and the cold and heat of the four seasons, the birth, growth, gathering in, and storing of all living things, the constant moral relations of the people's daily life, the victory and defeat, gain and loss in human affairs. And amid all of this prolific variety and phenomenal diversity there is a detailed order and an elaborate coherence which cannot ultimately be disturbed, and which is so even without our knowing why it is so. This is what is called principle. Principle is not a separate entity which depends on material force in order to exist or which "attaches to material force in order to operate."[57]

[53] Refers to heaven, earth, and man.

[54] *Tseng-hsiu Tung-lai Shu-shuo*, 26:8b. I am indebted to Wing-tsit Chan for identifying the source of this and the preceding quotation.

[55] Because it implies a dualism where one no longer exists. Cf. the contrasting view of Wang Yang-ming on the meaning of *ko* in Part 2 of the *Ch'uan-hsi lu*. See Wing-tsit Chan, trans., *Instructions for Practical Living*, sec. 137 (pp. 102–6).

[56] *Book of Changes*, "Discussion of the Trigrams" *(Shuo-kua)*, 9:2a.

[57] An explicit rejection of the language used by Chu Hsi in his statement (*Chu Tzu ch'üan-shu*, 49:4b) that, "Principle attaches to material force and thus operates."

The phrase, "There is in the changes the Great Ultimate,"[58] has led some to suspect that there is a single entity that acts as a controlling power amid the transformations of yin and yang. But this is not the case. "Change" is a collective name for the two primary forces, the four second-ary forms, and the eight trigrams. "The Great Ultimate" is a collective name for all principles taken together. To say that, "There is in the changes the Great Ultimate," means that manifold diversity takes its origin from a single source.[59] This is then extended to the process of "production and reproduction"[60] to clarify that the dispersal of the single source produces manifold diversity. This is certainly the working of nature, its unregulated regularity, and not something that can be sought in the tangible realm.

It was only the elder Master Ch'eng (Ch'eng Hao) who de-scribed this most incisively. The views of the younger Master Ch'eng (Ch'eng I) and Master Chu (Chu Hsi) seem to have been slightly different, and inasmuch as their theories all coexist, one must try to find a way to recon-cile them and recover the ultimate unity.

The elder Master Ch'eng quoted successive passages from the "Appended Remarks" as follows: "What is above physical form is called the Way. What is below physical form is called a concrete thing."[61] "Yin and yang are established as the Way of heaven, the weak and the strong as the Way of earth, and humanity and rightness as the Way of man."[62] "The succession of yin and yang is called the Way."[63] He elaborated this by saying, "Yin and yang are below physical form, and yet here they are called the Way. This expression distinguishes most clearly the meaning of 'above' and 'below.' From the beginning the Way is nothing but this. The impor-tant thing is that man must appreciate this in his own mind."[64] If the student meditates deeply and reflects carefully on these words, in the course of time he will naturally gain insight into what is meant.

The slightly different view held by the younger Master Ch'eng

---

[58] *Book of Changes*, "Appended Remarks," 7:17a.

[59] *Mencius*, 3A:5:3.

[60] *Book of Changes*, "Appended Remarks," 7:8a.

[61] *Ibid.*, 7:18b.

[62] *Book of Changes*, "Discussion of the Trigrams," 9:2a–b.

[63] *Book of Changes*, "Appended Remarks," 7:7a.

[64] *I-shu*, 11:1b. Translation adapted from Wing-tsit Chan, *A Source Book in Chinese Philosophy*, pp. 537–38.

is evidenced in these statements recorded by Liu Yüan-ch'eng:[65] "That whereby yin and yang come about is the Way."[66] Again, "That whereby closing and opening come about is the Way."[67] When one carefully analyzes the two words "that whereby," (_suo-i_), it is quite evident that they refer to what is above physical form, which inevitably insinuates the notion that [yin and yang and the Way] are two things. But when one views it from the standpoint of the elder Master Ch'eng's statement that, "From the beginning the Way is nothing but this," one will naturally perceive the subtle truth that they are wholly undifferentiated (_hun-jan_), and it would seem unnecessary to add the words "that whereby."

The slight differences in Master Chu's view are illustrated in statements like the following: "_Li_ and _ch'i_ are definitely two things."[68] "_Ch'i_ is strong and _li_ is weak."[69] "If there were no _ch'i_, how would _li_ find a place to reside?"[70] There are many such statements. Only in one of his letters to K'o Kuo-ts'ai[71] is there the statement, "Yin and yang succeeding one another in ceaseless alternation is the complete substance of the Way."[72] This statement is right to the point and is altogether consistent with the statements of Ch'eng Hao, but since one does not see many like it, one does not know which to take as his final conclusion.

12. When Master Chu was fifteen or sixteen he set his mind on the Way. He sought it from the Buddhists for nearly ten years, and it was only when he was twenty-four that he took Li Yen-p'ing[73] as his teacher. It was then

[65] Liu An-chieh (1068–1116), a disciple of Ch'eng I. For an account of him, see Huang Tsung-hsi and Ch'üan Tsu-wang, _Sung Yüan hsüeh-an_ (Philosophical Records of Sung and Yüan Confucians), _ch._ 32.

[66] _I-shu,_ 15:13b.

[67] _Ibid._

[68] Letter to Liu Shu-wen in _Chu Tzu wen-chi_ (Collection of Literary Works by Master Chu Hsi), 46:24a.

[69] _Chu Tzu yü-lei,_ 4:13b.

[70] _Chu Tzu yü-lei,_ 4:8a.

[71] K'o Han.

[72] Letter to K'o Kuo-ts'ai in _Chu Tzu wen-chi,_ 39:6b.

[73] Li T'ung (1093–1163). As a student of Lo Ts'ung-yen (1072–1135), Li T'ung carried on the tradition of the Ch'eng brothers. He was a friend of Chu Hsi's father, Chu Sung, who greatly admired him and urged Chu Hsi to become his student.

that he was greatly awakened to the errors of Ch'an Buddhism and completely abandoned his former practices. After Yen-p'ing died, Master Chu met and became friends with Chang Nan-hsien[74] and truly derived great benefit from this relationship.

Yen-p'ing once said in a letter to his friend Lo Po-wen,[75] "Yüan-hui (Chu Hsi) first began his endeavors with Ch'ien K'ai-shan,[76] and therefore his entire effort was devoted to achieving personal realization of the inner meanings of things. Now through our discussions and arguments he has gained insight into the essential tenets of Confucianism and is extremely adept at pointing out where he has erred. Since I saw you, sir, I have seen no one like this." He also said, "This gentleman has no other concern than to apply his mind persistently and deeply to this . . . Now he has gradually become capable of thorough understanding. He applies himself singlemindedly to daily affairs. If he gradually becomes adept at this, substance and function will be united."[77] Looking at this letter, one can see that Master Chu had achieved the goal of entering the Way. There are innumerable letters in which he argued back and forth with Nan-hsien, and in the last letter discussing equilibrium and harmony he elucidated the subtleties of the learning of the mind *(hsin-hsüeh)*[78] so that nothing was left unrevealed. Here too one can see the profundity of his achievement.

"Sincerity and intelligence advanced together,"[79] and in his writings he was also prolific. Those who followed him during his own lifetime and those in later generations who considered themselves to be his

---

[74]Chang Shih (1133–1180). Chang, Chu Hsi, and Lü Tsu-ch'ien were known as the "Three Worthies of the Southeast." For an account of Chang, see *Sung Yüan hsüeh-an*, ch. 50. Chu Hsi's letters to him are found in *Chu Tzu wen-chi*, ch. 24–25 and 30–32.

[75]Also known as Lo Tsung-li or Lo Tsung-yüeh (1116–1168). A brief account of him is given in *Sung Yüan hsüeh-an*, ch. 39, where he is identified as one of the two most intimate disciples of Li T'ung, the other having been Chu Hsi.

[76]His monastic name was K'ai-shan Tao-ch'ien. He was also known as Mi-an Tao-ch'ien and (after his native place of Chien-ning in Fukien) Chien-ning Tao-ch'ien. Little is known of him apart from the fact that he was a follower of Ta-hui Tsung-kao (1089–1163), who also gave him the name Chien-chou Tzu. See *Hsü Ch'uan-teng lu* 32 (T 51, 688b–689a).

[77]Letter to Lo Po-wen in *Li Yen-p'ing hsien-sheng wen-chi* (Collection of Literary Works by Master Li T'ung), 1:4b–5a.

[78]Letter in Reply to Chang Ch'in-fu in *Chu Tzu wen-chi*, 32:24b–26b.

[79]Alludes to the "Prose Poem on the Po-lu-tung [Academy]" in *Chu Tzu wen-chi*, 1:2b.

disciples number in the hundreds and thousands. It could not be that they were all inferior to our contemporaries, yet they all took delight in sincerely submitting to him. Could this have been owing to eloquence and an ingratiating manner? Scholars of today have generally not explored the matter in depth but, having casually read through the works of Lu Hsiang-shan a few times, heedlessly follow prevailing trends and stridently and unreasonably disparage [Chu Hsi]. Yet this merely expresses their own meanness and doesn't hurt Master Chu in the least.

> Note: Ch'ien K'ai-shan must have been
> an eminent monk; however, I have not yet
> investigated this.[80]

13. It has long been true that those who are committed to the learning of the Way (*tao-hsüeh*) have all honored and trusted Ch'eng and Chu. Recently those who prate about the learning of the Way arrogantly place themselves above Ch'eng and Chu, yet if one considers their attainments, they are things that the Ch'engs and Chu learned in their earlier years and later discarded. Isn't it a mistake to devote one's entire life to seeking the Way only to collect what able and virtuous men of an earlier day discarded, considering this as one's personal treasure and turning around and criticizing them?[81]

　　Although the learning of Ch'eng and Chu might be called complete, in their own minds they certainly never considered it complete. How can one know this? When the younger Master Ch'eng's *Commentary on the Book of Changes* (*[I-ch'uan] I chuan*) was finished, he would show it to no one. When someone asked him about it, he said, "In my own opinion my vital powers have not yet declined, and I still hope to see some slight improvement."[82] When Master Chu was nearing the age of seventy he la-

---

[80] Lo Ch'in-shun's original note.

　　[81] *Tao-hsüeh* was the term applied from Chu Hsi's time on to the learning practiced by Neo-Confucian scholars. In his *Hsüeh-p'u t'ung-pien* (General Critique of Obscurations of Learning), 1:7a–b, Ch'en Chien (1497–1567) quotes this paragraph, expressing the view that Lo intended it as a criticism of Wang Yang-ming.

　　[82] *I-ch'uan hsien-sheng nien-p'u* (Biography of Master Ch'eng I), in *I-shu*, Appendix, p. 12a. In *Ts'ui-yen* (Pure Words), 1:26a, it is indicated that Ch'eng I was over seventy at the time he made this statement.

mented that he was "still not able to see everything clearly."[83] They truly had insight into the inexhaustibility of moral principles, and in their minds they could not be contented. Nor were they simply being modest in what they said.

I have taken up all of the writings of Ch'eng and Chu, meditating deeply and reflecting carefully on them, reading them over and over again without putting them down. It is only in the case of the views of the elder Master Ch'eng that I feel not the slightest doubt. The writings and conversations of the younger Master Ch'eng and Master Chu are numerous, and they often probe the furthest depths and attain the utmost subtlety. Both sides of an argument are explored to the fullest.[84] The reason that I have doubts is that I have yet to see that they finally achieved unity (*ting yü i*). Can this be called "still not seeing everything clearly"? To search their statements for what is not yet unified can only be done by one who genuinely honors and trusts them. This is why I devote all my mind to this and dare not be neglectful.

14. In the Six Classics[85] discussion of the mind began with Emperor Shun.[86] Discussion of the nature began with T'ang the Accomplished.[87] The four sentences uttered by Shun did not include the term "nature," though the idea of the nature was definitely implied. It was T'ang who first clearly mentioned it, saying, "The Lord has bestowed on the common people a moral sense through which they have the potential of a constant nature. To cause them tranquilly to pursue the course which it would indicate is the work of the sovereign."[88]

Confucius spoke of it in greater detail, saying, "The succession

---

[83] *Chu Tzu yü-lei*, 104:10b.

[84] Alludes to *Analects*, 9:7.

[85] The *Books of Odes, History, Rites, Changes*, the *Chou-li* (Rites of Chou), and the *Spring and Autumn Annals*. The ancient Six Classics included the *Book of Music*, which is no longer extant, in place of the *Chou-li*.

[86] Refers to a statement attributed to Shun in the "Counsels of the Great Yü" in the *Book of History*. Shun advised Yü that, "The human mind is insecure . . ."

[87] Refers to the *Book of History*, "Announcement of T'ang." See Legge, *Shoo King, The Chinese Classics*, 3:185.

[88] Translation adapted from Legge, *Shoo King*, p. 185.

of yin and yang is called the Way. That which furthers it is good. That which brings it to completion is the nature. The humane perceive it and call it humane. The wise perceive it and call it wise. The people use it day by day and are not aware of it. Therefore the Way of the gentleman is rare."[89] He also said, "By nature men are nearly alike."[90] Tzu-ssu transmitted the idea, saying, "What Heaven has endowed is called the nature. Following one's nature is called the Way."[91] Mencius followed in this tradition and said, "The nature is good."[92] The sages and worthies of antiquity always discussed the nature in just such terms.

From Kao Tzu on there were none with utmost clarity of vision. They all made pronouncements on the basis of mere imagination, and the more pronouncements were made, the fewer were in conformity with the teachings of the sages and worthies. At last there was no one who could finally achieve unity. Then in the Sung there emerged Ch'eng, Chang, and Chu, who were the first to use different terms to explain what was the nature endowed by Heaven and what was the physical nature.[93] They formulated their theories with reference to Confucius and Mencius and verified them in terms of the human emotions, so that they were in this respect complete. But to a single nature they applied two names. Although [Ch'eng I] said, "It is wrong to regard [the nature and ch'i] as two,"[94] he was not yet able to see them as one. In the end the doubts of scholars were not resolved, so that right down to the present their endless debates are carried on in the world. How can one blame them?

Day and night I was immersed in this, seeking intently to achieve personal realization. I had devoted years to it when suddenly one day it

---

[89] *Book of Changes*, "Appended Remarks," 7:7a–b.

[90] *Analects*, 17:2.

[91] *Mean*, 1:1.

[92] *Mencius*, 3A:1:2 and 6A:6:4.

[93] Referring here to Ch'eng I, Chang Tsai, and Chu Hsi. The contrast is between *t'ien-ming chih hsing* and *ch'i-chih chih hsing*. See *Chang Tzu ch'üan-shu* (Complete Works of Master Chang Tsai), 2:18b–19a. "With the existence of physical form, there exists physical nature. If one skillfully returns to the original nature endowed by Heaven and earth (*t'ien-ti chih hsing*) then it will be preserved. Therefore in physical nature there is that which the superior man denies to be his nature." See Wing-tsit Chan, *A Source Book in Chinese Philosophy*, p. 511.

[94] *I-shu*, 6:2a.

seemed to me that the whole of it had become transparently clear. I submit that the subtle truth of the nature and endowment is summarized in the formulation, "Principle is one; its particularizations are diverse."[95] This is simple and yet complete, concise and yet utterly penetrating.

This [oneness of principle and diversity of its particularizations] owes nothing to compulsion or to contrivance, and by its nature it is utterly insusceptible to change. At the inception of life when they are first endowed with *ch'i,* the principle of human beings and things is just one. After having attained physical form, their particularizations are diverse. That their particularizations are diverse is nothing but natural principle, for the oneness of their principle always exists within diverse particularizations. This is the explanation for the subtle truth of the nature and endowment. In terms of its oneness, "every human being can become a Yao or a Shun,"[96] and in terms of its diversity, "only the very wisest and the very dullest do not change."[97] Were the sage to come to life again, he would certainly agree with what I have said.[98]

15. Having said that ["principle is one; its particularizations are diverse"] is concise and yet utterly penetrating, I should like to illustrate with reference to statements about the nature made from antiquity until recent times. "Having the potential of a constant nature,"[99] refers to the oneness of principle. "Causing them tranquilly to pursue the course which it would indicate,"[100] refers to the diversity of particularizations. That which, dwelling hidden within them, "brings [the Way] to completion is the nature,"[101] refers to the oneness of principle. "The humane [perceive it and call it humane], the wise [perceive it and call it wise], the people [use it day by

[95] A statement of Ch'eng I's found in *I-ch'uan wen-chi* (Collection of Literary Works by Ch'eng I), 5:12b.

[96] *Mencius,* 6B:2:1.

[97] *Analects,* 17:3.

[98] Paraphrasing the statement in *Mencius,* 3B:9:10 that, "When sages rise up again, they will not change my words."

[99] *Book of History,* "Announcement of T'ang." Legge, *Shoo King, The Chinese Classics,* 3:185.

[100] *Ibid.*

[101] *Book of Changes,* "Appended Remarks," 7:7b.

day and are not aware of it],"[102] and "[by nature, human beings are] nearly alike,"[103] refer to the diversity of particularizations. "What Heaven has endowed is called the nature,"[104] refers to the oneness of principle. "Following one's nature is called the Way,"[105] refers to the diversity of particularizations.

Note: This will be discussed separately below.[106]

"The nature is good,"[107] refers to the oneness of principle, but the statement was not extended to include the idea that particularizations differ. "The nature of some is good, and the nature of others is not good,"[108] refers to the diversity of particularizations, but the statement was not extended to include the idea of the oneness of principle.

Ch'eng [I] and Chang [Tsai] based their discussion of the nature on the views of Tzu-ssu and Mencius, and, since the primary emphasis had been on principle, they went on to develop their theory of the physical being, so that the diversity of particularizations was also dealt with most thoroughly. But when we speak of the nature endowed by Heaven, this already entails the physical being. And when we speak of the physical nature, isn't this the nature endowed by Heaven? To a single nature, they applied two names, and, moreover, spoke of the physical being and the endowment of Heaven as if they were opposed, so that in the final analysis their argument turned out to be unclear.

Master Chu was most fearful that people might regard [the physical being and the endowment of Heaven] as two things, and so he said that the physical nature is "the total substance of the Great Ultimate descended into the physical being."[109] But once he used the word "de-

---

[102] *Ibid.*

[103] *Analects*, 17:2.

[104] *Mean*, 1:1.

[105] *Ibid.*

[106] See below, *K'un-chih chi*, Part I, sec. 20.

[107] *Mencius*, 3A:1:2 and 6A:6:4.

[108] A statement advanced by Mencius' disciple Kung-tu, in *Mencius*, 6A:6:4.

[109] Letter in Reply to Yen Shih-heng ("Ta Yen Shih-heng") in *Chu Tzu-wen-chi*, 61:21b. See the discussion of this passage by Ch'ien Mu in *Chu Tzu hsin hsüeh-an* (A New Philosophical Record of Chu Hsi), 1:450.

scended," *li* and *ch'i* were inevitably sundered.[110] Only in "principle is one; its particularizations are diverse" is everything encompassed, nothing left uncomprehended. Isn't this the true meaning of the statement, "In the universe there is no single thing that lies beyond the nature"?[111]

16. The source of ultimate principle is simply the two phases of activity and tranquillity. As there is tranquillity, there is unity; as there is activity, there is manifold diversity. This is the same in Heaven (or nature) and in man.

The "Record of Music" (*Yüeh chi*) says, "Man is tranquil at birth; this is his Heaven-endowed nature. When, influenced by things, he begins to be active, this is desire arising from his nature."[112] The *Mean* says, "The state before the feelings of pleasure, anger, sorrow, and joy have been aroused is called equilibrium (*chung*). When these feelings have been aroused and have all been regulated so as to attain their due degree, this is what is called a state of harmony (*ho*)."[113] This is principle as it exists in man. If one does not seek it within activity and tranquillity, where will one find it? But tranquillity is characterized by formlessness, while in activity there are observable signs. That which has observable signs is easy to discern, while that which is without form is difficult to understand clearly. The important thing in probing principle is precisely the desire to understand clearly what is difficult to understand.

The equilibrium before the feelings have been aroused is "the moral sense bestowed by the Lord."[114] In the equilibrium of Heaven and earth which one receives along with life, could there be anything that is not good? It is only that the feelings of pleasure, anger, sorrow, and joy arise but are not necessarily regulated so as to attain their due degree, and this is why there is the distinction between good and evil. Regulation refers to the oneness of principle as it exists within diverse particularizations, while

[110]Lo denied that the two could be sundered. See below, *K'un-chih chi*, Part II, sec. 21, where he states that *li* and *ch'i* are "absolutely unsundered."

[111]Chu Hsi's statement, as recorded in *Chu Tzu yü-lei*, 4:5b.

[112]*Book of Rites*, "Record of Music." Cf. translation by James Legge in *Li Chi: Book of Rites*, 2:96.

[113]*Mean*, 1:4.

[114]*Book of History*, "Announcement of T'ang." Legge, *Shoo King*, p. 185.

attaining due degree refers to not losing Heaven's endowment as it originally is. What greater good can there be?

Even in the case of "those who go beyond it" and "those who
do not come up to it,"[115] they still preserve within themselves something
that may be called "good," and we cannot summarily call them evil. Only
when one contravenes what is natural do we consider it to be evil. To
contravene what is natural is "to love what other people hate and to hate
what they love."[116] Therefore the disparity between good and evil may be
such that "some are twice, some five times, some ten times, some a hundred
times, some a thousand times, some ten thousand times [as good or bad as
others]."[117] What is this if not manifold diversity? Thus, when the desires
are aroused and the emotions gain the upper hand, even if it should happen
that one "drifts with the current and forgets to return,"[118] the original substance of equilibrium is definitely as it was before. One cannot depart from
it for an instant.[119] How wrong it would be were I to claim to know the
nature without understanding this!

17. The desire, love, and hate spoken of in the "Record of Music"[120] together with the pleasure, anger, sorrow, and joy mentioned in the *Mean*[121]
are collectively termed the seven emotions. Their principles in each case
are rooted in the nature. Among the seven emotions, desire is relatively
important. Heaven (or nature) produces people with desires. By following
their desires people find pleasure. From the flouting of them they feel anger.
In fulfilling them they feel joy. And in finding them thwarted they know
sorrow. Therefore the "Record of Music" only speaks of "the desires arising
from the nature."[122] The desires cannot be spoken of as evil. They may be
good or evil depending solely upon whether or not they are regulated.[123]

---

115 *Mean*, 1:2.

116 *Great Learning,* Commentary, 10:17.

117 *Mencius,* 3A:4:18.

118 *Mencius,* 1B:4:7.

119 *Mean*, 1:2.

120 *Book of Rites*, "Record of Music." Legge, *Li-Chi: Book of Rites*, 2:96.

121 *Mean*, 1:4.

122 *Book of Rites*, "Record of Music." Legge, *Li Chi: Book of Rites*, 2:96.

123 This alludes to the passage in the "Record of Music" which in Legge's translation (*ibid.*) reads: "Things come to him more and more, and his knowledge is increased. Then

18. One principle exists in heaven (or nature) and man, but its particularizations are not the same. At the point when "man is tranquil at birth,"[124] principle exists in man, but the particularization belongs to heaven. When, "influenced by things, he begins to be active,"[125] principle issues from heaven, while the particularization belongs to man. That "the gentleman must watch over himself while alone,"[126] is because of this.

19. "Principle is one; its particularizations are diverse," derives from a statement made by Master Ch'eng in his discussion of the "Western Inscription" ("Hsi-ming").[127] These words are extremely simple, and yet when they are extended to the principles of the universe, there is nothing that is not comprehended. This is definitely true for heaven (or nature), it is likewise true for man, and it is true for all living things. It is equally true for the individual, for the family, and for the world. It is true for a year, for a single day, and for all time.

    If one discusses the nature on the basis of this statement, there will naturally be no need to postulate a dichotomy between the endowment of heaven and the physical being—this is unmistakably clear. Yet I-ch'uan did use such terms. He also thought that capacity (*ts'ai*) comes from *ch'i*.[128] Could it be that when he spoke of the diversity of particularizations he was referring only to *ch'i?* Master Chu, in responding to a disciple's question concerning *li* and *ch'i*, praised these words of I-ch'uan's,[129] though he finally came to regard *li* and *ch'i* as two things. This is precisely what I mean by suggesting that I doubt he finally achieved unity.

arise the manifestations of liking and disliking. When these are not regulated by anything within, and knowledge leads more astray without, he cannot come back to himself, and his Heavenly principle is extinguished."

[124] *Book of Rites*, "Record of Music." Legge, *Li Chi: Book of Rites*, 2:96.

[125] *Ibid.*

[126] *Mean*, 1:3.

[127] The "Western Inscription" is Chang Tsai's moving reflection on the unity of all being. It is found in *Chang Tzu-ch'üan-shu*, 1:1a–6b and translated by Wing-tsit Chan in *A Source Book in Chinese Philosophy*, pp. 497–98. Ch'eng I's discussion of its metaphysical significance is found in *I-ch'uan wen-chi*, 5:15b. For the background to this formulation in the thought of Tao-sheng and others, see Wing-tsit Chan, "The Evolution of the Neo-Confucian Concept of Li as Principle," in *Ch'ing-hua hsüeh-pao* (Tsing Hua Journal of Chinese Studies), NS IV, no. 2 (February 1964), p. 134.

[128] Ch'eng I in *I-shu*, 19:4b.

[129] *Chu Tzu yü-lei*, 1:1b.

20. "What heaven has endowed is called the nature."[130] This refers to the time when *ch'i* is first received. "Following one's nature is called the Way."[131] This refers to the time after physical form is attained. For after physical form has been attained, man follows his human nature and acts according to the way of man. Other things follow their natures and act according to the way of things.

"All are equally men,"[132] but their way is not exactly the same. "The humane perceive it and call it humane. The wise perceive it and call it wise. The people use it day by day and are not aware of it."[133] This is owing to the diversity of particularizations. From this it can be seen why it is said that "the Way of the gentleman is rare."[134] For the Way of the gentleman is "the harmony after [the feelings] have been regulated so as to attain their due degree." It is the universal Way of the world. Only if one devotes himself to the teaching [of the *Mean*] concerning the cultivation of the Way, can the way of the gentleman be attained and one's nature thereby fulfilled. "Being cautious and apprehensive"[135] and "watching over oneself while alone,"[136] are the means to cultivate the Way.

21. "The state before the feelings of pleasure, anger, sorrow, and joy have been aroused is called equilibrium."[137] These words of Tzu-ssu were extremely profound and incisive and thus served to enlighten later students. For the nature endowed by heaven has no physical form that can be seen, and no concrete substance that can be sought, and consequently it is very difficult for the student to understand it right away. Therefore Tzu-ssu clarified [the reality of the nature] in terms of the feelings of pleasure, anger, sorrow, and joy. Pleasure, anger, sorrow, and joy are common to all people and are easily observed without our knowing what is called "equilibrium"

---

[130] *Mean*, 1:1.

[131] *Ibid.*

[132] *Mencius*, 6A:15:1.

[133] *Book of Changes*, "Appended Remarks," 7:7b.

[134] *Ibid.*

[135] *Mean*, 1:2.

[136] *Mean*, 1:3.

[137] *Mean*, 1:4.

or what constitutes "the great foundation of the world."[138] Therefore Tzu-ssu especially pointed this out to show people and enable them to know that it is precisely there that the nature and endowment exist. When he spoke in the preceding text of "being cautious and apprehensive," the idea was to preserve and nourish them.

But before knowledge is complete, one's nourishing cannot be without error, and it may happen that one sinks into the emptiness and quietism of the Buddhists. Therefore Li Yen-p'ing taught that one must "achieve personal realization of the 'great foundation' in a state of tranquillity. If at the time before the feelings have been aroused, the disposition is distinguished clearly, then in managing affairs and responding to things, one naturally regulates the feelings so that they attain due degree."[139] These guidelines of Li's were obtained from Lo Yü-chang,[140] and Lo in turn obtained them from Yang Kuei-shan.[141] Yang having been an eminent disciple of the Ch'eng school, this line of thought is well established.

The elder Master Ch'eng once said, "The student must first of all understand humanity . . . [One's duty] is to understand this principle and preserve [humanity] with sincerity and seriousness, that is all."[142] The younger Master Ch'eng also said, " 'Neither forgetting nor helping things grow'1[143] is the method of nourishing *ch'i*. If one does not understand how to nourish and only talks about nourishing when there is some concrete object, how will one be able to nourish when there is no object!"[144] Viewed from this standpoint, how could one fail to make the effort of personal realization in the state of equilibrium before the feelings have been aroused?

[138] *Mean*, 1:4.

[139] *Li Yen-p'ing hsien-sheng wen-chi*, 3:18a.

[140] Lo Ts'ung-yen (1072–1135). At the age of forty he became a student of Yang Shih, from whom he learned of the teachings of Ch'eng I. After a visit to Ch'eng I, financed by selling his property, he returned to his native Fukien to resume his studies under Yang Shih. At the expiration of a term in office, he retired from public life and later died a recluse. For an account of him, see *Sung Yüan hsüeh-an*, ch. 39.

[141] Yang Shih (1053–1135). A student first of Ch'eng Hao and later of Ch'eng I, he is generally credited with having established the teachings of the Ch'eng brothers in south China. See *Sung Yüan hsüeh-an*, ch. 25.

[142] Ch'eng Hao's statement in *I-shu*, 2:3a–b.

[143] Alluding to *Mencius*, 2A:2:16.

[144] Ch'eng I's statement in *I-shu*, 18:18b.

Although the younger Master Ch'eng said that "one can preserve and nourish at the time before the feelings have been aroused," but that "one cannot
seek equilibrium in the state before the feelings have been aroused,"[145] this
was merely the way he expressed it when he was answering a question and
was not necessarily the final conclusion he arrived at through the course of
his life.[146] He also considered that "when one has thought, the feelings will
already have been aroused."[147] Here again his language suffered from exag-
geration. Thinking, being the link between activity and tranquillity, differs
from what is manifested outwardly. And when one goes on to examine
personal realization, it is essentially something that does not go beyond the
mind.

The elder Master Ch'eng once said, "[Although I have learned
some of my doctrines from others,] the concept of the principle of nature
(t'ien-li) has been realized directly by myself."[148] He also said, " 'The mean
(or equilibrium) is the great foundation of the world.' It is the correct principle of all under heaven which is central and straight. Any deviation from
it is wrong."[149] Had he not achieved direct realization through the effort of
a deep and patient mind, how could he have perceived this so clearly? The
student must truly approach the equilibrium before the feelings have been
aroused through the effort of personal realization. When I clearly perceive
its straightness as if it were truly an object before my eyes, then I can be
said to know the nature. By being cautious and apprehensive throughout[150]
one will not fall short of the profound idea intended by Master Tzu-ssu
when he handed down his teaching.

22. Preserving the mind and nourishing the nature are the life-long work
of the student. But the meaning is definitely different depending on whether

---

[145] Ch'eng I's statement in I-shu, 18:14b.

[146] Compare with the opinion of Wang Yang-ming on this subject in Ch'uan-hsi lu,
Part 1, in Wang Wen-ch'eng kung ch'üan-shu 1:37b–39a. Wing-tsit Chan, trans., Instructions
for Practical Living, secs. 75–76 (pp. 50–52).

[147] I-shu, 18:14b.

[148] Ch'eng Hao in Wai-shu (Additional Writings), 12:4a.

[149] I-shu, 11:11a. Translation adapted from Wing-tsit Chan, A Source Book in Chinese
Philosophy, p. 541.

[150] Alludes to the Mean, 1:1.

or not knowledge is already complete. In preserving and nourishing at the time when knowledge is not yet complete, unless one devotes his full attention to it, it is not adequate. Manipulating and grasping make it difficult to be tranquil and calm, and often when one has been at it for a while, one will tend to become weary. In preserving and nourishing after knowledge is complete, one does not need to make such a great effort. In a state of ease and spontaneity the vital inspirations flow out smoothly and irrepressibly, and the resonances are profound and long-lasting. But when one first undertakes to learn, unless there is constantly the effort of preserving and nourishing, and unless the faculty of the mind is not neglected, one will lack the means to bring knowledge to completion. When Master Chu spoke of "sincerity and intelligence advancing together,"[151] he meant that one should examine oneself in this way.

To pay special attention at the point when the feelings are about to be aroused[152] is what is known in the *Great Learning* as "being at peace and then deliberating."[153] But "being at peace and then being able to deliberate" is what follows "knowing what to abide in,"[154] so that there is great depth to what one attains. If one routinely engages in self-examination, what one finally attains will not be remotely comparable. On the whole, the primary task is preserving and nourishing, while self-examination is secondary.[155]

23. Mencius understood "neither forgetting nor helping things grow"[156] as the method of nourishing *ch'i*. *Ch'i* and the nature are one thing; there is only the difference that one is above form while the other is within form. Nourishing the nature is nourishing *ch'i*, and nourishing *ch'i* is nourishing

---

[151] "Prose Poem on the Po-lu-tung [Academy]" in *Chu Tzu wen-chi*, 1:2b.

[152] The question of whether examination could be carried on before the feelings were aroused was discussed in detail by Chu Hsi and his contemporaries. See *Chu Tzu wen-chi*, 53:18b–21a.

[153] *Great Learning*, 2.

[154] *Ibid.*

[155] For Wang Yang-ming's rather different view of the relation between preserving and nourishing and self-examination, see *Ch'uan-hsi lu*, Part 1, in *Wang Wen-ch'eng kung ch'üan-shu*, 1:25a. Wing-tsit Chan, trans., *Instructions for Practical Living*, sec. 36 (p. 34).

[156] *Mencius*, 2A:2:16.

the nature. Thus, although the terms are not the same, the methods are not distinct. Tzu-ssu's notion of "being cautious and apprehensive"[157] closely resembles the idea of "not forgetting," but Mencius' way of expressing it was more complete.

24. The investigation of things and the extension of knowledge are the beginning of learning. Subduing the self and returning to propriety are the end of learning.[158] The Way is originally inherent in man, and the fact that one cannot become completely identified with it is because things and the self are contraposed[159] so that one knows only that there is this self. As the consciousness of self grows stronger by the day, one becomes that much further removed from the Way. When things are investigated, it is no longer things but only principle that is perceived, and when the self has been subdued, it is no longer the ego but only principle that one follows.

The operation of the principle of nature is all-pervasive, and this is why people are humane. Its process is regular and orderly and permits no confusion, hence it is said, "He knows the utmost point to be reached, and reaches it . . . He knows the end to be rested in and rests in it."[160] It does happen that "a man's knowledge may be sufficient to attain,"[161] and yet his action may not be commensurate. But if one had never truly known what propriety is, wouldn't it be unlikely that he could return [to the Way] before having strayed far from it?

---

[157] Mean, 12.

[158] Alludes to Analects, 12:1:1, which in Legge's translation (The Chinese Classics, 1:250) reads: "Yen Yüan asked about perfect virtue. The Master said, 'To subdue one's self and return to propriety is perfect virtue. If a man for one day subdue himself and return to propriety, all under heaven will ascribe perfect virtue to him. Is the practice of perfect virtue from a man himself or is it from others?' "

[159] The language here echoes that of Chu Hsi's commentary on Mencius, 1A:1:3 in Meng Tzu chi-chu (Collected Commentaries on the Mencius) where Chu states: "The mind of profit arises through contraposing external things and the self (wu wo chih hsiang-hsing), and this is the selfishness of human desires." In Ssu-shu chang-chü chi-chu (KHCPTS ed.), 1:2. Also in Ssu-shu chi-chu (Shushigaku taikei ed.), 2:75.

[160] Book of Changes, ch'ien hexagram, 1:3a.

[161] Analects, 15:32:1, which in Legge's translation (The Chinese Classics, 1:303) reads: "The Master said, 'When a man's knowledge is sufficient to attain, and his virtue is not sufficient to enable him to hold, whatever he may have gained, he will lose again.' "

25. Yen Tzu's inquiry about "subduing the self and returning to propriety"[162] is surely not easy to discuss. For in what he said concerning propriety, he was already extremely astute in his insight.[163] Only in what he said about [the Master's teaching] being "like something to stand up right before me [but which I cannot lay hold of]"[164] there still remained a lingering trace of the self-conscious ego which had not yet been completely dispelled. When it has been completely dispelled, we are made one with principle without any differentiation. But this task is most difficult, and while one may be able to become great, he may yet be unable to transform.[165] People like us who lag behind both in natural endowment and capacity for learning can only follow the advice of Hsieh Shang-ts'ai[166] to "follow the nature and subdue the self in precisely those points where partiality is difficult to subdue."[167] This is the genuine task of daily life. "Scholars aspire to become worthies," and "worthies aspire to become sages."[168] There is indeed an orderly sequence.

26. That Yen Tzu still had a sense of ego is apparent in his statement, "I should like not to boast of my excellence, nor to make a display of my meritorious deeds."[169]

---

[162] *Analects*, 12:1:1–2.

[163] *Analects*, 12:1:2.

[164] *Analects*, 9:10:3 records Yen Tzu's statement about the teaching of Confucius, which in Legge's translation (*The Chinese Classics*, 1:220) reads: "When I wish to give over the study of his doctrines, I cannot do so, and having exerted all my ability, there seems something to stand up right before me, but though I wish to follow and lay hold of it, I really find no way to do so."

[165] This is the distinction between being a great man and being a sage, as suggested in *Mencius*, 7B:25:6–7. In Legge's translation (*The Chinese Classics*, 2:490), the passage reads: "He whose completed goodness is brightly displayed is what is called a great man. When this great man exercises a transforming influence, he is what is called a sage."

[166] Hsieh Liang-tso (1050–c.1120) was considered by Huang Tsung-hsi to have been the most eminent of the direct disciples of the Ch'eng brothers. See *Sung Yüan hsüeh-an*, ch. 24.

[167] *Shang-ts'ai hsien-sheng yü-lu* (Recorded Conversations of Master Hsieh Liang-tso), C:1a.

[168] Chou Tun-i, *T'ung-shu* (Penetrating the *Book of Changes*), ch. 10, in *Chou Tzu ch'üan-shu* (Complete Works of Master Chou Tun-i), p. 17. Wing-tsit Chan, *A Source Book in Chinese Philosophy*, p. 470.

[169] *Analects*, 5:25:3.

27. The transformations of heaven and earth, the life of human beings and
other living things, the beauty of ritual, the mysteries of positive and negative spiritual forces, the passage of time, the metamorphoses of life and
death, the circumstances of good and ill fortune, remorse and humiliation—
the theories about them are endless. Yet they may be summarized in a single
phrase: "yin and yang succeeding one another is called the Way."[170]

28. "The doings of high heaven have neither sound nor smell."[171] This
does not go beyond the sphere of the activity and tranquillity of the human
mind and the constant relationships and daily occurrences of human life.
When the Ode says,

> Great heaven is bright,
> And is with you wherever you may go,
> Great Heaven is clear,
> And is with you wherever you may wander[172]

this is its significance. "When the gentleman is reverent and not neglectful,"[173] he is close to fulfilling the Way of heaven. If the singleness of the
sage is likewise unceasing,[174] then he will assuredly become one with heaven.

29. Humaneness (*jen*) is extremely difficult to discuss. In answering questions about humanity, Confucius only spoke about the manner in which
one should exert effort. Nor did Mencius ever clearly explain its meaning.
When he said, "Humaneness is the human mind,"[175] he was referring to
one in order to clarify the other and to show that it is extremely important
to people and cannot be neglected. The idea is the same as that in the
subsequent passage which speaks of rightness being man's path.[176] Therefore
Li Yen-p'ing said that Mencius "was not defining humaneness in terms of

---

[170] *Book of Changes,* "Appended Remarks," 7:7a.

[171] Ode 235. The line is quoted in the *Mean,* 33:6.

[172] Ode 254.

[173] Alludes to *Analects,* 12:5:4.

[174] *Mean,* 26:10, describing the virtue of King Wen.

[175] *Mencius,* 6A:11:2.

[176] *Ibid.*

the word 'mind.' "[177] This is an excellent perception. Yet among scholars in general there are none who take account of it, and as a result they commonly miss the point. When one takes up the definitions offered by our Confucian predecessors, one finds that it was only the elder Master Ch'eng who, in speaking of "forming one body with all things without any differentiation,"[178] seems to have understood it fully. He also thought that "Rightness, propriety, wisdom, and faithfulness are all humaneness."[179] Thus all the distinct particularizations are brilliantly clear, and not one is omitted. It is precisely because not one is omitted that all in their wholeness and entirety constitute this one thing. This is what is meant by "without any differentiation." The general idea of Master Chang's "Western Inscription" is consonant with this. As to others who saw humaneness as impartiality[180] or love[181] and the like, everything can be understood if we infer from the idea of "forming one body."

30. "Holding fast" and "letting go" are similar to what we speak of in common parlance as "picking up" and "putting down." But constantly keeping hold of this mind and not letting it go astray is "holding fast."[182] "Holding fast" is being serious. Confucius once explained seriousness as "straightening the inner life."[183] When this mind is always held fast and preserved, there is no longer any room for selfishness. Without expecting one's inner being

---

[177] *Li Yen-p'ing hsien-sheng wen-chi*, 3:8b. Li Yen-p'ing urged that "humaneness" and "mind" were to be distinguished.

[178] Ch'eng Hao's phrase in *I-shu*, 2A:3a.

[179] *Ibid.*

[180] Refers to Chou Tun-i, who in *T'ung-shu*, *ch.* 21 and 38 discussed humaneness in terms of impartiality (*kung*).

[181] Hsieh Liang-tso, who himself discussed humaneness in terms of consciousness (*chüeh*), was somewhat wary of a tendency to discuss *jen* in terms of love (*ai*) and asked (in *Shang-ts'ai hsien-sheng yü-lu*, A:7a): "If one concentrates on love, how will one understand *jen?*"

[182] Alludes to *Mencius*, 6A:8, which in Legge's translation (*The Chinese Classics*, 2:409) reads: "Confucius said, 'Hold it fast, and it remains with you. Let it go, and you lose it. Its outgoing and incoming cannot be defined as to time or place.' It is the mind of which this is said!"

[183] *Book of Changes*, *k'un* hexagram, 1:16a.

to be straight, it is naturally straight of itself. Among Confucians of the
past there were some who spoke of "abiding in seriousness"[184] and "maintaining seriousness."[185] It seems that, while wanting to be precise, they
were, on the contrary, vague, thus prompting later scholars to be skeptical.[186] Furthermore, I don't know what their actual practice was really like.

31. The passage which speaks of "the hawk flying and the fish leaping,"[187]
truly shows "Tzu-ssu's concern for what it means to be human."[188] When
he continued by saying, "The Way of the gentleman has its origins among
ordinary men and women,"[189] he probed the matter to its very depths. That
ordinary men and women dwell together[190] is the source of the endless
process of production and transformation. "The nature which is endowed
by heaven"[191] is created through this, and the way of "following one's
nature"[192] emerges through this. The most obvious thing in the world is
really rooted in what is most subtle.[193] What the sages and worthies spoke
about were all actual realities. The Buddhists sever the root, so that the
source of production and transformation is cut off, and yet they still vocif-
erously contend that it is they who perceive the nature. What kind of thing
is this nature after all?

32. One who is committed to the Way must bypass the two barriers of
wealth and status, honor and glory, before he is able to enter. Failing this,
he will be here while the Way is over there, with a strong fence and a thick

---

[184] Ch'eng I in *I-shu*, 15:20a.

[185] Ch'eng I in *I-shu*, 3:5a.

[186] See, for example, Wang Yang-ming's comment about the task of seriousness in
Ch'uan-hsi lu, Part 1, *Wang Wen-ch'eng kung chüan-shu*, 1:64a–65a. Wing-tsit Chan, trans.,
Instructions for Practical Living, sec. 129 (pp. 86–87).

[187] *Mean*, 12:3 which in turn quotes Ode 239.

[188] Quoting Ch'eng Hao in *I-shu*, 3:1a. I am indebted to Professor Wing-tsit Chan
for pointing out the allusion here.

[189] *Mean*, 12:4.

[190] *Mencius*, 5A:2:1.

[191] *Mean*, 1:1.

[192] *Mean*, 1:1.

[193] *Mean*, 1:3.

wall between them and the separation growing greater by the day. When one performs a task, one will necessarily obtain the reward that goes with it; where the reality exists, the fame will naturally follow. The sages and worthies were not lacking in rewards and fame. But all that they did, being in accordance with the dictates of principle, had to be done and was not done for any ulterior motives. As to wealth and status that were not gained in accordance with the Way, they would not even accept them much less have sought them. If while one's mind is constantly chasing after profit and fame he prates about the Way and virtue so as to make a favorable impression, he will find it difficult to escape the charge of being what Hsieh Shang-ts'ai derisively termed "a parrot." [194]

33. *Kuei* and *shen* are the spontaneous activity of the yin and the yang. [195] They are always correct. Should there be anything that is not correct, such as disordered *kuei* or unaccountable events, these are nonetheless caused by yin and yang. It is just that when the yang *ch'i* is in the ascendancy, yang is dominant and yin is supportive, which makes for *kuei* and *shen* that are orderly. When the yin *ch'i* is in the ascendancy, yin is dominant and yang reverts to subserviency, which may cause unaccountable events which are not correct. Although these unaccountable events may do violence to *ch'i*, they could not occur without yang.

This principle is most profound. The main thing is that one must reflect carefully and understand it for himself. This is not something that can be fully expressed in words. When unaccountable events occur, it is always owing to a lack of clarity in administration or instruction. In the absence of support, yang daily disperses, while in the absence of restraints, yin daily expands. The action of the one and the response of the other are like the relation between shadow and form. Naturally there may be such unanticipated occurrences, but the way to dispel evil and promote good cannot be far off.

34. Master Shao said, "The alternation of activity and tranquillity is the consummate mystery of Heaven and earth. That which occurs in the course

---

[194] *Shang-ts'ai hsien-sheng yü-lu*, C:5a.

[195] Quoting Chang Tsai in *Cheng-meng* (Correcting Youthful Ignorance), "T'ai-ho" sec., no. 12, in *Chang Tzu ch'üan-shu*, 2:4a.

of the alternation of activity and tranquillity is the consummate mystery of heaven, earth, and man." [196] In this single phrase—the consummate mystery—the principle of the nature and endowment is fully expressed. How excellent his view is!

Among his poems there is also one that says,

> You must explore the crevices of the moon
> if you would know things
> Before having tracked the root of Nature,
> how can you know man? [197]

Master Chu selected these lines to praise him in a eulogy and also to give full expression to Master Shao's profundity. [198]

If the student does not seek within activity and tranquillity he will have no way to see the crevices in the moon and the root of Nature. And if the root of Nature and the crevices in the moon could not be known, then the words "consummate mystery" would amount to nothing more than an exclamation of admiration. Can the reader be indifferent to the profound ideas of our Confucian predecessors?

35. Not only do all people have the equilibrium before the feelings have been aroused, [199] but all things have it too. For equilibrium is "the great foundation of the world," [200] and it could not be different in human beings and in things. Although it is true that only a sage is capable of establishing

---

[196] Shao Yung (1011–1077) in *Huang-chi ching-shih shu* (Supreme Principles Governing the World), 5:16b. See also *Yü-ch'iao wen-tui* (Dialogue of the Fisherman and the Woodcutter) in *Shuo-fu*, 92:26b (Hsin-hsing shu-chü reprint, p. 1256). For Chu Hsi's comments on this passage, see *Chu Tzu yü-lei*, 100:6b–7a.

[197] "Kuan-wu yin," in *I-ch'uan chi-jang chi* (Striking an Earthen Instrument in the I River), 5:9b–10a (*Kinsei kanseki sōkan, shisō hen*, 4:446–47). The poem is also found in Chang Po-hsing, comp., *Lien-lo feng-ya* (Anthology of Poems from the Schools of Lien-hsi and Lo-yang), 3:13b. In his commentary on this poem in the *Chūgoku koten shinsho* ed. of the *I-ch'uan chi-jang chi* (p. 136) Ueno Hideto explains the "root of nature" (*t'ien-ken*) as "the vast earth." I am indebted to Conrad Schirokauer for drawing my attention to this edition with its useful commentary.

[198] *Chu Tzu wen-chi*, 85:9b and *Chu Tzu yü-lei*, 100:9a–b. In the *Yü-lei*, Chu interprets the "crevices of the moon" and the "root of Nature" to represent yin and yang.

[199] *Mean*, 1:4.

[200] *Ibid.*

the great foundation, one must nonetheless work at this in the course of learning. It is precisely this that "the people use day by day without being aware of it," and that Mencius was referring to when he said, "that whereby man differs from the lower animals is but small."[201]

Among Confucians of the past there were some who considered that ordinary people were lacking in the equilibrium before the feelings are aroused.[202] I am afraid that they were mistaken. Were there a distinction between those who had it and those who did not, how could it be that "all things are endowed with the entirety of the Great Ultimate?"[203] This idea is extremely refined and subtle and is definitely not subject to more than one interpretation.[204]

36. Master Ch'eng (Ch'eng I) criticized Lü Yü-shu[205] for not comprehending "the great foundation."[206] He did not say that a child lacks the equilibrium before the feelings are aroused, but simply that the child's mind cannot be devoid of activity, and that activity involves the defect of onesidedness and attachment, so that one cannot speak of "the great foundation." Yet in its original substance equilibrium certainly remains the same. Although there may be onesidedness and attachment, it is always perfectly unified

---

[201] *Mencius*, 4B:19:1.

[202] Chu Hsi responds to questions about the nature of equilibrium in sages and in ordinary people in *Chu Tzu yü-lei*, 62:25a.

[203] Chu Hsi in *Chu Tzu yü-lei*, 4:2a.

[204] Compare with Wang Yang-ming's view on this subject in *Ch'uan-hsi lu*, Part 1, in *Wang Wen-ch'eng kung ch'üan-shu*, 1:29a and 38a–39a. Wing-tsit Chan, trans., *Instructions for Practical Living*, sec. 45 (p. 39) and sec. 76 (pp. 51–52).

[205] Lü Ta-lin (1044–1090). He began as a pupil of Chang Tsai, becoming a student of the Ch'eng brothers after Chang's death. With Hsieh Liang-tso, Yu Tso, and Yang Shih, he was styled one of "the four disciples of the Ch'eng school." For an account of him, see *Sung Yüan hsüeh-an*, ch. 31.

[206] *I-ch'uan wen-chi*, 5:10b–11a, records a statement by Lü Ta-lin suggesting that "the equilibrium before the feelings have been aroused" of the Mean may be associated with "the child's mind" referred to by Mencius when he said (*Mencius*, 4B:12): "The great man is he who does not lose his child's mind." Ch'eng I rejected this idea, saying, "The state before the feelings of pleasure, anger, sorrow, and joy have been aroused is called equilibrium. The child's mind is aroused. Though it may not yet be far removed from equilibrium, to call it equilibrium means that one does not comprehend 'the great foundation.' "

and free from guile. That is why Mencius used this illustration,[207] and if one extrapolates from this one can come close to comprehending the meaning of equilibrium.

37. Principle (*li*) is one. Only in response to action will there be form. Once there is action, there is duality. Without duality, there would not be unity. Within heaven and earth, action and response are everywhere, and therefore principle is everywhere.

38. Spirit (*shen*) and transformation (*hua*) are the mysterious functioning of heaven and earth. Were it not for yin and yang, there would be no transformation in the world, and were it not for the Great Ultimate, there would be no spirit. However, to conclude from this that the Great Ultimate is spirit and that yin and yang are transformation would be invalid. For transformation results from the action of yin and yang, but yin and yang are not transformation. Spirit results from the action of the Great Ultimate, and yet the Great Ultimate is not spirit. The word "action" (*wei*) expresses what [Mencius] called, "that which is enacted without an agent" (*mo chih wei erh wei che*).[208]

      Master Chang said, "Unity is the condition for spirit. Duality is the condition for transformation."[209] The word "transformation" here refers to movement and action, whereas the word "spirit" refers to permanence and abiding. Although transformation involves duality, its action is always unitary. Spirit is originally unitary, and yet it is always present within duality. United, we call it spirit; divided, we call it transformation. Thus when one speaks of transformation, spirit is included, and when one speaks of spirit, transformation is included. Yin and yang include the Great Ultimate, and the Great Ultimate includes yin and yang. Unity implies duality and duality implies unity (*i erh erh; erh erh i*). The student must realize this so as to distinguish clearly between substance and function, for those who make the least error in this regard seldom avoid drifting in the direction of Buddhism.

     [207] *Mencius*, 4B:12.

     [208] *Mencius*, 5A:6:2.

     [209] Chang Tsai in *Cheng-meng*, "Ts'an-liang" sec., no. 2, in *Chang Tzu ch'üan-shu*, 2:5b.

39. Only after heaven and man, things and the self, have been clearly distinguished can one speak of the unity of principle. Failing that, one is merely repeating clichés.

40. What the Ch'eng brothers said about "the investigation of principle to the utmost, the full development of one's nature, and the fulfillment of destiny,"[210] pertained to the task of the great worthy and the sage. What Master Chang said about it pertained to the task of the student.[211] When things have been investigated and knowledge has been extended, the nature and destiny are perfectly understood, and there are no longer gradual stages. If one reaches the ultimate point, there are things that are not easy to explain.[212]

41. The younger Master Ch'eng answered a question of Su Chi-ming[213] saying, "What physical form (*hsing-t'i*) does equilibrium have? However, since it is called equilibrium, it must have some symbolic form (*hsing hsiang*)."[214] The elder Master Ch'eng said, " 'Equilibrium is the great foundation of the world.' It is the correct principle of all under heaven which is

---

[210] *Book of Changes*, "Discussion of the Trigrams," 9:1a. Wing-tsit Chan, *A Source Book in Chinese Philosophy*, p. 269.

[211] Ch'eng Hao (in *I-shu*, 11:3b) maintained that, "The investigation of principle to the utmost, the full development of one's nature, and the fulfillment of destiny are one thing." Ch'eng I's position was essentially the same. They were criticized for this by Chang Tsai, who believed that there were necessary stages of attainment and that the probing of principle had to precede the full development of the nature. Wing-tsit Chan (*A Source Book in Chinese Philosophy*, p. 540) has noted that, "Whereas in the *Book of Changes* and in Chang Tsai, for example, the fulfillment of destiny always follows the other two steps, the Ch'eng brothers stressed their simultaneity. They were the first ones to do so. But Chang criticized them as too high sounding, for according to him, the full development of nature involves the nature not only of oneself but of all men and even things, and therefore there must be a sequence."

[212] Wing-tsit Chan observes that this refers to the endowment or destiny (*ming*), which is sometimes not understood.

[213] Su Ping was a student of Chang Tsai for a long time before having become a disciple of the Ch'eng brothers. For an account of him, see *Sung Yüan hsüeh-an, ch.* 31.

[214] Ch'eng I in *I-shu*, 18:15a. Translation adapted from Wing-tsit Chan, *A Source Book in Chinese Philosophy*, p. 566, where *hsing-t'i* is rendered "physical form" and *hsing-hsiang*, "some feature."

central and straight."[215] What is this if not its symbolic form? Since every-thing that has symbolic form can be sought, why can one not seek equilib-rium in the state before the feelings have been aroused? I am sure that the younger Master's words did not represent a definitive view which he held throughout his life.

42. Between "symbolic form" (*hsing-hsiang*) and physical form (*hsing-t'i*) there is only one word of difference. The words "physical" and "form" are both concrete, whereas a symbol is in between the concrete and the abstract. But equilibrium as a symbol is, like the symbols of the *Book of Changes*, difficult to discuss in a general way. One must observe it attentively and comprehend it in silence.

43. Human beings are fundamentally alike at birth in sharing the unitary *ch'i* and the compassionate mind.[216] This is universal, and therefore "one accords his parents with affection, the people with humaneness, and other living things with kindness."[217] This is in accordance with the imperatives of principle. It is what one naturally must do, and not something that one is compelled to do by others. "The gentleman takes office and performs the righteous duties belonging to it."[218] It is through carrying out my duty that I fulfill my humanity. One who abandons himself to wealth and status and forgets all restraints is certainly not worth talking to, but one who rigidly adheres to a particular form of propriety and considers this to be noble, is also not worthy to be engaged in discussion of the Way of humaneness and rightness.

44. A discussion of the Way of governing must center on correcting the mind of the sovereign.[219] I Yin[220] helped T'ai-chia.[221] The Duke of Chou[222]

---

[215] Ch'eng Hao in *I-shu*, 11:11a.

[216] *Mencius*, 2A:6:3–4 and 6A:6:7.

[217] Alludes to *Mencius*, 7A:45.

[218] *Analects*, 18:7:5.

[219] *Mencius*, 4A:20.

[220] Famous minister of King T'ang, he helped T'ang to found the Shang dynasty (c. 1200–1044 B.C.).

[221] The grandson of King T'ang.

[222] The uncle and minister of King Ch'eng of Chou, he served as regent for his nephew and helped to consolidate the Chou empire.

helped King Ch'eng.[223] Both were able to cause their sovereigns to see the light so that they were able to perfect their virtue. That the Shang and the Chou endured for long was because of them. How magnificent they were! Later times have not been without their able and virtuous ministers, and for rectifying and redeeming events as they occurred they deserve much praise. But if we examine their total achievements, we see that there have not been many who could come anywhere near I Yin and the Duke of Chou. Before we can hope for the achievements of an I Yin or a Duke of Chou we must have the learning of a Yen Hui or a Mencius. Thus, cultivating talent is truly the urgent task of government. Wishing for the basis to be correct while ignoring this urgent task is like coming upon a river with neither boat nor oar. I cannot see how it is possible to cross.

45. The work of cultivating talent must be done through the schools. The instruction in present-day schools is solely devoted to classical study and is generally said to be good. But because of the selection of scholars by means of the civil service examination system, the scholar often puts priority on elegant language ahead of the cultivation of his own person and mind. This is why our talent does not compare with that of ancient times. If present-day schools were to implement Master Ch'eng's method of instruction and selection,[224] we might reasonably hope that the enterprise of cultivating talent might approach that seen in the flourishing periods of the Shang and Chou. Didn't the wisdom of Yao and Shun lie in "attending earnestly to what was important?"[225] Didn't it lie in this?

46. When the ancients established government it was in order to enable the people to have plenty.[226] Now when governments are established, it is only to enable the state to have plenty. As the government was run in

---

[223] The successor to King Wu, King Ch'eng was a child at the time of his accession and depended on the wisdom and acumen of his uncle, the Duke of Chou.

[224] Ch'eng I favored reduced reliance on examinations, which he felt served only to discover "the literary products and external deeds" of students, and greater emphasis on personal instruction, a longer period of study for potential officials, and financial support for students during their term of study. His proposals are found in I-ch'uan wen-chi, 3:1a–5b. See also Wing-tsit Chan, trans., Reflections on Things at Hand: The Neo-Confucian Anthology, pp. 223–24.

[225] Alludes to Mencius, 7A:46:1.

[226] Alludes to Analects, 12:9.

former times, it served to transform the people. As it is run now, there are some among the common people who criticize it. How can the people be transformed?

47. The reason that knowing men[227] is difficult is that their outward appearance does not correspond to what is in their minds. The mind of the gentleman is directed toward goodness, and he is definitely free of any trace of evil. The mind of the petty man is directed toward evil, but he always feigns humaneness and rightness in order to conceal his treachery. The more deeply implicated he is in treachery, the more thoroughly will he conceal it. Having the fortune to be thrown together [with righteous people], he becomes ever more ingenious in his concealment, so that, unless one sees through the workings of his mind, one may come to believe that he is a gentleman. He will inevitably meet defeat in the end, but the calamities he will have inflicted on the state may be beyond repair.

When one examines the history of former times, evidence for this will be found in every period. It is certainly not easy to know men. But if one is "clear within oneself,"[228] how can sincerity or guile be hidden? If one is obscured by selfishness and ensnared by desire so that one loses his inherent vision and insight, how can he be free from error? Thus the study of understanding men's words and the art of correcting their minds must truly be part of the effort undertaken by one who would "put men in their proper office."[229]

48. Those laws (fa) that should be changed must be changed because, if they are not, good government will not result. But if one wishes to change the laws, the essential consideration is to get hold of the right men [as officials]. Truly, if there are many who know the Way and respect virtue, they will have no regard for "self" and "other," but will follow only good-

[227] Alludes to the Book of History, "The Counsels of Kao-yao." Legge, Shoo King, p. 70. According to Kao-yao, the duty of the virtuous sovereign lies in "knowing men, and in giving repose to the people."

[228] Alludes to the Book of Rites, "Confucius at Home at Leisure." Legge, Li Chi: Book of Rites, 2:282.

[229] Book of History, "The Counsels of Kao-yao." In Legge's translation (Shoo King, The Chinese Classics, 3:70): "When a sovereign knows men, he is wise, and he can put men into their proper offices."

ness. Then, when it comes to laws that should be changed, their discussion of them will be excellent, and when the changes have been made, their upholding of them will be firm. When this happens, it is possible that the benefit will endure for at least several decades or as much as several centuries. Given the vastness of the empire, how could one possibly assume that there are none who know the Way? If one gets the right men to offer their example and leadership, influence and encouragement, things will naturally change from month to month and year to year. In five or ten years men of genuine talent should turn up one after another. Discussion of the Way and deliberation concerning the laws are not mutually contradictory but are, in fact, mutually complementary. Is there anything that cannot be undertaken in the space of a few years?

49. It may be observed from the vantage point of a single city that, if the administrator is not the right man, the people will quickly become intransigent. Even severe punishments and harsh laws will be to no avail. But as soon as one gets hold of a worthy man to govern them, they will be conscientious and united in their response to him. It does not take long for the people to know whether he is worthy or unworthy. They will already have understood this from his slightest gesture or expression. His reputation carries a momentum of its own, and the people will be spontaneously united in their sentiment of according with him or opposing him. This is a constant principle of action and response. Thus "the ruler holds to the practice of personal cultivation, and the empire is thereby at peace."[230] "The high official undertakes to rectify the ruler, and the empire is thereby secured."[231] "To recognize the immediate in the remote, the cause in the effect, and the manifest in the obscure,"[232] may be considered the task of governing. The Way of governing is in no sense separate from the Way of virtue.

---

[230] *Mencius*, 7B:32.

[231] *Mencius*, 4A:20.

[232] Alludes to the *Mean*, 33:1 which in Legge's translation (*The Chinese Classics*, 1:430–31) reads: "[The superior man] knows how what is distant lies in what is near. He knows where the wind proceeds from. He knows how what is minute becomes manifested. Such an one, we may be sure, will enter into virtue."

50. "To admonish loyally and lead skillfully"[233] is not only applicable to the way of friends but equally applicable to the way of officials who offer advice to the sovereign. Thus intransigence and incitement should be scrupulously avoided. For intransigence is not loyalty, and incitement implies lack of skill. Either will make it difficult to elicit the desired response. When incitement is prompted by loyalty and sincerity it may be countenanced. But if it is motivated by design or calculation, even if it should by chance have helped, what about the warning, "do not deceive"?[234]

51. Those who govern are constantly perturbed about a lack of talent, yet talent has certainly never been lacking. On the contrary, it has just not been sought in the right way. Each person should recommend those whom he knows, and the talent of the empire will all be utilized. As Confucius said to Chung-kung, "Raise to office those whom you know. As to those whom you do not know, will others neglect them?"[235] He meant that each person should recommend those whom he knows. At present the channels for recommending worthy men are extremely narrow. No one who has not held office gets recommended. For those who have held office, from provincial officials to district intendants—and if one counts those in just one circuit, they are quite numerous—the decision as to whether or not they are worthy is made on the word of one or two individuals. Under such circumstances, how is it possible to find all the talent throughout the entire empire? Unless changes are implemented, the lament over a "lack of talent" will be inevitable.

52. Only after institutions have been established is it possible to improve customs and increase material prosperity. But at present the resources of the empire are increasingly strained, and customs have become ever more degenerate. This is the result of the abandonment of institutions. From cloth-

---

[233] Alludes to Analects, 12:23. "Tzu-kung asked about friendship. The Master said, 'Loyally admonish [your friend], and skillfully lead him. If you find him unwilling, stop. Do not disgrace yourself.'" Translation adapted from Legge, The Chinese Classics, 1:261.

[234] Analects, 14:23. "Tzu-lu asked how a ruler should be served. The Master said, 'Do not deceive him, and moreover, withstand him to his face.'" Translation adapted from Legge, The Chinese Classics, 1:285.

[235] Analects, 13:2:1–2.

ing, food, dwellings, and transport, to capping, marriage, funerals, and sacrifices, there must be gradations according to status and distinctions based on rank. Then things will not be wasted, and prosperity may be increased; people will not misappropriate things, and customs may be improved. This principle is unchanging. But the reason the law is not carried out is that it is defied in high places. "The virtue of the sovereign is the wind, while the virtue of the ordinary man is the grass."[236] Everything depends on the court, that is all.

53. Circumstances are such that the well-field system[237] cannot be restored, and the system of delimiting landholdings is not readily implemented. But while landholdings throughout the empire cannot be completely equalized, it is nonetheless appropriate to seek means to adjust them, for otherwise the task of supporting people will never be carried out. At present in areas north and south of the Huai River[238] and in the western reaches of the Han and Mien Rivers[239] a great proportion of the land lies fallow, the population is scattered, and the soil is underutilized. At the same time the population of Kiangsu and Chekiang is especially dense, and many often have no land to cultivate. Were there some means to adjust this, the benefit involved would be considerable.

"Let the people be employed in a way which is intended to secure their ease, and though they be toiled, they will not murmur."[240] How could a gentleman who has studied the Way and loves the people[241] fail to remember this? Ch'ao Ts'o in the Han carried out his plans within

[236] Alludes to *Analects*, 12:19 which in Legge's translation (*The Chinese Classics*, 1:258–59) reads: "The relation between superiors and inferiors is like that between the wind and the grass. The grass must bend, when the wind blows across it."

[237] A landholding system in which land was to be divided into nine equal squares in the configuration of the Chinese character for well (*ch'ing*). The outer squares were to have been farmed by eight families for their individual support, while the central square was to have been worked jointly for the benefit of the government. The system was believed to have been operative in the early Chou period, though its actual historicity remains questionable.

[238] Northern Anhui and southern Honan.

[239] Southern Shensi and northern Szechuan.

[240] *Mencius*, 7A:4:3.

[241] Alludes to *Analects*, 17:4:3.

the borders,[242] while Ch'en Ching in the Sung failed to implement his theories in Ching-hsi.[243] The difference was determined by the intelligence and judgment of their superiors.

54. The proper approach to managing resources was dealt with thoroughly in four sentences in the Great Learning,[244] but in later ages this has rarely been heeded, with the result that both public and private interests have suffered. Now the tributary grain which was supposed to be delivered to the capital has become a monthly ration [for government personnel] and is in innumerable cases intercepted by the powerful and influential.[245] Those in

---

[242] Ch'ao Ts'o was prefect of the capital under Emperor Ching (r. 156–141 B.C.) of the former Han. According to his biography in Ssu-ma Ch'ien, Shih-chi, 101, he succeeded in having thirty new statutes added to the laws, though he was opposed by the feudal lords, whose territories he sought to curtail. See Burton Watson, trans., Records of the Grand Historian of China (hereafter abbreviated as Watson, Records), 1:527–32.

[243] When Sung T'ai-tsung (r. 976–997) called for deliberations on the equal field system, Ch'en Ching came forward with an elaborate proposal to reform the landholding system. The emperor acknowledged that Ch'en's proposal had merit, but he refused to implement it out of concern that tax revenues might be reduced. Ch'en was not even permitted to try out his plan in the area of Ching-hsi, the circuit located just west of the capital of Loyang. See Ch'en's biography in Sung-shih, 426:1b–4a.

[244] A reference to the Great Learning, Commentary, 10:7–9. "Virtue is the root; wealth is the result. If the ruler make the root his secondary object, and the result his primary object, he will only wrangle with his people and teach them rapine. Hence the accumulation of wealth is the way to scatter the people. Letting it be scattered among them is the way to collect the people." (Translation adapted from Legge, The Chinese Classics, 1:375–76.)

[245] Ray Huang observes that a substantial part of the tribute grain was used during this period as a food ration, distributed monthly. From 1472, approximately 3.7 million piculs of grain were delivered to Peking annually and used in large part to meet salary obligations. As he explains (Taxation and Governmental Finance in Sixteenth-Century Ming China, p. 59), "The distribution was effected through a rationing system. With few exceptions, all civil officials, army officers, and lesser functionaries received 1 picul per man per month regardless of rank, as part of their pay. Soldiers and artisans on duty received half this amount. By the late fifteenth century and early sixteenth century there were no fewer than 300,000 men eligible for the grain payment. The 1502 report by the ministry of revenue indicated that the annual amount payable was 3.38 million piculs. Whenever there was a shortage in grain delivery or an additional demand for payment, the capital granary incurred a deficit. Thus the tribute grain, which entailed such high delivery costs, contributed little to the empire's finances. While it solved the food supply problem in the capital, most of its recipients, being supernumeraries, performed no useful function in to the state." Professor Huang also points out that a substantial amount of this tribute grain was intercepted by persons occupying high positions, notably army officers and eunuchs (pp. 336–37, n. 80).

charge of the financial administration of the state are no longer informed about receipts and disbursements. Can this be called the administration of official business? Since revenues are not sufficient, unreasonable extortion of taxes frequently occurs. What is there to prevent the people from being impoverished and reduced to banditry? It was still possible for Emperor Te-tsung (r. 780–804) of the T'ang to receive a petition from Yang Yen (727–781) to transfer tax revenues to the Left Treasury.[246] What difficulty could there be for a heroic and perceptive sovereign? What one may infer from this is that by fully utilizing surpluses, "resources will be more than can be consumed."[247]

55. Many eminent officials of the T'ang and Sung periods were inclined toward Ch'an, and those who achieved consummate mastery of it derived ample benefits. For not only were they refined in their inborn endowment, they also thereby achieved purity and tranquillity of mind. If in addition they had the accomplishment that goes along with the study of antiquity, then their operations and dealings, even if they did not hit the mark, would nonetheless not be far afield. Moreover, those who engaged in this practice neither concealed the name nor disguised the reality of their practice, so that there was never a question of its damaging their integrity. Although the practice was mistaken, they were often enough praiseworthy. However, in later generations there are those who are nominally Confucian but actually Ch'an and who disguise the reality and make much of the name. I do not know what would happen if they were to return to their own minds.

56. The world is a great vessel. It is necessary to regard the world as one's standard before one can begin to move it. Talent cannot be relied upon,

---

[246] Yang Yen's memorial of 780 is found in *T'ang hui-yao*, 59, pp. 1015–16. According to *Chiu T'ang shu*, 105:8a, the Emperor Hsüan-tsung (r. 713–755) had large expenditures for gifts to concubines and palace ladies, and, to spare him the inconvenience of going to the Left and Right Treasuries (tso-yu ts'ang), an arrangement was made by Wang Hung to place vast amounts of money and treasure directly into the Palace Stores (nei-k'u). *Hsin T'ang shu*, 51:4b, states that during the An Lu-shan Rebellion the Revenue Commissioner Ti-wu Ch'i had all the tax revenues put into the Palace Stores and placed in the charge of eunuchs. This system continued until Yang Yen's request in 780 to have taxes paid into the regular treasury stores. See Edwin G. Pulleyblank, *The Background of the Rebellion of An Lu-shan*, pp. 132–33, n. 83.

[247] *Mencius*, 7A:23:2.

for one may have a surpassing talent without having heard of the Way of the gentleman, in which case the vessel will be too readily filled. What is not yet full is great. When one relies on greatness to move what is great, will it not be found to be ample?

57. The talent which we see displayed in the world is given over either to the learning of the Way *(tao-hsüeh)*,[248] to literary composition, or to the practice of government. Generally speaking, there are these three categories, and, among them, there are also differences in depth and distinction. Yet all are referred to as "talent." In my experience, however, the term *tao-hsüeh* finds little favor in the world. Those who have pursued the study of it have not necessarily done so in such a way that the name and the reality have corresponded. Then too there have been those who have not managed to avoid arrogance and intolerance, which in turn give rise to antipathy and invective. Now to study with the object of seeking the Way is naturally our responsibility. It is certainly unacceptable to shun others on this account and worse yet to be arrogant toward them. Once the first signs of this emerge, it spreads everywhere, as evidenced by the case of Ch'eng [I] and Su [Shih][249] in the Yüan-yu period (1086–1093).[250] Therefore one who

[248] For *tao-hsüeh*, see n. 81, above.

[249] Su Shih or Su Tung-p'o (1037–1101) was among the most famous writers and statesmen of the eleventh century. For an account of his influence on the culture of the Northern Sung, see Peter Kees Bol, "Culture and the Way in Eleventh Century China," Ph.D. dissertation, Princeton University, 1982.

[250] See the biography of Ch'eng I in *Sung-shih*, 427:10a–15b. Wing-tsit Chan's summary of the situation (*A Source Book in Chinese Philosophy*, p. 546, n. 14) is as follows: "[Ch'eng I] lived and taught in Lo-yang, and repeatedly declined high offices, including a professorship at the directorate of education in 1085. In 1086 he was appointed expositor in waiting, and he lectured in great seriousness on Confucian principles to the emperor. He did this for twenty months and attracted many followers. But his uncompromising attitude, his critical opinions, and his attack on many things created bitter enemies, particularly Su Shih . . . leader of the Szechuan group. This led to the bitter factional struggle between it and the Lo-yang group led by Ch'eng I. In 1087 he was appointed director of the directorate of education in the western capital but resigned a few months later. When he was supervisor of the directorate in 1092, censors repeatedly petitioned for his impeachment. He finally resigned and returned to Lo-yang. In 1097 his teachings were prohibited, his land was confiscated, and he was banished to Fu-chou in modern Szechuan. He was pardoned three years later and resumed his position at the directorate. By that time, government persecution of factions had

would be a scholar-official ought to put primary emphasis on cultivating real accomplishments, and one who seeks to employ scholar-officials must elicit their various strengths. In this way the talent of both great and small men will develop in due course. There will be no antipathy among them and mutual benefit will result. The good government of the empire will then be virtually ensured.

58. It was not that Emperor Kao of Han did not employ Confucians but rather that true Confucians were hard to come by. At that time the Emperor always accepted the counsel of men like Lu Chia[251] and Shu-sun T'ung[252] and permitted them to do as they saw fit. Their scope and capacity are quite apparent. Given the intelligence and discernment of Kao of Han, would he have lightly abandoned men who were even more worthy than these two? Two scholars of Lu refused the invitation of Shu-sun. Yang Tzu-yün[253] praised their potential to be high officials,[254] but I don't know what he had in mind when he said this.

    Now to say that "rites and music can only be set up after [a

---

become severe. Both he and Su Shih, along with several hundred scholars, were blacklisted. His followers left him. In 1103 his books were destroyed and teachings prohibited. He was pardoned again in 1106, a year before he died."

    [251]His biography is found in *Shih-chi*, 97. As a master strategist, Lu Chia was of particular service to Emperor Kao in persuading Chao T'o, the ruler of Yüeh, to declare his allegiance to the Han. On becoming a palace counselor, Lu Chia expounded the *Book of Odes* and the *Book of History*. Challenged by the emperor's criticism that, "All that I possess I have won on horseback," Lu countered, "Your Majesty may have won it on horseback, but can you rule it on horseback?" Counseling against excessive attention to military affairs, he wrote for Emperor Kao a work in which he expounded the essential principles of political survival and defeat. The work presumably bore Confucian influence. See Watson, *Records*, 1:275–83.

    [252]His biography is found in *Shih-chi*, 99. He served the second emperor of the Ch'in, later went over to Hsiang Yü, and finally attached himself to Liu Pang. When the latter became Emperor as Han Kao-tsu, Shu-sun T'ung arranged the titles and ceremonies to be used, and it was he who was later charged with formulating a new code of ritual for the Han. For this work he summoned some thirty scholars of Lu, though, as his biography records, two of the Lu scholars refused on principle to come. See Watson, *Records*, 1:291–98.

    [253]Yang Hsiung (53 B.C.–A.D. 18).

    [254]*Fa-yen* (Model Sayings), ch. 6. See *Tsuan t'u hu-chu Yang Tzu Fa-yen* (*Chung-kuo tzu-hsüeh ming-chu chi-ch'eng, chen-pen*, vol. 29), 6:2a–b (pp. 123–24).

dynasty] has accumulated virtue for a period of a hundred years[255] is not unreasonable, yet during this hundred-year period there must be ways of carrying on the affairs of government. How much more does this apply to the employment of rites and music, which the empire cannot be without for a single day? Were these two scholars really great worthies? They certainly must have had definite views concerning the appropriate order of priorities, but if they had had definite views, wouldn't it have been better to have come out and stated them? If their recommendations had really been practicable, and yet the Emperor would not comply with them, then whether they remained in office or retired would have been entirely up to them. And how did they know that their counsel would not be heeded? As they based their decision merely on the example of Shu-sun alone, didn't they idly allow an opportunity to be lost? In my humble opinion it was not that the two scholars had definitely heard the Way, but only that they were obstinately committed to their own limited view of it and found it lofty. Since they did not come forward, they remained two scholars. If they had come forward, they might have served in the manner of the four elders.[256] In either case I am afraid that they had not the capacity to serve as high officials.

59. The T'ang system of military prefectures most closely approximated the way of the ancients. Fan Wen-cheng[257] once proposed to revive it but was

---

[255]Lo alludes to the account in Shu-sun T'ung's biography in the *Shih-chi* of the refusal of the two Lu scholars to serve the Han. The following argument is attributed by Ssu-ma Ch'ien (Watson, *Records*, 1:294) to the two scholars: "Now the world has just been set at peace, the dead have not been properly buried, and the wounded have not yet risen from their beds, and yet you wish to set up rites and music for the new dynasty. But rites and music can only be set up after a dynasty has accumulated virtue for a period of a hundred years. We could never bring ourselves to take part in what you are doing, for what you are doing is not in accord with the ways of antiquity. We will never go! Now go away and do not defile us any longer!"

[256]Emperor Kao seriously entertained the possibility of changing the heir apparent so as to favor the son of his concubine, Lady Ch'i. He was dissuaded from this course by Chang Liang and Shu-sun T'ung, both tutors to the heir apparent. It was Chang Liang's plan to enlist the support of four old men whom the Emperor admired but had not succeeded in enlisting in the Han cause. The appearance of these four (the famous *ssu-hao*) in the service of the heir apparent impressed the emperor and persuaded him not to change the heir apparent. However, no sooner had the decision been made than the four quickly departed. See *Shih-chi*, 55; Watson, *Records*, 1:146–49.

[257]Fan Chung-yen (989–1052).

held back by the opinions of the other officials.[258] Truly, whether the Way declines or flourishes depends upon whether it is ordered.[259]

    I have looked into this with some degree of thoroughness and feel that the implementation of this system would have been clearly advantageous and not harmful. Neither in terms of human considerations nor in terms of strategic factors was there any reason it could not work. The system is elaborate in its reciprocal functions and complex in its interlocking details. It would require flexible application to be determined in accordance with particular circumstances, and this is not something that can be summarized in a word. The system would have to be extended to the entire empire, so that every prefecture and prefectural city without exception would be prepared and the system would be reliable in every contingency. Soldiers who were old or weak, feeble or idle, would be returned to farming. Naturally this would mean increasingly maximizing the wealth of the state and steadily improving the strength of the people. This is an obvious benefit, having nothing to do with the empty talk that comes of plying the brush or the tongue.

60. When Ch'u and Han were contending for the empire, Emperor Kao himself opposed Hsiang Yü[260] between Ying-yang and Ch'eng-kao and ordered Han Hsin[261] to ford the river to the north and seize Wei, Chao, Yen, and Ch'i. As the area of Hopei and Shantung was taken, Yü was thus surrounded by the Han. But the circle was not yet drawn because he could still count on the King of Chiu-chiang, Ch'ing Pu,[262] in the south. Then

---

    [258] As prime minister during the reign of Jen-tsung (r. 1023–1056) in the Northern Sung, Fan proposed a ten-point program of administrative reform, including revival of the militia system that had existed in the early T'ang. This is discussed in his memorial of Ch'ing-li 3 (1043) in *Fan Wen-cheng kung cheng-fu tsou-i* (Memorials on Government by Fan Chung-yen) (in *Che-shih chü ts'ung-shu*), ch. 1.

    [259] Paraphrases *Analects*, 14:38:2 which in Legge's translation (*The Chinese Classics*, 1:289) reads: "The Master said, 'If my principles are to advance, it is so ordered. If they are to fall to the ground, it is so ordered. What can Kung-po Liao do where such ordering is concerned?' "

    [260] The great opponent of Liu Pang. A long and moving biography of him is found in *Shih-chi*, 7; Watson, *Records*, 1:37–74.

    [261] His biography is found in *Shih-chi*, 92; Watson, *Records*, 1:208–32.

    [262] His biography is found in *Shih-chi*, 91; Watson, *Records*, 1:196–207.

Sui Ho caused Pu to join forces with the Han,[263] so that the encirclement was complete. How could Yü any longer escape? This was the general situation that pertained as the Han conquered the realm.

The successful deployment of troops requires first of all an understanding of circumstances. There are the circumstances of the empire, the circumstances of a given area, and the circumstances of a given battle. Understanding them will lead to success, while failure to understand them leads to defeat, and the benefit and harm involved in success and defeat are incalculable. At present few Confucians will discuss military matters, but, essentially, grain and military equipment are both our responsibility. How can we fail to discuss these matters?

For example, when in the T'ang, An Lu-shan[264] captured Loyang [in 756], leaving his family behind, Li [Kuang-] pi[265] and Kuo Tzu-i[266] requested that they first [be authorized to] "capture Fan-yang in order to destroy his lair."[267] This was truly a case of understanding circumstances. But Su-tsung (r. 756–762) was anxious about recapturing [the capital] and did not approve their plan. As a result the area of Hopei was lost and never regained during the whole of the T'ang. When Huang Ch'ao[268] made his incursion into Kuang [-chou] [in 879(?)][269] Kao P'ien[270] requested that troops be separately garrisoned in strategic places in the prefectures of Ch'en, Hsün,

---

[263] Sui Ho's mission is described in the biography of Ch'ing Pu in *Shih-chi*, 91; Watson, *Records*, 1:198–203.

[264] His biography is found in *Chiu T'ang-shu*, 200A:1a–5b, and *Hsin T'ang-shu*, 225A:1a–7a. See also Howard S. Levy, trans., *Biography of An Lu-shan*.

[265] The text reads Li Pi, but this is an apparent error. The biography of Li Kuang-pi is found in *Chiu T'ang-shu*, 110:1a–6b, and *Hsin T'ang-shu*, 136:1a–4b.

[266] His biography is found in *Chiu T'ang-shu*, 120:1a–12b, and *Hsin T'ang-shu*, 137:1a–7b.

[267] Quoting their memorial. See Ssu-ma Kuang, *Tzu-chih t'ung-chien* (A Comprehensive Mirror for Aid in Government), 218:6967.

[268] His biography is found in *Chiu T'ang-shu*, 200B:4b–9a and *Hsin T'ang-shu*, 225C.

[269] For a detailed discussion of the controversy over the dating of Huang Ch'ao's incursion into Kuang-chou, see Howard S. Levy, trans., *Biography of Huang Ch'ao*, pp. 113–16.

[270] His biography is found in *Chiu T'ang-shu*, 182:5b–11b and *Hsin T'ang-shu*, 224B:3a–11b.

Wu, Chao, Kuei, and Yung. He himself planned to attack him by crossing the Ta-yü ridge.[271] This was truly understanding circumstances. If his advice had been followed, Ch'ao would have been caught like a rabbit in a snare. But the rulers of the state failed to realize this. In the end Ch'ao erupted and spread his evil, and consequently the deluge mounted to heaven. Was this only in small part related to the matter of understanding circumstances?

61. In the Way of nature the sun, moon, stars, and the asterisms are the warp, and the wind, rain, thunder, clouds, frost, and dew are the woof. The warp and the woof are characterized by constancy wherein lies the wonder of origination, prosperity, advantage, and correctness.[272] It is through them that creation is completed. In the Way of man the relations between sovereign and minister, father and son, husband and wife, elder and younger, and friend and friend are the warp, while the feelings of pleasure, anger, sorrow, and joy are the woof.[273] The warp and the woof do not err, and the reality of humaneness, rightness, propriety, and wisdom are included within them. Their [excellent] virtue and [great] calling are fulfilled through this.[274]

62. In Master Chou's discussion of the nature there are points at which he was speaking of what is essential. Such was the case when he spoke of "the source of sincerity" and "the establishment of sincerity"[275] and when he said, "it is pure and perfectly good."[276] There are also points at which he

---

[271] His memorial is found in *Tzu-chih t'ung-chien*, 253:8216.

[272] "The sun, moon, stars, and the asterisms," alludes to the *Book of History*, "Canon of Yao." See Legge, *Shoo King, The Chinese Classics*, 4:81. In *Pacing the Void*, Edward H. Schafer interprets *ch'en* as "asterism" or "chronogram" (see esp. p. 5), and Legge's translation has been adapted accordingly. "Origination, prosperity, advantage, and correctness" are the opening words of the *Book of Changes, ch'ien* hexagram.

[273] The five human relationships are discussed in the *Mean*, 20:8, and the arising of the feelings of pleasure, anger, sorrow and joy in the *Mean*, 1:4.

[274] Alludes to the *Book of Changes*, "Appended Remarks," 7:8a.

[275] Chou Tun-i in *T'ung-shu*, 1a. For a complete translation of the *T'ung-shu*, see Wing-tsit Chan, *A Source Book in Chinese Philosophy*, pp. 465–80.

[276] *Ibid.*

was speaking of what is contingent. Such was the case when he said, "Strength may be good or evil. The same is true of weakness. The ideal is the Mean."[277] But the statements in the first chapter of the *T'ung-shu* (Penetrating the *Book of Changes*) form an integral whole and are very precise. If there is something that the reader has not yet studied, he may think that Master Chou was discussing the nature solely in terms of strength and weakness, good and evil.[278] This would be inaccurate.

63. The wonder of the Great Ultimate and yin and yang is such that, through careful observation, perfect understanding can be achieved by searching in the space of a single year. The observations may also be made in the space of a single day, though it is difficult to scrutinize something that is too near at hand. The observations may also be made in the course of a millennium,[279] though it is difficult to examine something that is too remote. Essentially, whether in the immediacy of a single day or in the remoteness of a millennium, emptiness and fullness, concentration and dispersal, mutually create the cycle of interaction which is principle. One may infer on the basis of what occurs in a single year and find nothing that is out of conformity. The *Book of Changes* says, "In the hexagram of return, one sees the mind of heaven and earth."[280] This clearly shows the origin of all this, and if one understands it, when one encounters the transactions of society and the transformations of the world, what need will there be to rely on anything external?

64. The nature is without form. Although there are apt analogies, it is in the end difficult to exhaust its mystery. Both Mencius and Master Ch'eng (Ch'eng Hao) selected the analogy of water, and what they had to say has an enduring quality. They considered that water is the same thing whether

---

[277] *T'ung-shu*, 5a.

[278] Chu Hsi's view, as found in *Chu Tzu yü-lei*, 94:28a, was that when Chou Tun-i discussed the nature in terms of strength and weakness, good and evil, he was speaking about the physical nature *(ch'i-chih chih hsing)*. This category was not accepted by Lo Ch'in-shun, who insisted that any division between an ideal and a physical nature was artificial.

[279] Literally, one *yüan*, a period of 129,600 years.

[280] *Book of Changes, fu* hexagram, 3:11b.

it "flows down" or is "forced uphill"[281] and whether it is clear or turbid.[282] But when it comes to explaining what it is that is not good, according to the first analogy, one causes water to be diverted by striking it, while, according to the second, it is the mud and sand that make it turbid. In this respect there is a slightly different conception. If, in one's own mind, one can combine the two theories, one may approach a complete understanding of the meaning of the nature.

Hsieh Hsien-tao (Hsieh Liang-tso) recorded Master I-ch'uan's saying that "The adherents of Ch'an discuss the nature on the analogy of containers which are arranged in the sunlight. The square ones differ from the round ones, and the large differ from the small. Pick one up and try to pour from one into another. When does the sunlight move?"[283] These words of I-ch'uan's served to demolish the errors of the Ch'an school. Yet he also said, "Man is to his nature like a container which receives light from the sun."[284] The word "receive" is certainly not the same as the word "pour," but after all the analogy is still inapt.

[281] Alludes to Mencius, 6A:2:2–3, which in Legge's translation (The Chinese Classics, 2:395–96), reads: "The tendency of man's nature to good is like the tendency of water to flow downwards. There are none but have this tendency to be good, just as all water flows downwards. Now by striking water and causing it to leap up, you may make it go over your forehead, and by damming and leading it, you may force it up a hill—but are such movements according to the nature of water? It is the force applied that causes them. When men are made to do what is not good, their nature is dealt with in this way."

[282] Ch'eng Hao in I-shu, 1:7b–8a. In Wing-tsit Chan's translation (A Source Book in Chinese Philosophy, p. 528) the passage to which Lo alludes reads as follows: "Actually, in our discussion of nature, we only talk about (the idea expressed in the Book of Changes as) 'What issues from the Way is good.' This is the case when Mencius speaks of the original goodness of human nature. The fact that whatever issues from the Way is good may be compared to the fact that water is always the same in all cases. Some water flows onward to the sea without becoming dirty. What human effort is needed here? Some flows only a short distance before growing turbid. Some becomes extremely turbid, some only slightly so. Although water differs in being clean or turbid, we cannot say that the turbid water (evil) ceases to be water (nature)."

[283] Ch'eng I in I-shu, 3:3b. Chu Hsi also referred to this as a Ch'an metaphor in Chu Tzu yü-lei, 97:19a and 126:22a. He said that to discuss the nature through the analogy of placing vessels in the sunlight was redolent of the notion of transmigration.

[284] I-shu, 3:6a. The passage concludes, "The sun is the thing that is fundamentally unmoving."

65. In the passage in which the elder Master Ch'eng discussed "What is inborn is the nature,"[285] he reiterated and elaborated, but the whole idea was that "principle is one; its particularizations are diverse." When explaining this to students, Master Chu may on occasion have been detailed or concise, but the general idea was the same. Yet since there would seem to be some slight differences, I should like to examine them.

When [Ch'eng Hao] said, "According to principle there are both good and evil in the ch'i with which man is endowed at birth,"[286] he was referring to the diversity of particularizations. When he said, "However, man is not born with these two opposing elements in his nature to start with,"[287] he was referring to the unity of principle. He said, " 'By nature man is tranquil at birth.' [288] The state preceding this cannot be discussed." [289] For the tranquillity at birth is the equilibrium before the feelings have been aroused[290] and the reality of the nature, which is unitary. This is so utterly profound that the forms of language are inadequate to describe it, and therefore he said, "it cannot be discussed." "What issues [from the successive movement of yin and yang] is good,"[291] refers to man's being influenced by things and becoming active.[292] Once there is activity, there is manifold diversity, and it is then that the particularizations of strong and weak, good and bad, first begin to appear. That particularizations differ widely is entirely in accordance with natural principle, and therefore he said, "It cannot be said that evil is not the nature."[293] Once we call the nature strong or weak, good or bad, we are no longer returning to the

---

[285] Ch'eng Hao's discussion of Kao Tzu's statement in Mencius, 6A:3, is recorded in I-shu, 1:7b.

[286] I-shu, 1:7b. Translation by Wing-tsit Chan in A Source Book in Chinese Philosophy, p. 528.

[287] Ibid.

[288] Alludes to the Book of Rites, "Record of Music." Cf. translation by Legge, Li Chi: Book of Rites, 2:96.

[289] I-shu, 1:7b.

[290] Mean, 1:4.

[291] I-shu, 1:7b. Ch'eng Hao was quoting from the Book of Changes, "Appended Remarks," 7:7b.

[292] Book of Rites, "Record of Music."

[293] I-shu, 1:7b.

fineness and purity of its original substance, and therefore he said, "As soon as we talk about the nature, it is no longer the [original] nature." [294]

In what follows he also used the metaphor of the clearness and turbidity of water, with clearness being used to denote its original substance, which is truly most tranquil, and turbidity being expressive of the material desires which are associated with movement and activity. The original substance is indeed extremely pure, yet we have no way of seeing it before it has left the mountain. It must flow before it can be seen. Inasmuch as some turbidity is inevitable, we cannot do without the effort of cultivation. Once the effort of cultivation is complete, the turbid part becomes settled, while the original substance remains ever clear. It would be impossible for anything either to augment or diminish it. Therefore he concluded with the line, "Shun possessed the empire as if it were nothing to him." [295]

One must carefully examine the words "the state preceding this" as they are used in this essay. They serve simply to differentiate the realm of activity from the realm of tranquillity. Just as when one takes activity as the point of reference, tranquillity becomes "the state preceding this," so also when we speak about "the state before the feelings have been aroused," what point is understood to be prior to their arousal? It can only be discussed in relation to "what has already been aroused."

Master Chu seems to have gone too far in his search. He thought that "the state preceding this" was "the time before living things are born." [296] I am afraid that this was not Master Ch'eng's original idea. For when Master Ch'eng quoted the phrase, "By nature man is tranquil at birth," he was referring specifically to the original nature. When he continued, "As soon as we talk about the nature, it is no longer the [original] nature," he was referring to what people have always talked about, namely, the activity of the nature, and not the nature in its origin. This idea is extremely clear, and if one lingers over it, one can perceive it for oneself. If one takes "the state preceding" man's being tranquil at birth to refer to the time before living things are born, one would be speaking of the endowment of heaven

[294] *Ibid.*

[295] *I-shu*, 1:8a, alluding to *Analects*, 8:18.

[296] Letter in Reply to Yen Shih-heng in *Chu Tzu wen-chi*, 61:22b. See also *Chu Tzu yü-lei*, 95:13a–b.

(*t'ien-ming*).[297] This does not take into account the words "[as soon as we talk about the nature] it is no longer the [original] nature."

66. The younger Master Ch'eng said, "In considering Mencius' discussion of the nature, one must take into account the context. He did not hold that Kao Tzu's statement that 'What is inborn is the nature,'[298] was wrong. This is also the nature. It was only that [Kao Tzu] spoke of the nature as something that comes into being after life has been endowed, and therein lay the difference between them. [Mencius] continued by asking, 'Is the nature of a dog like the nature of an ox, and the nature of an ox like the nature of a man?'[299] But there is no harm in considering them as one. When it comes to what Mencius described as good,[300] he was speaking of the nature in its most original state."[301]

If one examines Master Ch'eng's many statements concerning the nature, only this formulation is altogether complete. Within identity there are distinctions, and amid distinctions there is identity. The reality of the nature and endowment is without surplus or deficiency. However, I am afraid that there must have been some slight misunderstanding on the part of the person who recorded it in connection with the closing sentences in this passage. At the time they are first endowed with *ch'i*, the nature of a dog or an ox is always one with that of man, while after having taken on physical form, the nature of a dog or an ox is naturally not the same as the nature of man. When Master Ch'eng said, "there is no harm in considering them as one," he was referring to the nature in its origin and source. Where the text goes on to say, "When it comes to [what Mencius described as good . . .]" these words disrupted his train of thought so that it is somewhat lacking in coherence. This could only have been a misunderstanding on the part of the recorder.

67. In the teaching of the Ch'eng brothers, knowledge and comprehension were always regarded as primary. These words are found again and again in

[297] Alludes to Ode 267.
[298] Recorded in *Mencius*, 6A:3:1.
[299] *Mencius*, 6A:3:3.
[300] *Mencius*, 3A:1:2 and 6A:6:4.
[301] *I-shu*, 3:3b.

the *I-shu* (Written Legacy) and in what their disciples recorded. As it says in the *Great Learning*, "Wishing to make their thoughts sincere, they first extended their knowledge . . . Their knowledge being complete, their thoughts became sincere."[302] This is an order that cannot be changed.

Going on to examine the words of Master Chu, there is the statement, "[Hsieh] Shang-ts'ai said, 'One must first have knowledge and comprehension and nourish oneself with reverence. This is like first establishing one thing.' "[303] On another occasion he said, "When one is not yet able to comprehend, what can one cultivate?"[304] He frequently praised Ch'eng Ming-tao's statement that "The student must first comprehend humanity,"[305] describing these words as excellent.[306] When it came to Hu Wu-feng's[307] statement, "If one desires to be humane, it is first necessary to comprehend the substance of humanity,"[308] he expressed grave doubts and said that it was not necessary to cause scholars "first to comprehend the substance of humanity."[309] Since he first said one thing and later another, how is the student to know which to follow?

I have tried to discern an order of priorities in this and have concluded that it is essential first to have knowledge and comprehension, though to comprehend humanity is a very difficult task indeed. Ming-tao once said, "The concept of the principle of nature I have realized directly for myself."[310] This is the method by which one comprehends humanity. The effort of realizing for oneself must be wholehearted and careful. If it is incomplete in the slightest particular, one will miss the truth. Master Chu's words were usually intended to remedy a student's particular onesidedness,

---

[302] *Great Learning,* 4–5.

[303] *Chu Tzu yü-lei,* 101:11a, quoting Hsieh Liang-tso as recorded in *Shang-ts'ai hsien-sheng yü-lu,* A:4b

[304] *Chu Tzu yü-lei,* 9:4a.

[305] Ch'eng Hao in *I-shu,* 2A:3a.

[306] *Chu Tzu yü-lei,* 97:5a.

[307] Hu Hung (1106–1162).

[308] Quoted in *Hu Tzu chih-yen i-i* (Doubts Concerning Master Hu's Understanding Words) (in *Yüeh-ya-t'ang ts'ung-shu,* collection 10), 9b. See also *Chu Tzu wen-chi,* 73:46a.

[309] *Hu Tzu chih-yen i-i,* 10a, and *Chu Tzu wen-chi,* 73:46a.

[310] Ch'eng Hao in *Wai-shu,* 12:4a.

which explains the fact that he was not consistent in what he said. When I follow out the inconsistencies and attempt to reconcile them so as to recover the ultimate unity, I find that I have an abundance of teachers.[311]

68. The place where principle resides is called the mind. Therefore unless one preserves the mind, one will not have the means by which to probe principle to the utmost. That which the mind possesses is called the nature. Therefore unless one knows the nature, he will not have the means by which fully to develop his mind. When Mencius discussed the mind and the nature he distinguished them clearly, so why should it be that scholars often mistakenly identify them?

Seeking the lost mind[312] is only the preliminary work; fully developing the mind[313] is the culmination of the process. In between what is most important is to probe principle to the utmost. Probing principle to the utmost necessarily entails gradual stages. But fully developing the mind and knowing the nature[314] take place at once, and there is no longer a question of priorities. Before principle has been probed to the utmost, the mind, even though it may have been established, cannot be fully developed. When we devote ourselves to the mind, we naturally know upon reflection whether or not we have developed our mind to the fullest. If we suppose that we have developed our mind to the fullest without actually having done so, this is willingly deceiving ourselves rather than being truly committed to the Way.

69. Master Li Yen-p'ing said, "The activity and tranquillity, truth and falsity, good and evil which are spoken of as opposites are what the world calls activity and tranquillity, truth and falsity, good and evil, and not the activity and tranquillity, truth and falsity, good and evil of the nature. Only when one seeks tranquillity in the state before there was activity can the tranquillity of the nature be perceived. When one seeks truth in the state before there is falsity, the truth of the nature can be perceived. And when

---

[311] Alludes to *Mencius*, 6B:2:7.

[312] *Mencius*, 6A:11:2–4.

[313] *Mencius*, 7A:1:1.

[314] *Ibid.*

one seeks goodness in the period before there is evil, the goodness of the nature can be perceived."[315]

These words were the result of personal realization after conscientious and painstaking effort. We should not just read them hastily.

70. "In activity it is still; in tranquillity it is likewise still."[316] This is characteristic of the original substance of the nature. That which varies in accordance with the circumstances of activity and tranquillity is the mind. The sage turns mind into nature, so that his mind is principle, and principle is his mind. Its original substance is always naturally clear and without the slightest difference whether in activity or tranquillity.

The reason that the ordinary man is confused and distracted and without a moment's calm is that his mind is carried away by things, and his nature is beclouded. Although events and things are numerous, they are all inherent in our nature and allotment. If one responds to them according to their principle, one will naturally not be encumbered. But when one's intelligence is not completely illumined and his sincerity is not preserved, in the normal course of events one has nowhere to abide. When one is confronted with some important event, how can he know wherein lies its principle so as to be able to follow it? Therefore it is necessary that "sincerity and intelligence advance together."[317] When one has done the utmost in his endeavor he is in a position to speak about the calm of the nature, and this is what the student must strive to attain.

71. "When one does not know how to 'honor the virtuous nature,' how can one 'maintain constant inquiry and study'?"[318] It is not that this statement is incorrect, but I am afraid that if one errs in comprehending this "virtuous nature," his inquiry and study will truly be profoundly in error. And a failure of comprehension derives simply from the fact that one is deficient in his endeavor to carry out inquiry and study. It is necessarily as

[315] *Li Yen-p'ing hsien-sheng wen-chi*, 3:12a–b.

[316] Ch'eng Hao in *Ming-tao wen-chi* (Collection of Literary Works by Ch'eng Hao), 3:1a.

[317] "Prose Poem on the Po-lu-tung," in *Chu Tzu wen-chi*, 1:2b.

[318] Quoting Lu Hsiang-shan in *Hsiang-shan ch'üan-chi*, 34:4b–5a. Lu in turn quotes from the *Mean*, 27:6.

Mencius said, "In learning extensively and discussing minutely what is learned, the object is that one be able to go back and set forth in brief what is essential."[319] Only in this way will he learn well. If one's learning is not extensive and one's discussion is not detailed, his vision will be limited by the confines of his own mind, and however he may wish to be free from error, it will be impossible.

72. Master Ch'eng once said, "It is because human beings exist in a sea of perplexity and delusion or are stuck fast in a mire that they cannot influence events and have no place to stand."[320] These words certainly convey a keen warning to people, but they still may not know how to free themselves. In the foregoing text there is the statement that one should "give each thing its due."[321] But it is very difficult to reach this stage. How many of our rash and impetuous contemporaries,[322] without having investigated things or extended their knowledge, wildly imagine themselves to have reached this point!

73. "When one speaks about the mind, one is always referring to the state after the feelings have been aroused."[323] Master Ch'eng once made this statement. Later he felt that it was not correct, and so he changed it.[324] In Master Chu's writings there are points at which he relied on Master Ch'eng's earlier theory without including the subsequent correction. For example, in interpreting the statement in the *Book of History* concerning the human mind (*jen-hsin*) and the mind of Tao (*tao-hsin*),[325] he always referred to [the

---

[319] *Mencius*, 4B:15.

[320] Ch'eng I in *I-shu*, 19:13a.

[321] *Ibid.* Ch'eng I was criticizing what he took to be the influence of Buddhism on popular morality. The statement to which Lo alludes is: "People of today merely allow themselves to be used by things, and so they feel that their sufferings are many. If one gives each thing its due, then one will be using things."

[322] The term *k'uang*—wild, mad, arrogant, or impetuous—was coming to be applied particularly to adherents of the left wing of the Wang Yang-ming school.

[323] Ch'eng I in *I-ch'uan wen-chi*, 5:12a.

[324] *Ibid.*

[325] Chu Hsi never wrote a commentary on the *Book of History*, but his pupils later selected his sayings on the classic and published them as his commentaries. There were four of these, all having been lost. Chu's interpretation of the human mind and the mind of Tao is found in *Chu Tzu yü-lei*, 78:31b–35a, and in his Preface to the *Chung-yung chang-chü*.

human mind as] the state after the feelings have been aroused. When he said in the preface to his commentary on the *Mean* that "therefore their consciousnesses are different . . ."[326] he was also referring to the time after the feelings have been aroused. This is one of the points in Master Chu's thought which seems to me to involve inconsistency.

74. The principle which is endowed [in all living things] is one. By introducing the terms yin and yang, differences in particularization are indicated, and, extended to the utmost, these are the myriad forms. The principle of the nature is one. By introducing the terms humanity and righteousness, differences in particularization are indicated, and, extended to the utmost, these constitute all events. There is a plethora of forms, but one form contains the complete substance of the endowment. There are innumerable events, and yet in one event there is preserved the complete substance of the nature.

75. In the Way of nature everything is natural, and in the Way of man, everything is as it should be. The reason it is as it should be is that what is natural cannot be opposed. How does one know that it cannot be opposed? To accord with it is auspicious, and to oppose it is inauspicious. This is to say that nature and man are one in principle.

76. We Confucians are exclusively dedicated to following the naturalness of the principle of nature. The Buddhists and Taoists all rebel against nature and reject principle, and yet they have always made a pretext of "naturalness." Master Shao once said, "The Buddhists abandon the Way of the sovereign and minister, father and son, and husband and wife. Could this be in accordance with the naturalness of principle?"[327] With just a few words he was able to pass judgment on them. Remaining adept at evasive words, they hold that in Buddhism not one law[328] is rejected. But, having

---

[326] I.e., the consciousness associated with the mind of Tao and that associated with the human mind. See *Chung-yung chang-chü*, Preface, in *Chu Tzu wen-chi*, 76:21b. Also in *Ssu-shu chang-chü chi-chu*, p. 1.

[327] Shao Yung in *Huang-chi ching-shih shu*, 8B:38b.

[328] The term used here is *fa* or *dharma*. Clearly, the Sanskrit term *dharma* has a wider metaphysical and moral significance than is conveyed by the term "law," though this is the primary sense in which Lo uses it here.

completely abandoned the five relationships, what law will they not neglect?

> Note: From here on the old text suffered from
> redundancy, and I have simplified it.[329]

77. That within tranquillity there are things is the point of the elder Master Ch'eng's statement that "[The mean, or equilibrium] is the correct principle of all under heaven which is central and straight."[330] Master Chu thought that "in the state before thought and deliberation have arisen, consciousness is already present."[331] Here it seems that he should have mentioned the word principle. If the student understands this in terms of consciousness, he cannot avoid falling into error.

78. "The human mind possesses consciousness. The substance of the Way is inactive."[332] Anyone who dwells on these two sentences will be able to perceive the difference between the mind and the nature.

79. Master Chu criticized the *Su Huang-men Lao Tzu chieh* (Interpretation of the *Lao Tzu* by Vice Prime Minister Su Ch'e),[333] saying, "Although the terms *tao* and 'concrete things' (*ch'i*) are different, they are actually one thing. Therefore [Confucius] said, 'My Way has one thing that runs right through it.' "[334] This does not coincide with his view that, "*Li* and *ch'i* are

[329] This is Lo Ch'in-shun's own note.

[330] Ch'eng Hao in *I-shu*, 11:11a.

[331] Letter in Reply to Chang Ch'in-fu in *Chu Tzu wen-chi*, 32:25a. Chu Hsi's statement is that, "In the state before thought and deliberation have arisen, consciousness is already present. This is activity in the midst of tranquillity. 'Through the hexagram of return (*fu*) one sees the mind of heaven and earth.' When it comes to examination, the confused disorder of events and things is perfectly regulated. This is tranquillity in the midst of activity. 'Through the hexagram of keeping still (*ken*) one does not feel his body . . . and does not see his people.' " Chu is quoting the hexagram *fu* and the hexagram *ken* from the *Book of Changes*.

[332] Quoting Chu Hsi in *Lun-yü chi-chu* (Collected Commentaries on the *Analects*) in *Ssu-shu chang-chü chi-chu*, 2:118.

[333] Su Ch'e (1039–1112) was the younger brother of Su Shih. His *Lao Tzu chieh*, an attempt to reconcile Confucianism, Buddhism, and Taoism, is considered one of his most important works.

[334] "Su Huang-men *Lao Tzu* chieh" in *Chu Tzu wen-chi*, 72:24a. Chu Hsi was quoting *Analects*, 4:15:1.

definitely two things."[335] Shouldn't those who study his teachings seek a means to reconcile them and recover the ultimate unity?

80. *"Ch'ien* knows through what is easy. *K'un* exhibits its capacity through what is simple."[336] This is the source of man's innate knowledge and innate ability. But *ch'ien* begins things and *k'un* brings them to completion, so there is a natural order of precedence. When it comes to learning, the effort of extending knowledge and the effort of earnest practice must be carried on simultaneously. There is certainly no reason to wait until one's knowledge has been perfected before one engages in earnest practice, but at the same time one cannot be entirely confident concerning his actions before his knowledge is perfected. Everything depends on exerting oneself. What good is it to engage in consulting and deliberating which will merely result in idle talk?

81. Chang Tzu-shao[337] used Buddhist terms to explain Confucian texts[338] and "adopted a disguise"[339] to deceive the eyes and ears of the world. The wrong he did to the Confucian school was great indeed. Yet in recent times there are still those whose conversations about the Way reveal them as the covert heirs to his stale wisdom. Their habit is to borrow from Confucian texts to cover up the mistakes in Buddhist teachings. I know that, were we governed by the rule in the *Spring and Autumn Annals (Ch'un-ch'iu)* of judging the intent,[340] they would not escape punishment.

---

[335] Letter to Liu Shu-wen in *Chu Tzu wen-chi,* 46:24a.

[336] *Book of Changes,* "Appended Remarks," 7:2a.

[337] Chang Chiu-ch'eng (1092–1159). Originally a student of Yang Shih, he later turned to Buddhism, for which he was strongly criticized by Confucians.

[338] Quoting from the opening lines of Chu Hsi's critique of "Chang Wu-kou *Chung-yung* chieh" (Chang Tzu-shao's Explanation of the *Mean*), in *Chu Tzu wen-chi,* 72:27a–42a.

[339] *Ibid.* Chu Hsi was here quoting Chang Tzu-shao himself, but, obviously, turning his words to different effect.

[340] In the *Spring and Autumn Annals,* Duke Hsüan, second year, Chao Tun of Chin is assigned the responsibility for the murder of Duke Ling. Though the act was in fact performed by another, Chao Tun failed to punish the murderer, and accordingly the blame was found to rest with him. See Legge, *The Ch'un Ts'ew with The Tso Chuen, The Chinese Classics,* 5:289–90. The phrase "judging the intent" *(chu-hsin)* was later applied to this case in the *Hou Han-shu* (History of the Latter Han).

K'un-chih chi, Part II

1. I have read Academician Sung's[1] "Preface to the New Edition of the *Lankāvatāra Sutra*" (*Hsin-k'e Leng-chia ching hsü*), which contains the instructions of our first Emperor.[2] From this I realized that our first Emperor had a thorough comprehension of Buddhism. I have also read the inscription composed by the Emperor for the Shen-yüeh monastery. It says, "The way of immortality has always existed. It is no more than cultivating the person and maintaining purity, escaping transformation, moving about swiftly, and causing there to be no obstructions. This is its secret."[3] From this I realized that our first Emperor also had a profound understanding of Taoism.

As to the management of the affairs of government, he handed down instructions to future generations in which he exclusively followed the Way which the ancient sovereigns passed down from generation to generation and reverently put his faith in the writings of Confucius, Tseng Tzu, Tzu-ssu, and Mencius and the theories of Chou, Ch'eng, Chang, and Chu.[4] He placed human relations in proper order, leaving the evil and disobedient nowhere to exist. If his sons and grandsons observe [these instructions] as house laws, it is even possible that they may share in the longevity of heaven and earth. How magnificent was the vision of our great Emperor! It truly surpassed the ordinary by a hundred million times.

[1] Sung Lien (1310–1381). Having served as a Hanlin compiler under the Yüan dynasty, Sung Lien joined the cause of Chu Yüan-chang in 1360 and became tutor to the Ming founder's eldest son, Chu Piao. Between 1368 and 1370 he was associate director of the bureau established to compile the *Yuan History* (*Yüan shih*), and between 1370 and 1377 he served in a number of capacities, including that of chancellor of the Hanlin Academy. For a detailed and informative account of his active life, scholarly influence, and tragic death, see the biography by F. W. Mote in the *Dictionary of Ming Biography*. See also the discussion of his thought in John W. Dardess, *Confucianism and Autocracy*, pp. 156–73.

[2] In *Sung Hsüeh-shih ch'üan-chi* (Complete Writings of Academician Sung), Appendix (*Pu-i*), 2:1238–39.

[3] The inscription is recorded in *Chin-ling hsüan-kuan chih* (Monograph on the Taoist Temples of Nanking), 13:2b.

[4] I.e., Chou Tun-i, the Ch'eng brothers, Chang Tsai, and Chu Hsi.

2. In the formation of the *Book of Changes* (*I ching*) there are the remarks and the transformations,[5] the images and the auguries. The transformations and the images both derive from what is natural. Their principle is what is known as the principle of the nature and endowment (*hsing-ming chih li*). The Sage[6] appended the remarks. He purposely relied on and followed this [principle] and thus profoundly extended its significance to auguries of fortune and misfortune, remorse and humiliation. He considered it all as a plan for establishing the Way of man.

When transformations reach their utmost point, the images become fixed. Once the images have become fixed, transformation begins anew. The two (fixity and transformation) follow one another in endless succession. The "Commentary on the Words of the Text" ("Wen-yen") says, "The one who knows how to advance and how to retire, who knows both existence and annihilation and does not deviate from what is correct—he alone is a sage!"[7] To respond to transformation before it materializes is something that a sage is able to accomplish. Great worthies and those below them must rely on learning. It says in the "Appended Remarks" ("Hsi-tz'u"), "When the gentleman remains at rest, he observes the images and meditates on the remarks. When he starts any activity, he observes the transformations and meditates on the auguries. Therefore, he is protected by heaven. Good fortune. There is nothing from which he does not derive benefit."-[8] This is the ultimate accomplishment of studying the *Changes*.

What do we mean by auguries? The sage, at the point when transformation begins, anticipates it and infers on the basis of principle the state that will inevitably be reached. Therefore he offers instruction, wanting people to have foreknowledge of what they are to be vigilant about so as to avoid remorse and humiliation as well as misfortune. If he apprehended when the image was already complete, avoidance would be impossible. If he truly apprehends through observation and meditation, he is certainly able to adopt expedient measures, whereas if he apprehends through divination, he may avoid being lost on the path of escape and evasion. This

[5] I.e., the movement of lines whereby one hexagram changes into another.

[6] I.e., Confucius.

[7] *Book of Changes*, Commentary on the *ch'ien* hexagram, 1:12b.

[8] *Book of Changes*, "Appended Remarks" ("Hsi-tz'u"), 7:4b.

is the way he establishes himself as the ultimate standard for man.[9] Thus meditating on the auguries becomes the constant task of the gentleman. He never depends on divination. If his values were those that divination promotes, the gentleman would be no different from the rest of mankind. And wasn't this the motive of the sages in making the *Changes?*

3. Master Ch'eng said, "The most profound intentions of the Sage are all contained in the 'Appended Remarks,' "[10] Despite the statement of Tzu-kung that "[The Master's discourses concerning] the nature and the Way of heaven cannot be heard,"[11] they are actually explained quite fully in the "Appended Remarks." If the student is able to understand it, he will find that none of the principles in the world has been omitted. While all of the classics of the sages and worthies of antiquity are subtle in their language and profound in their significance, the naturalness, coherence, and unity of this one are such that, through it, one may acquire self-confidence. When one looks at heretical doctrines and heterodox theories, they are really like rivulets in comparison with the vast ocean or fake gems in comparison with fine jade. [Confucius read the *Book of Changes* so many times that] the leather stays broke three times.[12] If he had found that it was not suitable to expound learning that would serve the world, why would he have read it so many times?[13]

---

[9] Alludes to Chou Tun-i's description of the work of the sage in his "Explanation of the Diagram of the Great Ultimate" (*T'ai-chi-t'u shuo*), in *Chou Tzu ch'üan-shu* (Complete Works of Master Chou Tun-i), p. 17. See Wing-tsit Chan, *A Source Book in Chinese Philosophy*, p. 463.

[10] Ch'eng Hao in *I-shu* (Written Legacy), 2A:1a.

[11] *Analects*, 5:12.

[12] Ssu-ma Ch'ien records in *Shih-chi* (Records of the Historian), 47, that in his later years Confucius read the *Book of Changes* so many times that the leather stays that formed the binding of the work broke three times. See *Hsin-chiao Shih-chi san-chia chu*, 3:1937.

[13] In defending the interpretation of the *Book of Changes* in the light of principle, Lo is apparently agreeing with Ch'eng I, who took this view in his preface to the *I-ch'uan I-chuan* (Ch'eng I's Commentary on the *Book of Changes*) and differing with both Chu Hsi (see *Chu Tzu yü-lei*, 66:1a–18a) and Wang Yang-ming. *Wang Wen-ch'eng kung ch'üan-shu*, 3:20b–21a. Wing-tsit Chan, trans., *Instructions for Practical Living*, sec. 247 (pp. 210–211). Both Chu and Wang stressed the importance of divination.

4. Liu Pao-chai[14] followed Master Chu with respect to the powers, substance, and images of the hexagrams, while he followed Master Ch'eng (Ch'eng I) in respect to their transformations.[15] His interpretations are most incisive. For he traced the points at which their views are different, seeking to reconcile them so that they would ultimately be unified. He may be described as one who was earnestly dedicated to honoring and trusting Ch'eng and Chu.

5. There is no human emotion or attitude that is not given full expression in the three hundred poems in eleven sections of the *Book of Odes* (*Shih ching*). When one is at leisure and picks them up and recites and chants them, what they depict is as vividly present as if it were right before his eyes. How varied are the feelings they evoke, and how resonant and inspiring are such words as these:

> All ye princely men
> Know ye not his virtuous conduct?
> He hates none; he covets nothing.
> What does he which is not good?[16]

6. "Fully encompassing the transformations of heaven and earth, there is no deviation."[17] Master Ch'eng said of this passage that "The pattern emerges from heaven and earth in their totality and does not lie outside it."[18] According to this interpretation, the idea is that of being integrally joined with heaven and earth, and the matter of "not deviating" rests with the sage. Master Chu said, "The transformations of heaven and earth are limitless, but the sage establishes a compass for them and allows no deviation from the Way of the Mean. He is the one who 'regulates and brings to

---

[14] Liu Ting-chih (1409–1469). His name is given in most sources as Ai-chai. The work alluded to here appears to be Liu's *I-ching t'u-shih*; however, I have not had access to this work.

[15] See n. 5, above.

[16] Ode 33. Translation by James Legge, *She King, The Chinese Classics*, 4:52.

[17] *Book of Changes*, "Appended Remarks," 7:6b.

[18] Ch'eng Hao in *I-shu*, 11:1b.

completion.' "[19] According to this interpretation, one may suppose that "allowing no deviation" must refer to the transforming and nourishing [powers of heaven and earth].

I venture that the transformations of heaven and earth are nothing but dispersal and concentration, fullness and emptiness. Although their mysteriousness cannot be fathomed, their principle is constant. To say that the sage regulates and brings to completion means that he follows their seasons, accords with their principles, and establishes regulations and measures so as to further human interests. It is not that the sage could subtract or add [to the transformations]. The phrase "allows no deviation from the Way of the Mean" seems lacking in clarity, while Ch'eng's statement is simpler and clearer.

7. "To forego friends in the east and north ultimately brings rewards,"[20] is incisively interpreted in Ch'eng's *Commentary* [on the *Book of Changes*].[21]

---

[19]Chu Hsi in *Chou I pen-i* (The Essential Meaning of the *Book of Changes*), 7:4b. Where he speaks of the sage as the one who "regulates and brings to completion," Chu is alluding to the *Book of Changes*, hexagram *t'ai* (in *Chou I cheng-i*, 2:12b).

[20]*Book of Changes*, *k'un* hexagram, 1:13b.

[21]Ch'eng I's interpretation of the text in *I-ch'uan I-chuan*, 1:9a is as follows: "The function of *ch'ien* is carried out by yang, while the function of *k'un* is carried out by yin. When [the text of the 'Appended Remarks'] speaks of what is 'above form,' it refers to the Way of heaven and earth, and when it speaks of what is 'below form,' it refers to the working of yin and yang. The phrase 'taking the lead creates confusion; following assures attainment,' and the succeeding passage pertain to the way of yin. Asserting the lead would entail confusion through losing the way of yin. By following and harmonizing, [the yin] accords with [the yang] and attains its constant principle. The west and south are the directions of yin. Consorting with one's own kind means finding friends. The east and the north are the directions of yang. Parting with one's own kind means foregoing friends. When it parts with its own kind and consorts with yang, [yin] is able to complete the work of giving birth to living things, which ultimately brings rewards. By virtue of its origin, it moves with its own kind, while by virtue of its function, it consorts with yang. In its substance yin is unstable and yielding, and therefore it is by consorting with yang that it is able to rest in correctness, bring about good fortune, and participate in the boundlessness of the earth. But since yin [of itself] does not rest in correctness, how could it participate in the way of the earth? According to the Decision, boundlessness has three distinct senses. 'The excellence which is in harmony with the boundless' refers to the infinitude of heaven. 'Participating in the boundlessness of the earth' refers to the inexhaustibility of the earth. 'Traversing the earth without bound' refers to the fortitude of the mare."

In the case of the line, "The fetters should be removed,"[22] it is my judgment that [the interpretation of Chu Hsi in] the *Essential Meaning* [of the
Book of Changes] is more in harmony with the preceding and succeeding
text.[23]

In recent years I deeply love to read the *Changes*, but my spirit
is gradually becoming deficient, and it has become difficult to be thoroughly
steeped in the text. All those who read commentaries on the *Book of Changes*
should certainly devote thought to the points on which they agree and
those on which they differ.

8. When Confucius wrote the *Spring and Autumn Annals (Ch'un-ch'iu)* he
simply took up the broad outlines of each event in order to show its significance. The details were all contained in the histories. At that time the
historical records all existed, and attentive readers were readily able to per-

---

[22] *Book of Changes, meng* hexagram, 1:19b.

[23] Ch'eng I's interpretation of the text as found in *I-ch'uan I-chuan*, 1:17b–18a is
as follows: "In the beginning, living in a benighted state causes the ignorance of people of
inferior status. When the lines speak of dispelling it, they refer to the ignorance of people of
inferior status. One should make clear the punishments and restrictions in order to inform
them and cause them to know fear, and afterwards one may instruct and guide them. In
ancient times the Sage kings governed by instituting punishments to bring order to the masses
and by displaying a civilizing influence to cause improvement in public morals. First the punishments were established, and then the civilizing process was carried forward. Although the
sages valued virtue and not punishments, they never did away with one in favor of the other.
Therefore the first step in forming a government is to establish laws, and the first thing in
dealing with ignorance is to awe [the people] with punishments so as to remove the fetters of
darkness and ignorance. 'Fetters' means obduracy. Unless the fetters of darkness and ignorance
are removed, the remedial instruction will have no way to penetrate. Once one has led them
with punishments and restrictions, then, even if their minds are unable to comprehend, they
will nonetheless obey out of fear and awe and will not dare to display their dark and ignorant
desires. Then gradually it will be possible to cause them to know the Way of goodness and to
correct their bad hearts and to improve public standards and morals. If one were to use only
punishments in government, ignorance might be disturbed, but ultimately it could not be
dispelled. But if [the people] avoid punishment without any sense of shame, the transforming
influence cannot be effective. Therefore [the hexagram] says, 'to continue in this way brings
humiliation.' " Chu Hsi's interpretation of the passage as found in *Chou I pen-i*, 1:6a is: "The
yin line at the bottom is the extreme of youthful ignorance. When one who is divining encounters it, he must dispel his ignorance. The way to dispel it is to punish him severely and
temporarily release him and then see what happens next. If it continues without stopping,
there will be occasion for shame and regret. The one who, through divination, would convey
a warning must act in this way."

ceive the justice of [Confucius'] verdicts concerning right and wrong. Therefore [Mencius] said, "[Confucius] completed the Spring and Autumn Annals, and rebellious ministers and villainous sons were struck with terror."[24] Later the historical records were all lost, and it was only what the Sage had written that survived. Master Tso must have seen the historical records of the states, so that in each case these represented the provenance of his commentary.[25] Though it is difficult to believe in its entirety, it did after all have a documentary basis.

9. In the Book of History (Shang shu) there are portions which are difficult to understand. One really does not need to waste his mental effort on these because if one forces oneself to achieve an understanding, it may not necessarily be right. If one can learn something from a thorough reading of those parts that are clear and readily understandable, the benefit will be inexhaustible.

10. The Book of History speaks of "ordering one's affairs by means of rightness and ordering one's mind by means of ritual."[26] The Book of Changes speaks of "being serious in order to straighten the inner life and being right in order to square the outer life."[27] The basic meaning of both is essentially the same. But where it is a matter of ordering "by means of" rightness and ritual, the emphasis is placed on man, and man and principle still represent a duality. Where it is a matter of being serious and right "in order to" straighten the inner life and square the outer life, the emphasis is placed on being serious and right, and man and principle are one.[28] There must cer-

---

[24] Mencius, 3B:9:11.

[25] The Tso-chuan was traditionally attributed to Tso Ch'iu-ming, a contemporary of Confucius, and was regarded as the most important commentary on the Spring and Autumn Annals. It seems clear that Lo, while questioning some of the content of the Tso-chuan, accepted this view.

[26] Book of History, "The Announcement of Chung-hui." See Legge, Shoo King, The Chinese Classics, 3:182.

[27] Book of Changes, Commentary on the k'un hexagram, 1:16a.

[28] This rendering represents only a loose paraphrase of the Chinese text. Lo observes that in the Book of History, the particle i precedes i (rightness) and li (ritual or decorum): (i i chih shih, i li chih hsin). In the Book of Changes, the particle i follows ching and i (rightness): (ching i chih nei, i i fang wai). He suggests that the slight difference in grammatical structure reveals a significant difference in the conception of principle and the problem of cultivation.

tainly be a difference in terms of the intensity of the endeavor and the depth of the achievement that are involved.

11. The "Canon of Yao" ("Yao-tien") gives four examples of the ways in which [Yao] understood men. The first was [his recognition of his son Chu as] insincere and quarrelsome.[29] The second was [his recognition of the Minister of Works as one who] indulged in idle talk but did not act accordingly and who was respectful in appearance only.[30] The third was [his recognition of Kun, the father of Yü, as one who was] disobedient to orders and tried to injure his clan.[31] These are all instances of the way he understood inferior men. The fourth was [his recognition of Shun as one who was] able through filial piety to live in harmony [with his father who was unprincipled and his mother who was insincere].[32] This is the way he understood the gentleman.

Being insincere and quarrelsome and trying to injure one's clan are what is called "strength that is evil,"[33] while indulging in idle talk and being respectful in appearance only are what is called "weakness that is evil."[34] The qualities of the inferior man are certainly not fully subsumed in this, but one may generalize on the basis of these three examples. Filiality is the primary element in human behavior. In this respect the Han departed very little from antiquity, for they continued to use filial piety and integrity as the basis for selecting officials. Since [Shun] was able to cause an obstinate father, an insincere mother, and an arrogant brother all to be converted so that they did not proceed to wickedness, there are none in

[29] *Book of History*, "Canon of Yao." See Legge, *Shoo King, The Chinese Classics,* 3:23.

[30] *Ibid.*, pp. 23–24.

[31] *Ibid.*, pp. 24–25.

[32] *Ibid.*, pp. 26–27.

[33] Alludes to Chou Tun-i's *T'ung-shu* (Penetrating the *Book of Changes*), sec. 7 in *Chou Tzu ch'üan-shu*, p. 33. As translated by Wing-tsit Chan (*Source Book in Chinese Philosophy*, p. 468) the passage reads: "Righteousness, uprightness, decisiveness, strictness and firmness of action are examples of strength that is good, and fierceness, narrow-mindedness, and violence are examples of strength that is evil. Kindness, mildness, and humility are examples of weakness that is good, and softness, indecision, and perverseness are examples of weakness that is evil. Only the Mean brings harmony."

[34] *T'ung-shu*, sec. 7.

the world who cannot be converted. Had it not been for his abundant virtue, how could he have done it?

Aside from [the account of] calculating [the movements of the sun and moon] and delivering the seasons [to the people],[35] the "Canon of Yao" contains only these four [examples of Yao's achievement]. Yet his greatness in employing [the upright] and dismissing[36] [the crooked][37] was such that his way of employing on the one hand and dismissing on the other may serve for all time as an example to rulers of the realm. If rulers are able to take an example from this, good government will exist in spite of any contingency.

12. The *Spring and Autumn Annals* are by no means easy to read. Master Ch'eng spoke of "using the commentaries to examine the details of the events recorded in the classic and using the classic to distinguish truth from falsehood in the commentaries."[38] In the three instances discussed by Ou-yang Wen-chung,[39] including those of [Duke] Yin of Lu, Chao Tun, and Chih of Hsü, he was correct in saying that he sincerely believed in the classic of the Sage and would not be misled by the three commentaries.[40]

---

[35] *Book of History*, "Canon of Yao." See Legge, *Shoo King*, *The Chinese Classics*, 3:18.

[36] Reading *ts'o* for *ts'u*, as in other editions of the *K'un-chih chi*.

[37] Alludes to *Analects*, 12:22 which in Legge's translation (*The Chinese Classics*, 1:261) reads: "The Master said, 'Employ the upright and put aside all the crooked,—in this way the crooked can be made to be upright.'"

[38] Ch'eng I in *I-shu*, 20:1a and 21A:2b. The commentaries referred to are the *Tso-chuan*, the *Ku-liang chuan*, and the *Kung-yang chuan*.

[39] Ou-yang Hsiu (1007–1072), the great scholar, historian, and statesman.

[40] Three short essays by Ou-yang Hsiu on the *Spring and Autumn Annals* appear in his *Chü-shih chi*, ch. 18, in *Ou-yang Yung-shu chi*, vol. 1, book 3, pp. 31–36. In the first of these essays, Ou-yang Hsiu argues that many scholars, failing to believe wholeheartedly in the classic itself, are frequently misled by the commentaries. He adduces three examples. First, Yin of Lu is referred to by Confucius by the title of "duke," but this title is denied him by the commentators, who assert that he was only a "deputy" for his younger brother. See Legge, *The Ch'un Ts'ew with The Tso Chuen*, *The Chinese Classics*, 5:1–3. Second, in the *Spring and Autumn Annals*, Duke Hsüan, 2nd year, Chao Tun was assigned the responsibility for the murder of Duke Ling. According to the commentators, Chao Tun was not the actual murderer, but the blame rested with him because he failed to punish the true murderer, Chao Ch'uan. See Legge, *The Ch'un Ts'ew with The Tso Chuen*, *The Chinese Classics*, 5:289–91. Finally, in the *Spring and Autumn Annals*, Duke Chao, nineteenth year, it says that Shih, the heir of

Yet when Hu Wen-ting[41] wrote his *Commentary* [on the *Spring and Autumn Annals*][42] he relied heavily on the three commentaries and did not go along with His Excellency Ou. Why should the opinions of different individuals be so much at variance?

The wonders worked by the brush of the Sage are like the workings of nature, and one should not make simplistic or superficial observations concerning them. Yet by excessive probing one may end up missing his true idea. If only one has an open mind and a relaxed disposition and tries again and again to enter fully into the spirit of the work and to avoid being confused by different theories, one should naturally be able to achieve some understanding. The merits of the three commentaries cannot be dismissed, yet, given the possibility of errors resulting either from falsification or arbitrariness, how can they be considered completely reliable? I would submit that the views of His Excellency Ou cannot be disregarded. But if one were to reject the words of Master Ch'eng, there would be no way to read the *Spring and Autumn Annals.*

13. The sentence, "Those of ability practice cultivation and thus approach happiness,"[43] repeatedly appears in various editions [of the *Tso-chuan*] rendered, "Those of ability cultivate them so as to bring about happiness."[44]

Hsü, murdered his ruler, Mai, whereas the commentators all deny that he was guilty of a crime of commission. See Legge, *The Ch'un Ts'ew with The Tso Chuen, The Chinese Classics,* 5:673–74.) Ou-yang Hsiu argues that those who believe the commentaries in such cases are, in effect, rejecting the judgments of Confucius.

[41] Hu An-kuo (1073–1138).

[42] *Ch'un-ch'iu Hu-shih chuan* (Mr. Hu's Commentary on the *Spring and Autumn Annals*) in 30 *ch.*

[43] *Tso-chuan,* Duke Ch'eng, 13th year. See Legge, *The Ch'un Ts'ew with The Tso Chuen, The Chinese Classics,* 5:379–81.

[44] The context of this line is the statement of the Viscount of Liu, "I have heard that human beings receive at birth the equilibrium of heaven and earth, and this is what is called their endowment (*ming*). With activity, there are the rules of ritual propriety and of dignified demeanor which serve to establish their nature. Those of ability practice cultivation and thus approach happiness, while those devoid of ability become corrupt and thus bring on disaster." In the two versions given by Lo, the verbal difference is merely the position of the particle *i* before or after the word *chih.* In the first instance (*neng-che yang i chih fu*) the word *chih* has verbal force, whereas in the second (*neng-che yang chih i fu*) it functions as a particle. There is a slight difference of nuance in each case. In the former version it appears to be the person that is cultivated; in the latter version it is the rules of ritual propriety and dignified demeanor that are cultivated.

One of the characters having been transposed, the nuance and meaning are completely different. Not infrequently mistakes pile up in this way.

14. It is said in the "Record of Music" that "Man is tranquil at birth; this is his heaven-endowed nature. When, influenced by things, he begins to be active, that is desire arising from his nature."[45] This passage reveals moral principle in its very essence. Were the author not a sage, he could not have said it. That Lu Hsiang-shan should doubt it is wrong. He advanced the idea that the desires are evil.[46]

The fact that man has desires definitely derives from heaven. Some are necessary and cannot be repressed; some are appropriate and cannot be changed. If those that are irrepressible all conform to the principle of what is appropriate, how can they not be good? It is only heedlessly giving way to the passions, indulging the desires, and not knowing how to turn back that is evil. Confucians of the past often spoke about eliminating or restraining human desires and thought it necessary to resort to severe means in order to repress them. But their mode of expression seems one-sided and exaggerated. The desires, together with pleasure, anger, sorrow, and joy, are qualities of the nature. Can pleasure, sorrow, anger, and joy also be eliminated?

Hsiang-shan also said, "Nature too is characterized by both good and evil, as in such phenomena as eclipses of the sun and moon and evil stars."[47] This is, of course, true. But, despite the occurrence of eclipses of the sun and moon and the appearance of comets, it has never happened that nature has failed to return to its proper course. What could this be but the Principle of Nature? What matters in the Way of man is that he not stray far [from the Way] without returning.[48] And yet "under heaven there is none that is not swept along by the same flood."[49] This being the case, then, speaking in terms of what is fundamental, how is it possible that nature and man are not one? And yet, followed through to the ultimate conclusion, must they not also be two?[50]

---

[45] *Book of Rites,* "Record of Music." Legge, *Li Chi: Book of Rites,* 2:96.

[46] See *Hsiang-shan ch'üan-chi* (Complete Works of Lu Chiu-yüan), 34:1b.

[47] *Ibid.,* 35:23a.

[48] *Mean,* 13.

[49] *Analects,* 18:6:3.

[50] On the relation between nature and man and the issue of unity or duality, see also secs. 32 and 62, below.

15. In the "Questions of Tseng Tzu" ("Tseng Tzu wen")[51] [Confucius explained that] "If during the rites of marriage the presents of silk have already
been offered, and an auspicious day has been selected . . . and the father
or mother of the bridegroom should die, [his eldest paternal uncle] will,
following the interment, send word to the parents of the bride, saying,
'Because of the death of his parent, my child cannot at present become as
a brother [to your daughter].' . . . The parents of the bride concur [in the
offer of a release from the marriage contract], but they do not permit her to
marry another. This is according to ritual. When the period of mourning is
over, the father or mother of the bride sends someone to invite the bridegroom [to proceed with the marriage]. The bridegroom [for the moment]
does not accept, but thereafter the marriage takes place. This is according
to ritual. If the father or mother of the bride should die, the bridegroom
does likewise."[52]

It says in Ch'en Hao's *[Li chi] chi-shuo* (Collected Explanations
of the *Book of Rites*),[53] "After the bridegroom has carried out the sacrificial
services [for his deceased parent], the parents of the bride send someone to
invite the bridegroom to proceed with the marriage. If the bridegroom adheres to the earlier agreement [to dissolve the marriage contract] and does
not accept, the woman is then to be married into another clan."[54] And if
"the bride enters mourning, the parents of the groom send someone to
invite her [to proceed with the marriage following the end of the mourning
period]. If the family of the bride does not concur, then the bridegroom
takes another as his wife."[55]

This interpretation is entirely out of keeping with moral principle and with human feelings. It is so wrong! How is it possible that, the
marriage agreement having been settled, and the requisite three years having passed on account of the death, one could then marry another husband
or take a different wife? The [bridegroom's] "not accepting" or the [bride's]
"not concurring" would occur at the beginning of the mourning period be-

---

[51] The "Questions of Tseng Tzu" ("Tseng Tzu wen") is a section of the *Book of
Rites*. Lo's quotation from it is accurate but not complete in that Tseng Tzu's question is here
elided with Confucius' response.

[52] Cf. translation by James Legge, *Li Chi: Book of Rites*, 1:320–21.

[53] A work by the Yüan Confucian, Ch'en Hao (1261–1341).

[54] *Li-chi chi-shuo*, 4:9b.

[55] *Ibid.*, 4:10a.

cause one could not bear to return so soon to wearing festive clothing [for the marriage ceremony]. Thus the invitation would be declined, this being called "declining according to ritual." Thereafter it is necessary that [invitations] be sent back and forth and the marriage ceremony should be accomplished. Though the Sage never spoke about this, one can reasonably infer it. [Ch'en] Hao's *Collected Explanations* are not without merit, yet he often made slight mistakes, and nothing could be more injurious to principle or inimical to proper education.

16. In each hexagram and line of the *Book of Changes* there is an image, and each image has one principle. The images themselves are not identical, and this is true of their principles as well. But in the final analysis, the non-identity of the images is bound up with the fact that they are truly not one, whereas principle, while not identical, is yet everywhere one. Therefore it is said, "The same destination is reached by different roads. One thought embraces a hundred deliberations."[56] Who but one who knows the Way can realize this?

17. Mencius' statements, "In the nature there is the endowment . . . In the endowment there is the nature,"[57] are all-inclusive in their significance. This is precisely what is meant by the expression, "Principle is one; its particularizations are diverse."[58] At that point Mencius was discussing the nature with Kao Tzu and refuting each of Kao Tzu's statements in turn, so that he had no opportunity to formulate this. Had he been able to get Kao Tzu to appreciate this concept, who knows but that Kao Tzu might have been jolted into true understanding, in which case he would have submitted.

18. Master Tung[59] said, "The nature is the substance that is inborn."[60] If one looks at Kao Tzu's discussion of the nature, one finds that he made

---

[56] *Book of Changes*, "Appended Remarks," 8:6a.

[57] *Mencius*, 7B:24:1–2.

[58] Ch'eng I's formulation in *I-ch'uan wen-chi* (Collection of Literary Works by Ch'eng I), 5:12b.

[59] Tung Chung-shu (179?–104?B.C.), the Han Confucian chiefly responsible for influencing Emperor Wu to make Confucianism the state doctrine in 136 B.C.

[60] *Ch'un-ch'iu fan-lu* (Luxuriant Gems of the *Spring and Autumn Annals*), 10:3b.

several different statements but never departed from his general idea of the nature as "the substance that is inborn."[61] Master Tung understood and respected Confucius and may also have understood the theories of Mencius, and yet he agreed with Kao Tzu. Could he have gotten his idea from any other source?

19. There can be no question about Master Chu's interpretation of the term *wu-chi* (the Infinite), which appears in the opening line of Master Chou's "Explanation of the Diagram of the Great Ultimate" (*T'ai-chi-t'u shuo*).[62] But I can only be skeptical when it comes to the statement that "When the reality of the Infinite and the essence of yin, yang, and the Five Agents (*erh-wu*)[63] come into mysterious union (*miao-ho*), integration (*ning*) ensues."[64] Things must be two before they can be said to come into union. Are the Great Ultimate and yin and yang really two things? If they are really two things, where was each one prior to their integration? Throughout his life Master Chu regarded *li* and *ch'i* as two things, and this was the source of his idea.

    For my own part I have spent several decades engaged in the effort to comprehend this point, and until now I have not dared to think that I may be right. I have studied Master Chu's words, including his statement that, "*Ch'i* is strong and *li* is weak, so that *li* cannot control it."[65] If this were true, then how could the Great Ultimate be "the pivot of creation and the ground of being of concrete things"?[66] Unfortunately, there was at

---

[61] Kao Tzu's theories about the nature are set forth in his dialogue with Mencius, recorded in *Mencius*, 6A:1–4.

[62] Chu Hsi's commentary on the "T'ai-chi-t'u shuo" (in *Chou Tzu ch'üan-shu*, p. 16) opens with the statement, " 'The doings of high heaven have neither sound nor smell' and yet are the pivot of creation and the ground of being of concrete things. Therefore he [Chou Tun-i] said, 'The Infinite and yet the Great Ultimate.' It is not that outside of the Great Ultimate there is something else called the Infinite."

[63] I.e., water, fire, wood, metal, and earth. For a discussion of the origin and meaning of the theories of yin and yang and the Five Agents (or Five Elements), see Joseph Needham, *Science and Civilisation in China*, 2:232–44.

[64] "Tai-chi-t'u shuo" in *Chou Tzu ch'üan-shu*, p. 17. Translated by Wing-tsit Chan in *A Source Book in Chinese Philosophy*, p. 463.

[65] *Chu Tzu yü-lei*, 4:13b.

[66] See above, n. 62.

that time no one who questioned Master Chu about this, and so I have recorded it to await the Master Chu of a later age.

20. Master Chu said that the entire text of the *T'ung-shu* (Penetrating the *Book of Changes*) was devoted to elucidating the inner meaning of the Great Ultimate.[67] But there is not a word to be found in this work about the "Infinite" *(wu-chi)*,[68] so that I do not really know what he meant by this statement.

21. The *T'ung-shu* in forty sections is refined in meaning and precise in language, and there can be no doubt that the work is by Master Chou's own hand. Take, for example, the words, "The Five [Agents] represent their differentiation, while the Two (yin and yang) constitute their reality . . . The one reality is differentiated in the many."[69] Here he illumines the wonder of creation in all its aspects. Root and branch are fully comprehended; words and concepts are perfectly coherent. *Ch'i* is *li* (*ch'i chi li*); they are absolutely unsundered. The passage is thoroughly in accord with the Commentary [on the *ch'ien* hexagram] in the *Book of Changes*, which says, "The Way of the Creative works through change and transformation so that each thing receives its proper nature and endowment."[70] But it is quite different from the statement [in the "Explanation of the Diagram of the Great Ultimate"] that "[When the reality of the Infinite and the essence of yin, yang, and the Five Agents] come into mysterious union, integration

---

[67] This statement was made by Chu Hsi in various contexts. See, for example, his "T'ai-chi-t'u T'ung-shu tsung hsü" in *Chou Tzu ch'üan-shu*, p. 28, and also *Chu Tzu yü-lei*, 93:7a and 94:20b.

[68] The observation that the term *wu-chi* was not found in the *T'ung-shu* had been made by Lu Chiu-shao and his brother Lu Hsiang-shan in letters to Chu Hsi. Chu Hsi, in a letter to Lu Hsiang-shan ("Ta Lu Tzu-ching") in *Chu Tzu wen-chi* (Collection of Literary Works by Master Chu Hsi), 36:8a, defended Chou Tun-i's use of the term despite the fact that it was of Taoist origin. Later the debate shifted to the question of the authenticity of the "T'ai-chi-t'u shuo," with some writers alleging that the absence of the term *wu-chi* from the *T'ung-shu* suggested that the former work, with its evidently Taoist cast, was not by Chou himself.

[69] *T'ung-shu*, sec. 22.

[70] *Book of Changes*, *ch'ien* hexagram, 1:4a.

ensues."[71] I wonder what the gentleman who understands words will think about this?

22. In the passage from Master Chang's *Cheng-meng* (Correcting Youthful Ignorance), "From the Great Vacuity (*t'ai-hsü*), there is heaven . . ."[72] *li* and *ch'i* are regarded as two things. I do not doubt the depth of his inquiry, but his language is arbitrary and forced and fails to convey the natural principle of the nature and endowment.

I have examined the statements of the elder Master Ch'eng on this subject, and they include the following: " 'The workings of high heaven have neither sound nor smell.'[73] As substance, it is called change; as principle, it is called the Way; in its functioning, it is called spirit; as an endowment in human beings, it is called the nature."[74] Employing only a few words, he was utterly incisive and incomparably intelligent.

If the student gets to this point and is still unable to understand, I am afraid that he will always be confused by various theories and cannot expect to resolve them into unity.

23. In the *Cheng-meng* it says, "Whether integrated or disintegrated, it is my body just the same. One is qualified to discuss the nature of man when he realizes that 'death is not annihilation.' "[75] It also says, "In its disintegrated state, *ch'i* is scattered and diffuse. Through integration, it forms matter (*chih*), thereby giving rise to the manifold diversity of men and things.

---

[71] "Tai-chi-t'u shuo" in *Chou Tzu ch'üan-shu*, p. 17.

[72] *Cheng-meng*, "T'ai-ho" sec. no. 9, in *Chang Tzu ch'üan-shu*, 2:3b. As translated by Wing-tsit Chan (*A Source Book in Chinese Philosophy*, p. 504), the entire passage reads as follows: "From the Great Vacuity there is Heaven. From the transformation of material force, there is the Way. In the unity of the Great Vacuity and material force, there is the nature (of man and things). And in the unity of nature and consciousness, there is the mind."

[73] *Mean*, 33:6, quoting Ode 235.

[74] Ch'eng Hao in *I-shu*, 1:3a–b. An almost identical statement appears in *Ts'ui-yen* (Pure Words), 1:1b and 2:22a.

[75] *Cheng-meng*, "T'ai-ho" sec., no. 4, in *Chang Tzu ch'üan-shu*, 2:2a, quoting *Tao-te ching*, 33. Translation by Wing-tsit Chan in *A Source Book in Chinese Philosophy*, p. 501.

Yin and yang follow one another in endless succession, thereby establishing the great norms of heaven and earth."[76]

Now human beings and things experience life and death, while from the point of view of the universe, ten thousand aeons are as one. Through the integration of *ch'i*, there is life, and when there is physical form, there is existence. When there is this thing, there is this *li* (principle). Upon the disintegration of *ch'i*, there is death, and ultimately the thing returns to nothingness. When there is no longer this thing, there is no longer this *li*. How could there be this so-called "death without annihilation"? If in the natural course of the universe, the ten thousand aeons are as one, what death and life, existence and annihilation could there be?

If one adopts the analogy of a tree, human beings and things are the flowers and leaves, while heaven and earth are the trunk and roots. When the flowers fade and the leaves wither, they are blown away and scattered. The spirit of life of the trunk and roots is as before, but how can what is blown away and scattered have any further connection with the trunk and roots? Can one say that they are not annihilated? Master Chu said of this statement of Master Chang's that "What it implies is a great process of transmigration."[77] But because he clung so tenaciously to this view, he did not realize the nature of his mistake.

24. "In its disintegrated state, *ch'i* is scattered and diffuse. Through integration, it forms matter, thereby giving rise to the manifold diversity of men and things. Yin and yang follow one another in endless succession, thereby establishing the great norms of heaven and earth."[78] This is perfectly summarized in two phrases in the *Mean:* "The smaller energies are river currents; the greater energies are mighty transformations."[79]

---

[76]*Ibid.*, no. 15, in *Chang Tzu ch'üan-shu*, 2:4b. Cf. translation by Wing-tsit Chan in *A Source Book in Chinese Philosophy*, p. 505.

[77]Chu Hsi's commentary in *Chang tzu ch'üan-shu*, 2:1b.

[78]*Cheng-meng*, "T'ai-ho" sec., no. 15, in *Chang Tzu ch'üan-shu*, 2:4b.

[79]*Mean*, 30:3.

25. That Tseng Tzu [on the point of death] had the mat changed[80] was an expression of humanity. That Tzu-lu tied the cords of his cap[81] was an expression of courage. I am afraid that the two are not commensurate.

26. There is no great harm in having slight differences in interpreting the classics, but when it comes to the foundations of moral principle, there must not be even the slightest discrepancy.

27. The discussion in the *Cheng-meng* of the "Li-ch'i" (Rites in the Formation of Character) and the "Li-yün" (Evolution of Rites) [chapters of the *Book of Rites*] is very detailed,[82] but in the final analysis it does not go beyond the concepts of "substance" (*t'i*) and "function" (*yung*). When the substance is established, the function will be effected. By embodying truthfulness, one inspires universal accord.[83]

28. The *Cheng-meng* says, "As the yin and yang *ch'i* revolve in their cycle of alternation, they react upon one another through integration and disintegration, pursue one another in their rise and fall, and encounter one an-

---

[80] In this poignant incldent recorded in the "T'an Kung" chapter of the *Book of Rites*, Confucius' disciple Tseng Tzu was gravely ill and on the point of death when he heard a servant observe that his sleeping mat, which was patterned and brilliant in hue, was of the sort appropriate only to a high official. Tseng Tzu agreed and insisted that the mat be changed. When his sons protested that his condition was too precarious to allow the change to be made, Tseng Tzu said, "Your love for me does not compare with the servant's. The love of a sage for others always tends in the direction of virtue, while the love of the ordinary man tends in the direction of indulgence. What more do I seek than to die in the course of doing what is right?" Hardly had the mat been changed when Tseng Tzu expired. See James Legge, trans., *Li Chi: Book of Rites*, 1:128–29.

[81] According to the account in the *Tso-chuan*, Duke Ai, 15th year, Tzu-lu met his death when he was cut down by Shih Ch'i and Yü Yen, who, in killing him, also cut the cords of his cap. "Tzu-lu said, 'The superior man does not let the cords of his cap fall to the ground when he dies.' With this, he tied the cords again and died." See James Legge, trans., *The Ch'un Ts'ew with The Tso Chuen, The Chinese Classics*, 5:843.

[82] *Cheng-meng*, "Chih-tang" sec. in *Chang Tzu ch'üan-shu*, 3:1b.

[83] Alludes to the final sentences of the "Li-yün" section of the *Book of Rites*: "The sovereigns of antiquity were able to practice ritual so as to extend rightness and to embody truthfulness so as to inspire universal accord." See James Legge, trans., *Li Chi: Book of Rites*, 1:393.

other as generative forces. They include and determine one another. They seek to be one but cannot. This is why there is no limit to their contraction and expansion and no respite in their movements and operations. There being no agent which causes this, it can only be called the principle of the nature and destiny."[84]

The conceptualization found in this passage is extremely refined. It is quite different from that of the so-called Great Vacuity and the transformations of *ch'i*.[85] For he came to understand this through the most intense contemplation and earnest inquiry as time went on. He wrote down some sections first and others later, and, as they were not done at the same time, they are also not alike in their depth and subtlety. The reader may choose between them.

29. A point of convergence in the Way of the Six Classics[86] is found in the crucial importance attached to rites and music. But the ancient *Book of Rites* and the ancient *Book of Music* have long since been lost. The few passages which survive have barely been preserved, and only a few scholars are capable of reading the texts proficiently, deeply appreciating their meaning, thoroughly discerning their significance, and carefully considering the way they might actually have been performed. Thus the rites and music of the former kings could not be revived for over a thousand years, and most of the attempts to foist them on the present age derive from nothing more than obstinate and uncomprehending illiberality. This is indeed regrettable.

30. From the study of numbers, Master Shao [Yung] was able to extend his sights to ultimate principle. The scope of his vision was superlative, in which respect he was no different from the Ch'eng brothers. And yet he never really won their approval. This was because neither in his premises nor his conclusions did he ever depart from numbers. Since numbers function differently, they assumed that number must inevitably be distinct from

---

[84]*Cheng-meng,* "Ts'an-liang" sec., no. 12, in *Chang Tzu ch'üan-shu,* 2:9b.

[85]*Cheng-meng,* "T'ai-ho" sec. in *Chang Tzu ch'üan-shu,* 2:3a–b.

[86]Refers to the *Books of Odes, History, Rites, Changes,* the *Chou-li,* and the *Spring and Autumn Annals.* The ancient Six Classics included the *Book of Music,* now lost, instead of the *Chou-li.*

principle. Therefore whether in public life or in reclusion, in words or in silence,[87] if he were judged according to the Way of the great Mean and of the utmost rectitude, he might occasionally be not quite up to it. The elder Master Ch'eng once said to a student, "Seeing me like this, you know that I exert a great deal of effort."[88] One must "reflect on oneself and be sincere"[89] if one is to create "the learning of all-pervading unity"[90] of the school of the Sage.

31. It is certainly true that the transformations of the Way of Nature come to completion through spring, summer, autumn, and winter, while the transformations of the way of the world come to completion through the august sovereign, emperor, king, and hegemon.[91] Yet in the course of a year the four seasons are always in balance, so that, following winter, spring returns, and, following spring, the summer. Why should it be that from the Three August Sovereigns[92] down to the present day more than four thousand years have passed, and during this time the way of the hegemon has survived so long? Could it be true that, in the Way of Nature, what departs must return, while in the Way of the world, what has once departed is never to return again?

There can be only one explanation. Although the way of the king and the way of the hegemon are different, yet the hegemon must assume the way of the emperor and the king. The Han, T'ang, and Sung all endured for many years, and surely in that time the way of the emperor

---

[87] The phrase *ch'u ch'u yü-mo* alludes to the *Book of Changes*, "Appended Remarks," 7:10b.

[88] Ch'eng Hao as quoted in *Shang-ts'ai hsien-sheng yü-lu* (Recorded Conversations of Master Hsieh Liang-tso), A:21b.

[89] Alludes to *Mencius*, 7A:4:2.

[90] Alludes to *Analects*, 4:15:1.

[91] Shao Yung proposed an elaborate correlation between the four seasons, the way of the august sovereign, emperor, king, and hegemon; the *Book of Changes*, *Book of History*, *Book of Poetry* and *Spring and Autumn Annals*; the virtues of humaneness, rightness, decorum, and wisdom; the nature, feelings, form, and substance; the sage, worthy, man of talent, and strategist, etc. See *Huang-chi ching-shih shu* (Supreme Principles Governing the World), *ch.* 5–6, esp. 5:9a–b, 14a; 6:8a–b, 14a–15a.

[92] Fu-hsi, Shen-nung, and the Yellow Emperor.

and the king was to some limited extent tried in the world.. Thus it is still possible to designate them as eras of the emperor and king.

32. Seeing, hearing, thinking, deliberating, moving, and acting are all [functions of] heaven (or nature, *t'ien*). Man has only to recognize through them what is true and what is false. Basing one's actions on heaven is true; basing one's actions on man is false. Heaven and man do not represent a duality in any fundamental sense. It is only because man has this substantial form[93] that he is on a different level from heaven. When this substantial form is discarded, he is entirely merged with heaven. How can this substantial form be discarded? It is only by overcoming my egoistic sense of personal identity that it can be discarded.

33. Master Shao said, "The Mean is not concerned with what is conferred by heaven or what is produced by earth. Rather it understands true achievement to lie in determining the principles of things, estimating the feelings of men, and acting to bring about their repose."[94] I humbly submit that it is through what is conferred by heaven and produced by earth that the principles of things and the feelings of men find their repose. When Tzu-ssu composed the *Mean* he began the opening section with the phrase, "What heaven has endowed is called the nature,"[95] and he concluded with the words, " 'The doings of high heaven have neither sound nor smell.' "[96] In between the scope was broadened to include all things. And is there any one among them that does not derive from heaven? Thus when "the gentleman accords with the course of the Mean,"[97] he is only following heaven. He does not allow selfish calculation to play any role in it.

Given the lofty intelligence of Master Shao, he certainly had the most perfect comprehension of the interfusion of heaven and man, and yet he made a statement of this kind. Could it have been that he was

[93] The term *hsing-t'i* in this context refers to the concrete form which, experienced in terms of personal identity, marks the individual off as distinct from others.

[94] Quoting Shao Yung in *Huang-chi ching-shih shu*, 8B:26b.

[95] *Mean*, 1:1.

[96] *Mean*, 33:6, quoting Ode 235.

[97] *Mean*, 11:3.

anxious to lead students on and thus show them the truth that is near at
hand? Such a statement is also found in the *Book of Rites*,[98] but its most
profound thought did not lie in this.

34. The *Tso-chuan* provides the most detailed evidence concerning facts
which are recorded in the *Spring and Autumn Annals*. Although Master Tso
did not explain to any great extent what the Sage intended by what he
included and what he deleted, later students of the *Spring and Autumn Annals* still have his facts as a basis for probing and understanding the meaning
of the classic of the Sage. In this sense its value is considerable.

    Take, for example, the case of the crime of Shang-ch'en,[99] the
heir of Ch'u. Were it not for the detail contained in the *Tso-chuan*, how
would one know what motivated the crime? And unless one knows what
motivated the crime, the intentions of the Sage in handing down his warning would be quite unclear. It is not the case that whenever Confucius
recorded the killing of a sovereign it was only in order to hand down a

---

[98] A reference to the *Book of Rites*, "Questions about Mourning Rites." In Legge's
translation (*Li Chi: Book of Rites*, 2:379) the statement reads: "It does not come down from
heaven, it does not come forth from the earth; it is simply the expression of the human
feelings."

[99] *Spring and Autumn Annals*, Duke Wen, 1st year. The text of the *Spring and
Autumn Annals* records only that, "In winter, in the tenth month, on Ting-we, Shang-shin,
heir-son of Ts'oo, murdered his ruler, Keun." Legge, *The Ch'un Ts'ew with The Tso Chuen*,
The Chinese Classics, 5:229. The *Tso-chuan* provides the following background to the event:
"At an earlier period, the viscount of Ts'oo, intending to declare Shang-shin his successor,
consulted his chief minister Tsze-shang about it. Tsze-shang said, 'Your lordship is not yet old.
You are also fond of many [of your children]. Should you degrade him hereafter, he will make
disorder. The succession in Ts'oo has always been from among the younger sons. Moreover,
he has eyes [projecting] like a wasp's, and a wolf's voice;—he is capable of anything. You
ought not to raise him to that position.' The viscount did it however. But afterwards he wished
to appoint his son Chih instead, and to degrade Shang-shin. Shang-shin heard of his intention, but was not sure of it. He therefore told his tutor P'wan Ts'ung, and asked him how he
could get certain information. Ts'ung said, 'Give a feast to her of Keang [The viscount's sister],
and behave disrespectfully to her.' The prince did so, when the lady became angry, and cried
out, 'You slave, it is with reason that the king wishes to kill you, and appoint Chih in your
place.' Shang-shin told this to his tutor, saying, 'The report is true.' Ts'ung then said, 'Are
you able to serve Chih?' 'No.' 'Are you able to leave the state?' 'No.' 'Are you able to do the
great thing?' 'Yes.' In winter, in the 10th month, Shang-shin with the guards of his palace,
held the king in siege. The king begged to have bear's paws to eat before he died, which was
refused him; and on Ting-we he strangled himself." Legge, *The Ch'un Ts'ew with The Tso
Chuen*, *The Chinese Classics*, 5:230.

warning to ministers and sons. He also intended to hand down a warning to sovereigns and fathers. According to one theory, when a sovereign does not behave like a sovereign, ministers will not behave like ministers, and when fathers do not behave like fathers, sons will not behave like sons. According to another theory, even if a sovereign does not behave like a sovereign, a minister must behave like a minister and even if a father does not behave like a father, a son must behave like a son. If sovereigns behave like sovereigns, ministers behave like ministers, fathers like fathers, and sons like sons,[100] the bonds will be correct and all things will fall into place. Thus the *Spring and Autumn Annals* has value for all time.

Someone said, "When the *Spring and Autumn Annals* recorded that someone murdered his sovereign, the murder in itself was a crime. What is the need of inquiring into its details?"[101] But if one takes such a view, the final result of reading the classic would only be to elicit from the reader a prolonged sigh. How then could it be a work that will provide benefit for all time? And in that case, why would the Sage have written the *Spring and Autumn Annals*?

---

[100] Alludes to *Analects*, 12:11:2–3.

[101] An allusion to a comment by Wang Yang-ming recorded in Part 1 of the *Instructions for Practical Living*. Wang argued that a superfluity of writing after the Spring and Autumn period contributed to chaotic conditions in the world. He rejected the suggestion of his disciple Hsü Ai that the *Tso-chuan* was one example of indispensable writing: "To say that the *Spring and Autumn Annals* can only be illuminated with a commentary is to regard it as a puzzle with the last part left out. Why should Confucius write in such difficult and abstruse terms? Much of the *Tso-chuan* is from the original text of the history of Lu. If the *Spring and Autumn Annals* depends on it to be understood, then why should Confucius have abridged it? . . . When he recorded that so-and-so murdered his ruler, the murder in itself was a crime. What is the need of inquiring into its details? Military expeditions against the feudal state should proceed from the king. When he recorded that such-and-such a feudal lord invaded a state, the invasion in itself was a crime. What is the need of inquiring into its details? The primary purpose of Confucius' transmitting the Six Classics was purely to rectify people's minds, to preserve the Principle of Nature, and to eliminate selfish human desires. He did discuss these matters. Sometimes when people asked him, he would talk to them according to their ability to understand. But even then he would not talk much, for he was afraid that people would try to seek truth in words only. This is why he said, 'I do not wish to say anything.' How could he be willing to tell people in detail all these things that would release selfish human desires and destroy the Principle of Nature? That would be to promote disorder and induce wickedness." *Wang Wen-ch'eng kung ch'üan-shu*, 1:14a–b. Wing-tsit Chan, trans., *Instructions for Practical Living*, sec. 11, p. 20.

35. *Li* must be identified as an aspect of *ch'i*, and yet to identify *ch'i* with *li* would be incorrect. The distinction between the two is very slight, and hence it is extremely difficult to explain. Rather we must perceive it within ourselves and comprehend it in silence. It is one thing to speak of "identifying *li* as an aspect of *ch'i*" and another to speak of "identifying *li* with *ch'i.*" There is a clear difference between them. If this is not apparent, there is no point in explaining further.

36. Someone asked Yang Kuei-shan [102] whether the statement, "There is in the changes the Great Ultimate," [103] should not be taken to refer to what is called "equilibrium." "He said, 'That is correct.' 'If that is so, then it is fundamentally lacking in a fixed substance, so that the Great Ultimate is everywhere?' He said, 'That is correct.' 'Then how is it that, through it, the two forces, the four images, and the eight trigrams come into being?' He said, 'Once there is the Great Ultimate, there are also above and below. When there are above and below, there are also left and right, front and back. Given the four directions of left and right, front and back, there are also the four cardinal points. This is all natural principle.' " [104]

This explanation of Kuei-shan's is expressed in the simplest terms and shows true discernment in the discrimination of principle and the Great Ultimate. But what the student should understand here is that when the Sage spoke of the Great Ultimate, it was from the standpoint of the changes. He represented principle in concrete terms in order to make it apparent to people. He was not theorizing in a void. In order to be able to appreciate this, the student must make a careful effort in personal realization.

37. Hsieh Shang-ts'ai [105] said, "The mind which explores things to the utmost has its limits, whereas heaven is limitless. This being the case, how can the mind encompass heaven?" [106]

[102] Yang Shih (1053–1135). See above, Part I, n. 141.

[103] *Book of Changes,* "Appended Remarks," 7:17a.

[104] *Yang Kuei-shan hsien-sheng yü-lu* (Recorded Conversations of Master Yang Shih) (in SPTK *hsü-pien*), 4:15b–16a.

[105] Hsieh Liang-tso (1050–c.1120). See above, Part I, n. 166.

[106] *Shang-ts'ai hsien-sheng yü-lu,* A:18a.

I do not know what prompted him to make this statement. The substance of the human mind is the substance of heaven. Originally they are one thing, so that "encompassing" is unnecessary. It is only that what takes command in me is called the mind. If there are limits to the mind's exploring things to the utmost, it is only that it has not yet arrived in its exploration, whereas when things are investigated, the mind is limitless. To be limitless means to be fully developed. This is what is called developing the mind to the fullest.[107] When the mind is developed to the fullest, it is one with heaven. If they were ultimately two different things, how could the power of human intelligence manage to "encompass"?

38. The elder Master Ch'eng once said, " 'The myriad things are all complete in me,'[108] applies not only to human beings but to all living things."[109] The Buddhists also say that even crawling and wriggling creatures have the Buddha nature.[110] Their general idea is about the same, and yet Master Ch'eng did not accept their view. I have searched for the reasons for his rejecting it, but in the end they elude me.

What the Buddhists refer to as the nature is consciousness (*chüeh*), while what we Confucians refer to as the nature is principle. There is no need to get into the question of who is right and who is wrong in this instance, since, at birth, human beings and other living things all possess both principle and consciousness. Speaking in terms of consciousness, how could it be that the lowliest of living things is different from the Buddha? It is extremely rare to find such inconsistencies in Master Ch'eng's statements on any specific point, and so I have examined them repeatedly and explored their implications thoroughly in the hope of reconciling them and recovering the ultimate unity.

[107] Alludes to *Mencius*, 7A:1:1.

[108] *Mencius*, 7A:4:1.

[109] Ch'eng Hao's statement in *I-shu*, 2A:16a.

[110] In *Ch'uan-hsin fa-yao* (The Essential Method of the Transmission of the Mind) (T 2012A, 48:380b) the Ch'an master Huang-po Hsi-yün says: "Crawling and wriggling creatures are one and the same substance with the Buddha and bodhisattvas."

39. In the early years of our dynasty there were few who were profoundly versed in the learning of principle,[111] while many were versed in Ch'an. Though the fact that the Confucian Way has not flourished may have been a matter of destiny, the responsibility nevertheless rests with us. At that time Sung Ch'ien-hsi[112] was head of the civil bureaucracy. The influence of his writings and opinions at court and their wide currency throughout the empire are beyond recounting. Yet if you consider what it was that sustained him throughout his life, it was nothing but Ch'an. If, given his intelligence and experience, he had had a genuine inclination to be engaged in our Way and to go from broad learning to what is essential,[113] he would certainly have attained the ultimate standard. His achievements would have been so remarkable that he would have been considered the foremost Confucian of his day. But he discarded a Chou bronze and treasured a broken tile.[114] I cannot help but grieve deeply for Ch'ien-hsi.

40. In the final analysis Ch'an learning is superficial. If one first gains an insight into our Way and then examines their theories in detail, nothing will elude him.

41. The differences and similarities between Chu and Lu[115] are not something I should dare to discuss lightly, and yet if one is disinterested and fails to discriminate between them, he will not know which he ought to follow. In the matter of discrimination there are instances when one should proceed in spite of himself. And if, "while one is not yet clear in his discrim-

---

[111] *Li-hsüeh* was one of several terms by which Neo-Confucian philosophy was designated in the Sung period and thereafter.

[112] Sung Lien (1310–1381). See above, n. 1.

[113] Alludes to *Mencius*, 4B:15.

[114] Recalls a phrase from the "Funeral Oration for Ch'ü Yüan" by Chia I (201–169 B.C.). The idea is to cast off a treasure and treasure a cast-off.

[115] For Wang Yang-ming's views on this subject, see his two letters of 1522 to Hsü Ch'eng-chih ("Yü Hsü Ch'eng-chih") in *Wai-chi* (Additional Writings), 3 (*Wang Wen-ch'eng kung ch'üan shu*, 21:9b–17b). For an English translation of these letters, see Julia Ching, trans., *The Philosophical Letters of Wang Yang-ming*, pp. 70–78. Wang's general point of view was that Chu Hsi and Lu Hsiang-shan were not so far apart philosophically as had been generally assumed and that Lu was seriously maligned by those who described him as a Ch'an Buddhist.

ination, he does not intermit in his labor,"[116] there will surely be a time when he is clear. How can we avoid the charge of discussing our Confucian predecessors lightly if it means confusing the alternatives and bequeathing a great falsehood to future generations in the world?

The reason that the Way is not manifest in the world is that it is confused with Ch'an. With only an infinitesimal mistake at the beginning, why is it that there is an infinite error at the end?[117] It is because the adherents of Ch'an are content with a very limited view and know nothing whatever about our Way. Among students of the Way there are also some who have never entirely understood Ch'an and have no way of truly knowing wherein it actually differs from our Way.

Upon inquiry I find that the Ch'eng brothers, Master Chang, and Master Chu all studied Ch'an in their early years and were able to investigate it to the core. But only when they had acquired a grasp of our Confucian Way did they become greatly awakened to the errors of Ch'an and give it up entirely. Not only did they give it up, but they earnestly assailed and thoroughly controverted it. They were concerned lest people might become enmeshed in it and unable to extricate themselves, thereby compounding the casualties suffered by our Way. The language that they consistently used in assailing and controverting Ch'an allows us to comprehend their inner natures and to experience the sense of urgency they felt in their hearts. This was in no sense something that emanated from selfish contrivance or imagination. The fact that Master Chu regarded Hsiang-shan as an adherent of Ch'an was the result of careful scrutiny of his views. Would he have applied this designation simply out of dislike and jealousy and the desire to implicate him on trumped up charges?

From the time I began my education I was only aware of the instructions of the sages and worthies and knew nothing whatever about Ch'an. Then when I was employed in the capital, I encountered an old Buddhist priest and questioned him casually about how to become a Buddha. With equal casualness the priest[118] resorted to Ch'an language in his

---

[116] Alludes to the *Mean*, 20:20.

[117] Alludes to *I-wei t'ung-kua yen* (Apocryphal Treatise on the *Book of Changes*: On Understanding the Verification of Divination), A:5b.

[118] This edition of the text reads "I," but this has been corrected in other editions to read "the priest."

reply, saying, "The Buddha is in the pine tree in the courtyard."[119] I supposed that there must be something in what he said and gave it my undivided thought until dawn. As I grasped my clothing and was about to arise, I became suddenly enlightened and was unaware that my entire body was bathed in perspiration. Later I obtained the "Song of Enlightenment" (*Cheng-tao ko*). [120] Reading it, I found that it accorded perfectly with my own experience. I regarded this as most wonderful and mysterious and thought that in all the principles of the world there was nothing to add to it.

Later when I held office at the Imperial University in Nanking, I never put the books of the sages and worthies out of my hands for even a day. I entered into the spirit of the books and savored them over a long period of time, gradually realizing their truth. Only then did I understand that what I had perceived on that former occasion was the mysterious activity of the mind's pure spirituality and not the principle of the nature. From this point on, with day following upon day, I devoted my mind and my most painstaking effort to careful inquiry and personal realization. Only when I was approaching the age of sixty did I finally attain clear insight into the reality of the mind and the nature and truly acquire the basis for self-confidence.

Until then I had barely been able to discriminate clearly between the learning of Chu and Lu. I was truly obtuse. For having scrutinized the writings of Hsiang-shan in their entirety, I found that for the most part they dealt with the theory of clarifying the mind (*ming-hsin*). He himself had said that his learning was what he had realized for himself through study of the *Mencius,* and at that time there was someone who commented that, "Aside from the saying, 'First build up the nobler part of your nature,'[121] Hsiang-shan had nothing clever."[122] He himself considered this to be true.[123] But I came to realize that the words of Mencius were different

---

[119] Alludes to *Wu-men kuan* (The Gate Without a Door), T 2005, 48:297c.

[120] The "Song of Enlightenment" (*Cheng-tao ko*) (T 2014, 48:395–96) is commonly attributed to the Ch'an Master Yung-chia Hsüan-chüeh (665–713). There are various translations, including one by Charles Luk in *Ch'an and Zen Teaching,* Third Series, pp. 116–145.

[121] *Mencius,* 6A:15:2.

[122] Recorded in *Hsiang-shan ch'üan-chi,* 34:5a.

[123] *Ibid.*

from the teachings of Hsiang-shan. The fact that up to then I had been unable to discriminate this point clearly meant not only that I had not understood Hsiang-shan, but also that I had not understood Mencius.

Mencius said: "When the senses of hearing and seeing are used without thought, they are obscured by things. When one thing comes into contact with another, the senses are led astray. The function of the mind is to think. By thinking, the mind apprehends; in not thinking, it does not apprehend. This is what heaven has granted to us. If we first uphold the nobler part of our nature, the inferior part will not be able to overcome it." [124] The language of this statement is extremely clear. What is it that is important in "first building up the nobler part of our nature"? It is being able to think. That which is capable of thought is the mind. What we apprehend through thought is the principle of the nature. Mencius was emphatic that behaving like a human being could be summarized in the word "thought." Thus on another occasion he said, "Humanity, rightness, propriety, and wisdom are not infused in us from without. We possess them inherently. Failure to realize this is due to lack of thought." [125]

What Hsiang-shan teaches is, on the contrary, that "If this mind merely exists, this principle will illuminate itself. In a situation in which one ought to be compassionate, one will naturally be compassionate. In a situation in which one ought to feel shame and dislike, one will naturally feel shame and dislike. When one ought to be yielding, one will naturally be yielding. Confronted with right and wrong, one will naturally be able to discriminate between them. He [126] further said that when one ought to be generous and compliant, one will naturally be generous and compliant. When one ought to be bold and resolute, one will naturally be bold and resolute." [127]

If this were true, one would have no need for thought. But this is not the basic idea contained in Mencius' statement that we should "first build up the nobler part of our nature." To apprehend without thought [128]

[124] Mencius, 6A:15:2.

[125] Mencius, 6A:6:7.

[126] I.e., Mencius. Lu suggests that this was Mencius' view of the "four beginnings" (ssu-tuan).

[127] Hsiang-shan ch'üan-chi, 34:2a.

[128] Alludes to the Mean, 20:18.

is within the capacity of the sage, but how can the student attain to the state of one who is born with knowledge?[129] If one learns but does not think, he will lack the wherewithal to apprehend principle. If one naturally behaves just as he should in any given circumstance, this is naturally the result of the mysterious activity of the spiritual consciousness. But in matters of discretion and judgment[130] there is no way to be precisely right; one will either be excessive or deficient. Thus getting hold of the spiritual consciousness and considering this to be the ultimate Way can only be called Ch'an.

It is extremely difficult to be clear about the mind and the nature, and Hsiang-shan's mistake lay precisely in this. Consequently, in his exposition of the essentials of the mind he usually expended thousands of words, going on interminably, but when it came to the nature, he had little to say. Occasionally his disciples had questions, so that he was compelled to speak of it, but his statements were evasive, vague, and utterly devoid of substance. Since he was imprecise in his views, it was impossible for him to discuss it.

I have studied his pronouncements, which include statements such as the following: "The mind is principle."[131] If this is so, what is the nature? Again, "In heaven it is the nature; in man it is the mind."[132] If that is so, does the nature not after all reside in man? Since he did not recognize the nature for what it is, he could only identify the Way in terms of spiritual consciousness. Can there be any doubt that this is Ch'an?

There are some who construe Hsiang-shan's letters to Wang Shun-po[133] to mean that he had not adopted Ch'an. What they do not realize is that Hsiang-shan outwardly eschewed the name but inwardly employed its substance. How can this be known? In his letter he merely said that the teachings of the two schools were different in their point of departure.[134] He never explicitly said that there were differences between the

---

[129] Alludes to *Analects*, 16:9 and the *Mean*, 20:9.

[130] Literally, "weighing and measuring" (*ch'ing-chung ch'ang-tuan*).

[131] *Hsiang-shan ch'üan-chi*, 11:6a.

[132] *Ibid.*, 35:10b.

[133] Wang Hou-chih (*chin-shih*, 1166). A brief account of him is found in *Sung Yüan hsüeh-an*, ch. 58. Lu's letters to Wang are contained in *Hsiang-shan ch'üan-chi*, 2:1a–4b.

[134] Lu's first letter to Wang in *Hsiang-shan ch'üan-chi*, 2:2a. The two schools are Buddhism and Confucianism.

two ways. Is it conceivable that Confucianism and Buddhism are not two ways and that what defines the learning of the Confucian is merely his "concentrating on ordering the affairs of the world" (*ching-shih*) [135] and thus being public-spirited and righteous? When I say that he "inwardly employed the substance [of Ch'an]," I refer to this [failure to distinguish the two ways].

There are also some who observe that Hsiang-shan spoke of "exercising thought," "investigating things," and "probing principle to the utmost," and who therefore suppose that he did not turn his back on the instructions of the school of the sage. What they do not realize is that, although the words may be right, the connotation he gave them was wrong. For example, he said, "In investigating things and extending knowledge, one investigates this thing and extends this knowledge . . . In probing principle to the utmost, one probes this principle." [136] " 'By thinking one apprehends it,' means that one apprehends this. In 'first build up the nobler part of your nature,' one builds up this." [137] All these passages are based on the classics and commentaries. But when he quotes a phrase such as "one builds up this," the word *this* refers in every case to the mind. Do the "investigation of things" and the "probing of the principle to the utmost" spoken of in the classics of the Sage really refer to the mind? Thus the extensive quotations he proffers and the ample evidence he adduces are nothing but a contrivance to promote his theory of clarifying the mind. If one searches out the original ideas of the sages and worthies, one finds that his theory is in conflict rather than in harmony with them. If there are some who still do not agree with this, I beg to substantiate my contention with facts.

There was Yang Chien, [138] an eminent disciple of Hsiang-shan's. He once raised a question about the "original mind" (*pen-hsin*). When Hsiang-shan at that point made a pronouncement on it, he suddenly realized the

[135] Quoting from Lu's letter to Wang Shun-po in *Hsiang-shan ch'üan-chi*, 2:1b.

[136] *Hsiang-shan ch'üan-chi*, 19:9a.

[137] *Ibid.*, 1:1a.

[138] Yang Chien (1141–1226) was also known as Master Tz'u-hu from the name of the lake near which he lived. He was famous for his reflections on the identity of the self and the universe. Yang was criticized by Chu Hsi and many later thinkers of the Ch'eng-Chu school for what they saw as an inclination toward Ch'an Buddhism. Lo Ch'in-shun wrote an extended critique of Yang, which appears in *K'un-chih chi hsü* (Supplement to the *K'un-chih chi*), ch. 4.

purity of this mind. "He suddenly realized that this mind has no beginning or end and that it penetrates everywhere."[139] There was Chan Fou-min,[140] who was a follower of Hsiang-shan. [He recorded that,] ". . . I sat quietly with closed eyes, exerting myself to hold fast and preserve [my mind] . . . I did this for half a month, and one day while coming downstairs, I suddenly realized that my mind had been restored to purity and brightness . . . Hsiang-shan met me with his eyes and said, 'This principle is already manifested [in you].' "[141]

It is only in Ch'an that they have such devices as this. If one examines the exchanges in which Confucius, Tseng Tzu, Tzu-ssu, and Mencius took part, does one find a single phrase that resembles this? The evidence they offer is so clear and the inner coherence so compelling that even those with good powers of discrimination are usually unable to break free. What the two disciples perceived was no different from the vision that I perceived long ago.[142] This has enabled me to recognize their error and discuss it in detail, not daring to resort to language that is evasive or ambiguous.

Alas! Hsiang-shan possessed a superlative endowment far surpassing that of other people, and he met with associates who were intelligent and upright. Had he been able to proceed with an open mind and an easy temperament, disregarding the shortcomings of others and adopting their strengths so as to reach the utmost correctness, his attainment would have been matchless. However, he was deluded by the strangeness and singularity of the vision and forgetful of the fineness and subtlety of moral principle. Although he was diligent in seeking the Way, he did not discriminate as to its direction. To the end of his life he never knew how [the mind] comes into being. Isn't this lamentable? The transmission of his teaching has been uninterrupted down to the present day, and people who honor and trust it appear time and again in the world. As Tu Mu-chih[143] said, "One influences one's successors and also gives them cause to la-

---

[139] Recorded in *Hsiang-shan ch'üan-chi*, 36:7a.

[140] A brief account of him and his relation to Lu Hsiang-shan is found in *Sung Yüan hsüeh-an, ch.*, 77.

[141] Recorded in *Hsiang-shan ch'üan-chi*, 35:28b.

[142] See above, pp. 137–38.

[143] I.e., Tu Mu (803–853), the famous T'ang poet.

ment."[144] I have been moved to the depths by these words and cannot allow myself to fail to discriminate.

42. Master Ch'eng said, "All the words of the sages and worthies are designed to lead man to get hold of his lost mind[145] and cause it to return and reintegrate with his body. Having accomplished this, he will be able to direct his inquiries to a higher plane and 'through study of lower things advance to the higher.' "[146]

Hsi Wen-t'ung[147] says in the Introduction to his *Ming-yüan lu* (Plea for the Redress of Injuries), "Mencius' words were grasped by Master Ch'eng. After Master Ch'eng, Master Lu grasped them."[148] But when he quoted Master Ch'eng's words, he only got as far as "return and reintegrate with his body." The most important part lies in the two phrases, "be able to direct his inquiries to a higher plane" and "through the study of lower things advance to the higher." These he eliminated and did not use. What is the explanation for this? Given such a view, he is not only unable to redress an injury to Hsiang-shan, but I am afraid that he inevitably does injury to Master Ch'eng.

43. Master Ch'eng said, "The nature is principle."[149] Hsiang-shan said, "The mind is principle."[150] "What is ultimately as it should be returns to

---

[144]"O-fang-kung fu" (Prose Poem on the O-fang Palace) in *Fan-ch'uan wen-chi* (Collection of Literary Works of Tu Mu) (SPTK ed.), 1:2b.

[145]Alludes to *Mencius*, 6A:11:2–4.

[146]Ch'eng I in *I-shu*, 1:4a, quoting *Analects*, 14:37:2.

[147]Hsi Shu (1461–1527). He evidently respected both Wang Yang-ming and Lo Ch'in-shun, though, philosophically, he seems to have had a greater affinity with Wang. When Wang was in exile in Kuei-chou, Hsi, then Vice Commissioner of Education in Kueichou, invited him to come and teach in the provincial capital, Kuei-yang. In doing so, he risked the ire of the powerful eunuch, Liu Chin, who had been responsible for Wang's exile. At the end of his career in 1527, Hsi recommended Lo Ch'in-shun to become his successor as Minister of Rites, but Lo declined. In the interim Hsi had served in a number of high posts, including Governor of Hu-kuang, Vice Minister of War in Nanking, and Minister of Rites in Peking. See the biography by Chou Tao-chi in the *Dictionary of Ming Biography*, 1:523–25.

[148]I have not had access to this work.

[149]Ch'eng I in *I-shu*, 22A:11a.

[150]*Hsiang-shan ch'üan-chi*, 11:6a.

unity; what is perfectly right harbors no duality."[151] If one is right, the other is wrong, and vice versa. How can we fail to discriminate clearly between them?

When our Master[152] compiled the *Book of Changes* he spoke repeatedly about the nature. He said, "The Way of *ch'ien* works through change and transformation so that each thing receives its proper nature and endowment."[153] He said, "That which brings to completion is the nature."[154] He said, "The sages made the *Book of Changes* so that it would be in conformity with the principles underlying the nature and destiny."[155] He said, "[The sages taught] probing principle to the utmost and fully developing one's nature until the destiny is fulfilled."[156] If only one dwells on these statements, it will be clear that the nature is principle.

He also spoke repeatedly about the mind. He said, "The sages cleansed their minds by means of this."[157] He said, "[The gentleman] composes his mind before he speaks."[158] He said, "[The sages] were able to rejoice in their minds."[159] Thus he said of the mind that one cleanses it, one composes it, and one rejoices in it. With respect to cleansing the mind, he said that it is "by means of *this* [knowledge of the changes]." If one dwells on these statements, is it valid to say that the mind is principle? Moreover, Mencius said, "Moral principles are as agreeable to my mind as the flesh of grass- and grain-fed animals is to my mouth."[160] This is extremely clear and easy to perceive.

Thus if one carries on his studies without reference to the classics and is utterly arbitrary and opinionated, it is inevitable that he will be

---

[151] *Ibid.*, 1:3b.

[152] I.e., Confucius.

[153] *Book of Changes*, *ch'ien* hexagram, 1:4a.

[154] *Book of Changes*, "Appended Remarks," 7:7b.

[155] *Book of Changes*, "Discussion of the Trigrams," 9:2a.

[156] *Ibid.*

[157] *Book of Changes*, "Appended Remarks," 7:16a.

[158] *Ibid.*, 8:8b.

[159] *Ibid.*, 8:13b.

[160] *Mencius*, 7A:7:8.

misled. It is wrong to allow oneself to be misled, worse yet to mislead others.

44. Hsiang-shan said, "When at fifteen Confucius 'set his mind on learning,'[161] he at that time already knew the Way. Yet despite what he knew, he inevitably experienced departures and returns, clarity and obscuration. At times he was vigilant and at others lax, at times he was active and at others he took his rest. When he reached thirty and 'stood firm,' there was no longer any distinction between departing and returning, clarity and obscuration, vigilance and laxity, activity and rest. But he was not yet able to perceive things and events with perfect clarity. Only upon reaching forty did he 'no longer have doubts.' "[162]

Now when he first set his mind on learning, he already had a reputation for knowing the Way. Why should it have been that even after he "stood firm," his perception of events and things was still not perfectly clear? And if this were true, just what was the Way that he already knew? And what were the things that he had not yet perceived? Isn't it true that knowing how to preserve the mind is equivalent to knowing the Way? Moreover, Hsiang-shan definitely said, "If the mind is preserved, principle will naturally be clear."[163] If, given the endowment of the Sage, it still required twenty-five years before he was able to perceive with perfect clarity, there must be some inconsistency involved in these statements. How could the learning of our Sage have been such that what he "knew" was one thing and what he "perceived" was another?

I do not presume to discuss our Confucian predecessors lightly. "But if I do not correct his error, then the Way will not be perceived,"[164] and if anyone wanted to blame me, I could not be excused.

---

[161] Here and in what follows Lu was discussing the progress of Confucius as recorded in *Analects*, 2:4.

[162] *Hsiang-shan ch'üan-chi*, 35:32b–33a. See also *Hsiang-shan ch'üan-chi*, 12:1b, 21:5a–b, 34:26a, 35:6a, 14b, 25a.

[163] *Hsiang-shan ch'üan-chi*, 34:2a.

[164] Quoting *Mencius*, 3A:5:2.

45. Wu K'ang-chai[165] may be considered singleminded and earnest in his commitment to the Way. There is no real basis on which to assess the depth of his achievement, and if one is to judge by the "Ten Exhortations" that he submitted to the emperor after declining to accept his appointment,[166] one finds that they are strung together with quotations from the sages and worthies and offer little in the way of thematic unity. Thus in terms of Mencius' instruction to "go back and set forth in brief what is essential,"[167] his attainment may be considered somewhat wanting. Yet his declining to accept an official appointment was in itself an event so exemplary that it could serve to "make the corrupt become pure and the weak acquire determination."[168]

An examination of his original motivation indicates that it was not that he considered it noble not to serve. Rather he needed some time in which to make his contribution and to see whether or not it would be suitable before he could decide whether or not to accept an appointment. But the situation which prevailed at that time was far from normal, and the circumstances presented numerous obstacles. It was difficult to make a judgment at so critical a juncture, and consequently the officials in charge, who probably judged on the basis of what they observed, did not insist on his remaining. Through his resolute departure K'ang-chai gained a great deal.

The account of one or two events of K'ang-chai's later years recorded in [Yin] *Chien-chai's Interlocking Record (Chien-chai so-chui lu)* is

---

[165] Wu Yü-pi (1392–1469). He was the first major figure in the Ch'eng-Chu school of the early Ming and the teacher of Hu Chü-jen (1434–1484) and Ch'en Hsien-chang (1428–1500), among others. Declining to hold office, Wu devoted his entire life to teaching and farming. An account of him is found in *Ming-ju hsüeh-an, ch.* 1. For a discussion of his life and thought, see M. Theresa Kelleher, "Personal Reflections on the Pursuit of Sagehood: The Life and Journal *(Jih-lu)* of Wu Yü-pi (1392–1469)," Ph.D. dissertation, Columbia University, 1982.

[166] In *K'ang-chai chi* (Collected Works of Wu Yü-pi), 8:4a–12a. The "Ten Exhortations" ("Ch'en-yen shih-shih") have to do with 1) honoring the will of the sages; 2) promoting the learning of the sages; 3) exalting the virtue of the sages; 4) treating the people as one's children; 5) being cautious in issuing commands; 6) furthering education; 7) employing worthy officials; 8) managing affairs of state; 9) promoting lines of communication to the throne; 10) being of one mind with one's ministers.

[167] *Mencius,* 4B:15.

[168] *Mencius,* 5B:1 and 7B:15.

not necessarily slanderous.[169] But how many are there who can compare with K'ang-chai in their love of learning and dedication to moral principles? We should recognize his strengths and overlook his weaknesses, for surely this is the way of the gentleman.

46. The *Record of My Reading (Tu-shu lu)* by Hsüeh Wen-ch'ing[170] affords ample evidence of his effort to achieve realization through personal experience. He examined every subject with thoroughness, and I find that there are unanticipated points of agreement between his views and my own. Yet how true it is that it is difficult to achieve unity.

It says in the *Record*, "Li and *ch'i* are inseparable, and therefore it is said, 'Concrete things are the Way, and the Way is also concrete things.' "[171] This statement is correct. But I can only be skeptical in respect to his repeated attempts to prove the theory that *ch'i* is characterized by integration and disintegration whereas *li* is not characterized by integration and disintegration.[172] For if one were so characterized and the other were not, the separation between them would be considerable. How could one then say, "Concrete things are the Way, and the Way is also concrete things"? Wen-ch'ing always regarded *li* and *ch'i* as two things,[173] and therefore the occasional contradiction inevitably showed up in his words.

---

[169] In Wu Yü-pi's biography in *Ming shih* (History of the Ming Dynasty), 282:3171–72, the derogatory account by Yin Chih (1427–1511) of several incidents in Wu's later life is accepted as true. Lo here indicates that he was not persuaded that it was untrue. However, Fang Chao-ying, Julia Ching, and Huang P'ei, in their biography of Wu in the *Dictionary of Ming Biography* (2:1497–1501), are of the opinion that "The anecdotes about Wu, as told in the *Chien-chai so-chui lu*, must be pronounced untrue," and that their currency in Wu's own time may be explained in terms of a prevailing prejudice in favor of those holding the *chin-shih* degree, which Wu never earned.

[170] Hsüeh Hsüan (1389–1464). Leader of the Ho tung school, so named after his native place in Shansi, he was a prominent adherent of the Ch'eng-Chu school in the early Ming. An account of him is found in *Ming-ju hsüeh-an*, ch. 7.

[171] Hsüeh Hsüan, *Tu-shu lu* (Record of My Reading), 6:5b. The statement that "Concrete things are the Way, and the Way is also concrete things," is usually attributed to Ch'eng Hao. See *I-shu*, 1:3b.

[172] *Tu-shu lu*, 4:16b–17a, 5:8a, 6:3b.

[173] Hsüeh Hsüan repeatedly states the view that principle and material force are one and inseparable and denies that *li* has any priority over *ch'i*. Yet he retains the Sung view of *li* and *ch'i* as ontologically distinct, arguing, as in *Tu-shu lu*, 4:25b, that "Material force is constantly changing and varied; principle is forever fixed and immutable."

Li, being subtle, profound, and mysterious, is extremely difficult to discuss, and if one misses the truth by the slightest bit, there will be no way to avoid contradictions, no matter how great his desire to do so. Thus the instruction of our Master was to "enter the spirit through the purest of thought."[174] When one arrives at the point of "entering the spirit," one penetrates everywhere. This is not something that I can attain, and yet I devote all my thoughts to this end.

I would venture that the integration of ch'i is itself the li of integration and that the disintegration of ch'i is itself the li of disintegration. It is merely the fact that there is integration and disintegration that we refer to as li. Inferentially, it is the same in the case of the growth and decline of all creation and transformation and the beginning and end of all affairs and things. Discussed in this way, it is naturally clear, and there are no contradictions. Though one may seek to discover a separation [between li and ch'i], it will be utterly impossible. I wonder what the gentleman who understands words will think about this?

47. The scholarship of Hsüeh Wen-ch'ing was pure and correct, and he was genuine and earnest in his practice. Whether in service or in private life, in advancing or retiring, he was satisfied only when rightness was obtained. Though some of his statements may warrant skepticism, an examination of his attainment reveals that there are few who can match him. He deserves to be called "a scholar after the manner of the gentleman."[175]

48. It says in the Record of My Reading, "Such men as Han Wei Kung[176] and Fan Wen-cheng[177] all had hearts that were loyal and faithful to the state. Consequently their achievements were obvious, and their names inspired confidence throughout the world. In later ages men's conduct is governed by selfish thoughts and petty wisdom, and their desire is to be honored for their achievements. It is difficult for them to measure up to the worthies of the past."[178]

[174] Book of Changes, "Appended Remarks," 8:6a.

[175] Alludes to Analects, 6:11.

[176] Han Ch'i (1008–1075).

[177] Fan Chung-yen (989–1052).

[178] Tu-shu lu, 5:17a.

This statement is entirely correct. Because Hsüeh Wen-ch'ing had such a heart, he was not merely able to make such a statement but, more broadly, to make his study a matter of "abiding in loyalty and faithfulness."[179] This in turn required that he be loyal and faithful in serving the ruler. The loyalty with which one serves the ruler must already have been fixed on the day of learning.

49. Though Ch'en Pai-sha[180] was among the influential advocates of the learning of the Way (*tao-hsüeh*) in recent times,[181] I am afraid that errors in scholarship also began with Pai-sha. "From the utmost nothingness comes action, and what is nearest at hand is most spiritual,"[182]—this is what Pai-sha called the wonder of "acquiring for oneself" (*tzu-te*).[183] But, as I have stated previously,[184] this is merely perceiving what is "most spiritual" and assuming that the Way lies in this, without being able to "reach the depths" or "study the subtle activating forces"[185] [of all things]. Although my statement was not intended for Pai-sha, I am afraid that Pai-sha's error lay precisely in this.

[179] Alludes to a phrase repeated in *Analects*, 1:8:2, 9:24, and 12:10.

[180] Ch'en Hsien-chang (1428–1500). The founder of the Chiang-men school, named after his native place in Kwangtung, Ch'en spent most of his life as a teacher in Kwangtung. Briefly a student of Wu Yü-pi, he later rejected the approach of the Ch'eng-Chu school in favor of a philosophy which emphasized the individual human mind, acquiring the truth for oneself (*tzu-te*), and a lyrical appreciation of nature and the natural. For a discussion of his life and thought, see Jen Yu-wen, *Pai-sha tzu yen-chiu* (A Study of Ch'en Hsien-chang).

[181] When the biographies of the Sung Neo-Confucians, which had appeared in *Sung shih* (History of the Sung Dynasty), ch. 427–30, under the designation *tao-hsüeh*, were published in the Ming as a separate book, Ch'en wrote a preface for it under the title "Tao-hsüeh chuan hsü" (Preface to the Biographies of the Adherents of the Learning of the Way). It appears in *Pai-sha tzu ch'üan-chi* (Complete Works of Master Ch'en Hsien-chang), vol. 2, ch. 1, pp. 17b–18b.

[182] "Ta Chang nei-han T'ing-hsiang ssu kua erh ch'eng shih ch'eng Hu Hsi-jen t'i hsüeh," in *Pai-sha tzu ku-shih chiao-chieh*, A:10b (in *Pai-sha tzu ch'üan-chi*, vol. 10).

[183] For an analysis of Ch'en's use of this term, see Jen Yu-wen, *Pai-sha tzu yen-chiu*, pp. 194–232. See also his article, "Ch'en Hsien-chang's Philosophy of the Natural," in Wm. Theodore de Bary, ed., *Self and Society in Ming Thought*, pp. 81–85.

[184] *K'un-chih chi*, Part I, sec. 2. See above, p. 50.

[185] *Book of Changes*, "Appended Remarks," 7:15a.

Chang Feng-shan[186] once told me all about [Pai-sha's] learning, which he definitely regarded as Ch'an.[187] Hu Ching-chai[188] attacked Pai-sha even more trenchantly.[189] Their statements about him were well-founded. What is common opinion throughout the world cannot be regarded as slander.[190]

50. His excellency Ch'iu Wen-chuang[191] did not like Ch'en Pai-sha. In his [*Supplement to the*] *Extended Meaning of the Great Learning Elaborated (Ta-*

---

[186]Chang Mou (1437–1522). Known as an adherent of the Ch'eng-Chu school, Chang served in a number of high posts, including that of Chancellor of the Imperial University from 1504–1507. Like Lo, he spent many years of his life in retirement and had a reputation for integrity and commitment to a simple and abstemious style of life.

[187]Statements to this effect are found in *Feng-shan Chang hsien-sheng yü-lu* (Recorded Conversations of Master Chang Mou). See especially 1:6a, where Chang says of Ch'en Pai-sha, "I am afraid that by exclusively concentrating on abiding in tranquillity and seeking to 'acquire for himself,' *(tzu-te),* he inevitably drifted into Ch'an."

[188]Hu Chü-jen (1434–1484). A student of Wu Yü-pi and another upholder of the Ch'eng-Chu tradition, Hu was a staunch critic of heterodox teachings in any form.

[189]*Chü-yeh lu* (Record of Occupying One's Sphere of Activity), 1:36a, 2:33a, 3:22a.

[190]Ch'en's most outstanding student, Chan Jo-shui (1466–1560) had contended that the widespread accusations that Pai-sha was deeply involved in Ch'an were unfair and slanderous. Though Chan's letters to Lo Ch'in-shun are apparently no longer extant, it is clear from Lo's letter to Chan in *K'un-chih chi fu-lu,* 6:23a–25a, that this was a point of contention between them and that Chan had been concerned to defend Ch'en against the charge.

[191]Ch'iu Chün (1420?–1495). According to his biography in *Ming shih,* 181:2122–23, he was left fatherless at an early age but was taught to read by his mother. Since the family was too poor to afford books, he walked great distances to borrow them. After attaining the *chin-shih* degree, he served in the Hanlin Academy, was made Chancellor of the Imperial University in 1477, and in 1480 was elevated to Right Vice Minister of Rites. He became Grand Secretary in 1491. Ch'iu was known as a contributor to the Ch'eng-Chu tradition of Neo-Confucianism. A polymath, he was the author of numerous books on history, geography, political economy, education, medicine, philosophy, and poetry, among other subjects. His monumental *Ta-hsüeh yen-i pu* in 164 *ch.* represented an attempt to broaden the scope of the *Ta-hsüeh yen-i* by the Sung Neo-Confucian Chen Te-hsiu (1178–1235) so that its principles might apply not only to individuals and households but to the whole realm of public affairs. The work devotes considerable attention to economic affairs, bureaucratic recruitment, government organization, and law. In their biography of Ch'iu in the *Dictionary of Ming Biography,* 1:249–52, Chi-hua Wu and Ray Huang explain: "Opinions about his character differ. His critics charge him with being selfish and treacherous. His admirers insist that he was straightforward and uncompromising. That Ch'en Hsien-chang was unable to obtain an official post at court, the critics assert, was entirely because Ch'iu, fearful of competition, elbowed him out of Peking. Ch'iu's supporters not only hold the accusations to be false, but also present corre-

hsüeh yen-i [pu]) there is a passage in which he examines and ridicules heterodox teachings, and apparently it was Pai-sha that he had in mind.[192] His Excellency certainly merited a considerable reputation for his literary accomplishments, and yet he was unable to win over the mind of Pai-sha. When he died, Pai-sha honored him with a eulogy,[193] though it gives the impression of being something less than wholehearted in its sentiment. This may have been because, as Master Ch'eng said, "Overcoming oneself is most difficult."[194]

51. The marked resemblance between Hu Ching-chai and Yin Ho-ching[195] is primarily established through the word "reverence" *(ching)*. The discussion of reverence in the *Record of Occupying One's Sphere of Activity (Chü-yeh lu)* is very through,[196] and it was because Ching-chai embodied it within himself that his discussion of it was so personal and affecting. He also devoted his attention to probing principle to the utmost, but in this case he seems to have been lacking in thoroughness. For example, he said, "Ch'i is what is produced by *li*,"[197] and, again, "The Way of man is produced by humaneness and rightness."[198] Again, "That which brings about the Great

spondence and poems exchanged between the two learned men from Kwangtung to evidence their lasting friendship." Clearly Lo Ch'in-shun's position was somewhat different in that, while a defender of Ch'iu, he was also convinced that there had been genuine antipathy between him and Ch'en Pai-sha.

[192] There are a number of points in the *Ta-hsüeh yen-i pu* at which Ch'iu Chün criticized heterodox methods or teachings or distinguished between orthodoxy *(cheng-hsüeh)* and heterodoxy *(i-hsüeh)*. See 63:18a, 64:7a–b, 64:15b–16b, 65:12a–13b, 71:20b–21a, and 72:11a–b. While it is difficult to be certain which passage Lo had in mind, Professor Liu Ts'un-yan suggests that 71:20b–21a and 72:11a–b "hit the point Lo raised very well."

[193] "Ts'un Ch'iu Ko-lao wen," in *Pai-sha tzu ch'üan-chi*, vol. 4, 5:20b–21a.

[194] Ch'eng Hao in *I-shu*, 11:8b.

[195] Yin T'un (1071–1142). He was a disciple of Ch'eng I and, like Hu Chü-jen, put great stress on reverence or seriousness *(ching)*. See his *Yin Ho-ching chi* (Collected Works of Yin T'un).

[196] Reverence or seriousness is an important focus of attention in the *Chü-yeh lu*. See for example, 2:30b: "Reverence is the basis of the teachings of the Sage. Through reverence one can banish licentiousness, correct depravity, eliminate promiscuity, and establish a great foundation." Also, 2:31a: "The one is sincerity. Concentrating on the one is reverence. It is through reverence that one becomes sincere."

[197] *Chü-yeh lu*, 1:35a.

[198] *Ibid.*, 2:1b.

Harmony (*t'ai-ho*) is the Way." [199] "First there is *li* and then there is *ch'i.*" [200] "The changes are produced by the Way." [201] But a careful reader of the "Appended Remarks" [in the *Book of Changes*] will see for himself whether or not these theories are in conformity with it.

Although Master Chu regarded *li* and *ch'i* as two things, his statements were characterized by the utmost breadth and balance. None of his successors reached the same standard in their speculations, and so these qualities have been lost. The *Book on the Nature* (*Hsing shu*) by Yü Tzu-chi [202] affords an extreme example. He says, "*Ch'i* can lend beauty to *li*. Will not *li* save *ch'i* from decline?" [203] On one occasion I happened to re-mark that I had not realized that *li* and *ch'i* offered each other so much charitable assistance.

52. Hu Ching-chai vigorously attacked Ch'an, for he was committed to distinguishing it from the Way of the Sage. [204] But he apparently did not inquire deeply into Ch'an learning as a whole and often summarily judged it to be "imagination." [205] How could he have won their minds? What we Confucians have apprehended is certainly a genuine perception, and what is apprehended by the adherents of Ch'an is also a genuine perception. It is only that what is perceived is different and that judgments concerning right and wrong, gain and loss are made on this basis. What they perceive is that the mystery of "pure intelligence and consciousness" [206] is naturally clear and untrammeled. One cannot dismiss this as "imagination." But, once having achieved this perception, they believe that everything is complete.

---

[199] *Ibid.*, 2:20b.

[200] *Ibid.*, 2:30b and 2:51b.

[201] *Ibid.*, 2:35a.

[202] Yü Yu (1465–1528) was the son-in-law of Hu Chü-jen.

[203] The *Hsing-shu* is, to my knowledge, no longer extant; however, the author's views can be at least partially reconstructed on the basis of *Fu Yü Tzu-chi lun Hsing-shu* (Reply to Yü Yu on his *Book on the Nature*) by Wei Chiao (1483–1543). See *Ming-ju hsüeh-an, ch.* 3. Huang Tsung-hsi's criticisms of Yü's understanding of *li* and *ch'i*, also found in *Ming-ju hsüeh-an, ch.* 3, suggest that Yü's conception was basically dualistic.

[204] *Chü-yeh lu*, 1:12b, 1:43a, 2:21a.

[205] *Ibid.*, 1:12b, 1:43a, 2:21a, 4:36b, 4:46b.

[206] See above *K'un-chih chi*, Part I, sec. 5.

They are entirely free in all their activities and thus behave madly and recklessly, so that ultimately they cannot be brought into the Way of Yao and Shun. This is what I call perceiving the mind but not perceiving the nature,[207] which is a judgment I will stand by. If they truly perceived the principle of the nature and destiny, they would not come to the point of mad and reckless behavior.

The mind and the nature are extremely difficult to understand, and many have been mistaken about them. They may be called two things, and yet they are not two things. They may be called one, and yet they are not one. If one does away with the mind, there is no nature, and if one does away with the nature, there is no mind. It is only when a distinction is made within a single thing, allowing two things to emerge, that one can speak of "knowing the nature." Until our study has come to the point where we know the nature, the opinions of the world will not be readily understood.

53. It says in the *Record of Occupying One's Sphere of Activity:* "Lou K'o-chen,[208] having seen that a hauler of wood had grasped its law, said, 'this is the Way.' This is like 'carrying water and hauling brushwood,'[209] in that it suggests that the stirring of consciousness is the nature. This is why he said what he did. The Way is everywhere, of course, but one must be in accord with moral principle and free of selfishness before it can be considered to be the Way. But how could a hauler of wood be capable of this? If he were capable of it, this would be the work of a Confucian. In his mind he would necessarily consider that there was nothing that was not the Way Yet if in his hauling of wood he were not in accord with what is right, could this still be called the Way?"[210]

When I read this passage I found myself sighing sadly and

---

[207] *Ibid.*

[208] Lou Liang (1422–1491). A student of Wu Yü-pi, Lou adopted a philosophy that emphasized "abiding in reverence." Accounts of Wang Yang-ming's life indicate that, having met Lou in his youth, he was influenced by him to study the writings of the Sung Neo-Confucians.

[209] A Ch'an expression found in *P'ang chü-shih yü-lu* (Recorded Sayings of Layman P'ang) in ZZ, 2,25,1,1:28a.

[210] *Chü-yeh lu*, 1:29b.

thinking that it has never been easy to probe moral principles. Now law (or method, *fa*) is another name for the Way, and laws exist in everything. If one grasps a law, one is in accord with principle, and this is the Way. The wood hauler certainly did not know what the Way is, but by doing this one thing, he was spontaneously and unconsciously in accord with the wondrousness of the Way. It is the same in the case of the ordinary man and woman or the wayward person who can also act and know.[211] The Way is everywhere. If grasping the law through hauling wood is not to be called the Way, doesn't this imply that there is a void in which the Way is not present? There might be something which was not right in the way one came by the wood, but this would then be the responsibility of the owner. How could it be the fault of the hauler? If the hauler is himself the owner, then his grasping the law is the Way. Or if his grasping[212] is not right, it is naturally not the Way. Is it right to accept this in one instance and reject it in a hundred others? What is expressed in Ch'an as "carrying water and hauling brushwood" is nothing but the wondrous functioning [of consciousness]. But they differ from Confucians in that they regard being able to haul and to carry as the ultimate Way, without first having asked whether or not the law has been grasped.[213] Although K'o-chen may have been an adherent of Ch'an, his words were nevertheless not incorrect. For Ching-chai to have come along and criticized them was wrong.

54. Wang Po-an's[214] style of learning is all there in the *Instructions for Practical Living (Ch'uan-hsi lu)*.[215] His exchanges with Hsiao Hui and Lu Yüan-ching[216] entitle him to say, "I conceal nothing from you,"[217] and the

---

[211] Alludes to *Mean* 12:2.

[212] The character printed *te* (virtue) in this edition is amended to read *te* (grasp, attain) in accordance with other editions.

[213] The character printed *hou* in this edition is amended to read *te* (grasp, attain).

[214] Wang Yang-ming.

[215] Lo presumably refers to Part 1 of the *Instructions for Practical Living*, though it is likely that he had also had access to some of the material in the present Part 2, which was published in 1524.

[216] *Instructions for Practical Living*, Part 1, secs. 122, 124, and 126 (*Wang Wench'eng kung ch'üan-shu*, 1:58b–60b, 61a–b, 61b–62a) record exchanges between Wang and Hsiao Hui. Sections 15–94 (*ibid.*, 18b–43b) were recorded by Lu Yüan-ching (Lu Ch'eng, cs. 1517).

[217] Alludes to *Analects*, 7:13.

whole of the *Instructions* is in everything quite substantial. But he "changes and moves and adheres to no fixed place,"[218] so that if one reads it rapidly, one may not be able to tell where he stands. Yüan-ching was quite skillful in posing questions, and he was consummately capable of thinking and searching.[219] But I wonder whether in the end he found himself in agreement?

55. I have read through several works of Chan Yüan-ming[220] and observed that, in the vigor and refinement of his style, he bears a striking resemblance to Yang Tzu-yün.[221] He too wants to form his own school.[222] But Yüan-ming's self-esteem is so high and his self-confidence so great that he probably would not condescend to be associated with Tzu-yün. There are many points at which I find my humble opinions to be at variance with his, and I regret that there has been no opportunity to discuss this with him in detail personally. In the hope of recovering the ultimate unity, I have set forth the following few points.

56. That "the succession of yin and yang is called the Way,"[223] was stated by our Master when he commented on the *Book of Changes*. Yüan-ming

---

[218] *Book of Changes*, "Appended Remarks," 8:11a.

[219] This may have been more than a casual observation on Lo's part. See, for example, the comment by Ch'ien Te-hung following Wang's letter in reply to Lu Yüan-ching which appears in *Wang Wen-ch'eng kung ch'üan-shu*, 2:36a–51b. Wing-tsit Chan, trans., *Instructions for Practical Living*, Part 2, secs. 151–67 (pp. 131–50). Ch'ien also speaks of Lu's "skillful questions," but the comments of Wang's which he records suggest that Wang felt that Lu was too much oriented toward book learning and textual understanding.

[220] Chan Jo-shui (1466–1560). Chan was the outstanding disciple of Ch'en Hsien-chang. In 1505 when Chan passed the *chin-shih* examination, Lo Ch'in-shun was one of the examiners. Chan served in the Hanlin Academy and from 1524–27 was Chancellor of the Imperial University. He served in a number of high posts in the Ministry of Personnel in Nanking and the Ministry of Rites in Peking, and in the 1530s served in Nanking successively as Minister of Rites, Minister of Personnel, and Minister of War. In his biography of Chan in the *Dictionary of Ming Biography*, 1:36–41, Fang Chao-ying observes that Chan was the founder of at least thirty-six academies, each with a shrine to Ch'en Hsien-chang.

[221] Yang Hsiung (53 B.C.–A.D. 18), the eminent Han essayist and poet. His philosophical contribution lay mainly in his theory of human nature as a mixture of good and evil and his theory of the Great Mystery (*t'ai-hsüan*).

[222] Yang Hsiung was criticized for having wanted to form his own school, which was considered presumptuous. Lo suggests similar presumption on the part of Chan Jo-shui.

[223] *Book of Changes*, "Appended Remarks," 7:7a.

said, "What issues in the midst of yin and yang is called the Way."[224] Could there have been something omitted in the words of the Sage? This is quite unlikely.

57. In the hexagrams of the *Book of Changes* there are 384 lines. There are sixty-four that are both central and correct, and another sixty-four that are central but not correct. Those that are correct but not central number 128, and those that are neither correct nor central also number 128.[225] Yüan-ming said, "Through contemplating the great *Book of Changes* I know that the Way and concrete things cannot be two. That the lines are yin and yang and strong and weak is *ch'i.* Their attaining centrality and correctness is the Way."[226]

        What he says about concrete things is most clear. But when he considers only attaining centrality and correctness to be the Way, he is referring to no more than sixty-four lines. There are another 320 lines remaining, and, if he considers that these are not the Way, then it is impossible that the Way and concrete things should not be a duality. If he considers that they are the Way, they have certainly not attained to centrality and correctness. I do not understand by what resort Yüan-ming finally resolved this.

58. Yüan-ming said, "The nature of a dog or an ox is not the nature of heaven and earth."[227] This shows that he did not know where the dog and the ox get their nature. His view would only be correct if within Heaven and earth there were two foundations *(erh pen).*[228]

[224] *Chan Kan-ch'üan hsien-sheng wen-chi* (Collected Literary Writings of Master Chan Jo-shui), 2:15a.

[225] Among the six lines that form the sixty-four hexagrams of the *Book of Changes,* the second and fifth (counting from the bottom) are called "central" *(chung).* When a yang line occupies a yang position, and a yin line occupies a yin position, the formation is called "correct" *(cheng).* The first, third, fourth, and top lines are called "not central" *(pu-chung).* When a yang line occupies a yin position, and a yin line occupies a yang position, the formation is called "not correct" *(pu-cheng).* This is explained and diagrammed in Morohashi Tetsuji, *Dai Kanwa jiten,* 1:509.

[226] *Chan Kan-chüan hsien-sheng wen-chi,* 1:2a.

[227] "Hsin-lun," in *Chan Kan-ch'üan hsien-sheng wen-chi,* 2:15b. I am grateful to Ann-ping Chin for identifying the source of this quotation.

[228] Refers to the *Mean,* 1:4, which says, "Equilibrium is the great foundation of the world . . ." Lo takes the view that, in an ultimate sense, the nature of all living things must be one.

59. The oneness of principle (*li*) must always be understood from the stand-point of the diversity of its particularizations before it can be truly and thoroughly perceived. The reason that what the Buddhists perceive is par-tial is that they have never realized that there is this diversity of particular-izations. This is why they seem to be correct but are actually wrong. Their saying that one cannot engage in loose generalities about true suchness (*chen-ju*) or be vague about the Buddha-nature,[229] is for the most part merely to admonish those who are dull and uncomprehending and has nothing to do with the diversity of particularizations. They regard both phenomena (*shih*) and principle as obstructions[230] and merely wish to eliminate these two obstructions so as to arrive at the ultimate Way. How is it that they do not consider this to be overly general and vague?

Ch'en Pai-sha said to Lin Ch'i-hsi:[231] "This principle . . . ex-tends everywhere and operates at every moment . . . If one gets a grip on this handle, what other task is there?"[232] He had a lot to say about this and finally said in conclusion, "From this point on, there is also the matter of the diversity of particularizations which must be comprehended."[233] I am afraid that in first grasping this handle [of the oneness of principle] without having comprehended the diversity of its particularizations he was not free from excessive generality and vagueness. This was all the more true of his effort to comprehend the diversity of particularizations, for it is apparent from the way he carried on his own study and the way he instructed others that it was altogether insubstantial. Would he have deliberately made this statement had it not been for the fact that he wanted to distance himself just slightly from Ch'an? In the tomb inscription which Chan Yüan-ming wrote for him when he was reburied,[234] the phrase "[the diversity of parti-

---

[229] The phrase occurs in the biography of Ssu-hsin Wu-hsin ho-shang in *Hsü ku-tsun-su yü-yao*, ZZ 2,23,5,1:431b. See also the fifth of five stories about Le-t'an Chan T'ang-chun ch'an-shih in *Chia-t'ai p'u-teng lu*, ZZ 2B,10,2, 26:184a. I am indebted to Wing-tsit Chan for identifying the sources for this allusion.

[230] Alludes to the *Sutra of Comprehensive Enlightenment* (*Yüan-chüeh ching*), T 842, 17:916b, where both phenomenal reality (*shih*) and noumenal reality (*li*) are characterized as "obstructions" (*chang*).

[231] Lin Kuang.

[232] Letter to Lin Chün-po ("Yü Lin Chün-po") in *Pai-sha tzu ch'üan-chi*, vol. 4, 4:12a.

[233] *Ibid.*

[234] In *Pai-sha tzu ch'üan-chi*, vol. 9, *chüan mo*, pp. 27a–29b.

cularizations] must be comprehended" was not used. This must have been contained in his oral teachings or in his transmission from mind to mind.[235]

60. Among the poems in the first section of the opening chapter of Pai-sha's *Instructions through Poetry (Shih-chiao)* there is one that was composed at a time when he was gravely ill in order to instruct Yüan-ming. Why was it that he cited no more than one or two passages from classical texts before going on to the beating and shouting of the Ch'an school? Probably it was because he was so accustomed to it that it was difficult to forget.[236] When he said, "[Te-shan] never struck," and "[Lin-chi] never shouted,"[237] he was merely inverting a set expression. And there is a marked resemblance between, "Once one is enlightened, all dharmas are empty,"[238] and

> To be learned is really to be without learning,
> To be enlightened is really to be without
>   enlightenment.[239]

The analogy of the golden needle also derives from the Buddhists, being a metaphor for the method of the mind.[240] When he asked, "Who obtains

[235] The version of Chan Jo-shui's tomb inscription which appears in this edition of the *Pai-sha tzu ch'üan-chi* does, in fact, contain the phrase "[the diversity of particularizations] must be comprehended," though it is possible that it did not appear in the version which Lo saw. The implication of Lo's remark would seem to be that Chan Jo-shui, sensitive to the charge that Ch'en Pai-sha's teachings were close to those of Ch'an Buddhism, wished to emphasize those elements in Pai-sha's thought that were Confucian and to minimize those that may have betrayed Ch'an influence. However, the true character of Pai-sha's teaching was revealed in the fact that he stressed the unity of principle and slighted the importance of the diversity of its particularizations.

[236] Ch'en himself acknowledged that the language of his poetry resembled that of Ch'an, but he denied any Buddhist inclination. See, for example, his poem, "Tz'u yün Chang Tung-hai," in *Pai-sha tzu ch'üan-chi*, vol. 6, 8:78b–79a.

[237] "Shih Chan Yü," in *Pai-sha tzu ku shih-chiao chieh*, A:3b (in *Pai-sha tzu ch'üan-chi*, vol. 10). The Ch'an master Te-shan Hsüan-chien (d. 865) was the teacher of I-ts'un Hsüeh-feng, who in turn was the teacher of Yün-men Wen-yen, founder of the Yün-men (Japanese, Unmon) tradition of Ch'an. Te-shan was known for his use of the stick in Ch'an practice. Lin-chi I-hsüan (d. 867) was the heir of Huang-po Hsi-yün (d. ca. 850), and the founder of the Lin-chi (Japanese, Rinzai) tradition of Ch'an. He was known for his shout. "Te-shan's stick and Lin-chi's shout" had become a conventional phrase.

[238] A Ch'an expression.

[239] *Pai-sha tzu ch'üan-chi*, vol. 10, A:3b.

[240] A commentary on the poem (in *Pai-sha tzu ku shih-chiao chieh*, A:4a) explains that the golden needle refers to the mind itself.

[the golden needle]?"[241] it was probably because those who understood were very few indeed, and he had Yüan-ming very much in mind. Consider the lines,

> Do not say the golden needle will not be handed down,
> Deep in the moon and breeze of Chiang-men[242]
>   the Tiao-t'ai[243] lives on.[244]

His meaning here is quite apparent, and, though the commentary says that he was "deeply committed to clarifying orthodoxy in order to expose the errors of Buddhism,"[245] one may well question whether or not this was the case.

The moral principle which is "all-embracing and wide, deep and unceasingly springing, coming forth at all times,"[246] is natural, and this mode of expression is also natural. To say "it is hidden, and only later is it revealed,"[247] conveys the idea of contrivance and is in no way comparable.

"The four beginnings are within us,"[248] means that there is no time or circumstance in which they are not manifest, and "knowing how to develop and complete them"[249] means genuinely exerting effort. But now [Pai-sha] wants "to cultivate the beginnings in the midst of tranquillity."[250] How can one discover the four beginnings through the practice of quiet-sitting and disengagement from events and things? When one has suppressed his mind for a sustained period of time, he may suddenly attain

---

[241] *Pai-sha tzu ku shih-chiao chieh*, A:3b.

[242] The Chiang-men school (i.e., the school of Ch'en Pai-sha) took its name from the place where Pai-sha lived.

[243] The Tiao-t'ai was an elaborate lecture hall near Hsin-hui in Kwangtung and was the center of Pai-sha's school.

[244] *Pai-sha tzu ch'uan-chi*, vol. 8, 10:36b.

[245] *Pai-sha tzu ku shih-chiao chieh*, A:4b.

[246] *Mean*, 31:2.

[247] "Fu Chang Tung-po nei-han," in *Pai-sha tzu ch'üan-chi*, vol. 3, 3:11a.

[248] *Mencius*, 2A:6:7. Mencius stated that the "four beginnings" of virtue—namely, the sense of pity and commiseration, the sense of shame and dislike, the sense of modesty and yielding, and the sense of right and wrong—were innate and could be developed into the four virtues of humaneness, rightness, decorum, and wisdom.

[249] *Ibid.*

[250] "Yü Ho K'o-kung Huang-men," in *Pai-sha tzu ch'üan-chi*, vol. 3, 3:12b.

some insight, but it will be nothing more than a vision which emerges from the mind's pure spirituality.[251]

Through his teaching about "hearing [the Way] in the morning and dying [without regret] in the evening,"[252] our Master showed people that they ought to be so fully occupied with seeking the Way that they would not have lived this life in vain. Thus Master Ch'eng explained his meaning as follows: " 'Hearing the Way' means that one knows what it means to act as a human being. 'Dying [without regret] in the evening' means that this life has not been wasted."[253] Now, however, [Pai-sha] understands this statement to refer to the way of dealing with old age, illness, and death.[254] Wasn't he demeaning the words of the Sage?[255]

The Way is constituted of principles shared in common by heaven and earth and all things and is not something that I alone possess. On this the classics of the sages and worthies are as clear as the sun and the stars. Is there a single word in them to the effect that "the Way is myself" or "I am the Way"? It is only the Buddhists who are given to such wild statements as, "Above heaven and below, I alone am to be revered."[256] Now a poem [of Pai-sha's] says:

> [The years of heaven and earth are infinite.]
> Infinitely I shall also exist.[257]

And another says:

---

[251] Lo alludes to his own experience of a "vision" (kuang-ching), which followed his conversation with a Ch'an monk about the attainment of Buddhahood. See above, K'un-chih chi, Part II, sec. 41.

[252] Statement attributed to Confucius in Analects, 4:8.

[253] Ch'eng Hao in Wai-shu (Additional Works), 2:1b (in Erh-Ch'eng ch'üan-shu).

[254] "Yü Jung I-chih," Pai-sha tzu ch'üan-chi, vol. 4, 4:26a. In this letter Pai-sha says, "The ancients had a way of dealing with old age. They had a way of dealing with illness. They had a way of dealing with death. The Master said, 'Hearing the Way in the morning, one may die in the evening.' This is the way they dealt with these things."

[255] Alludes to Analects, 16:8:1–2.

[256] The statement is one commonly attributed to the Buddha on his birth and is found, with slight variations, in a number of sources, including Hsiu-hsing pen-ch'i ching (T 184, p. 463c); Fang-kuang ta-chuang yen ching (T 187, p. 613c); and Hsien-yü ching (T 202, p. 418c).

[257] "Ying Chen," in Pai-sha tzu ch'üan-chi, vol. 5, 6:26a.

> The Jade Terrace lends form to me,[258]
> What form have I?[259]

Where he says "me" and "I," the notes consistently indicate that he is referring to the Way. What is the basis for this? Thus he says, "Once I attain awareness, then I am great and things are small. Things are limited, but I am limitless."[260] This is precisely the theory that "I alone am to be revered." [Pai-sha] could certainly form his own school. The difficulty arises because of his determination to force an accord between [his school] and the Way of our Sage.

61. Yang Fang-chen[261] said in a letter in reply to Yü Tzu-chi,[262] "If one speaks about unity, then not only is *li* one, but *ch'i* is also one. If one speaks about multiplicity, then not only is *ch'i* manifold, but *li* is also manifold."[263] These words are altogether appropriate, and yet I feel somewhat uneasy about the word "also."

62. The *ch'i* involved in human breathing is the *ch'i* of the universe. Viewed from the standpoint of physical form, it is as if there were the distinction of interior and exterior, but this is actually only the coming and going of this unitary *ch'i*. Master Ch'eng said, "Heaven (or nature) and man are

---

[258] Master Jade Terrace (Yü-t'ai chü-shih) was a sobriquet of Ch'en Pai-sha.

[259] "Shen Shih-t'ien tso Yü-t'ai t'u t'i-shih ch'i shang chien chi tz'u yün i fu," in *Pai-sha tzu ch'üan-chi*, vol. 8, 10:16b. The poem here quoted was apparently written on the occasion of Pai-sha's receiving from the famous landscape painter Shen Chou (1427–1509) a picture of the Jade Terrace. The poem suggests that Shen Chou had represented Pai-sha in the painting and that Pai-sha had been surprised on seeing it. I have been unable to locate any other reference to the painting, however, and Professor Richard Edwards, an expert on Shen Chou, reports that he has not encountered it in the course of his studies.

[260] "Yü Lin Shih-chu," in *Pai-sha tzu ch'üan-chi*, vol. 4. 4:34a.

[261] Yang Lien (1452–1525). Yang was a scholar of considerable breadth and, like Lo, considered himself a defender of the Ch'eng-Chu tradition. The two men were friends, both holding high office in Nanking during the early years of the sixteenth century. In 1515 Yang was appointed Junior Vice Minister of Rites in Nanking, while Lo was made Junior Vice Minister of Personnel. Yang was promoted to be Minister of Rites in Nanking in 1522 but retired from office in 1523, as did Lo Ch'in-shun. In accordance with one of Yang's last requests, Lo wrote an epitaph for him. It is preserved in *Huang Ming wen-hai*.

[262] Yü Yu (1465–1528) was the son-in-law of Hu Chü-jen.

[263] I have been unable to determine whether the letter is still extant.

basically not two. There is no need to speak of combining them."[264] This is also the case with *li* and *ch'i*.

63. There are several passages in Ts'ai Chieh-fu's[265] *Beginner's Guide to the Mean (Chung-yung meng-yin)*[266] in which he discusses *kuei* and *shen*.[267] These are most profound. Throughout his entire life he engaged in the work of probing *li* to the utmost, and, what is more, he had the capacity to put his learning into practice. He was truly eminent among Confucians.

64. The various classics of immortality are all modeled on the five thousand words of the *Lao Tzu*, and if one studies them in detail, one will find no real discrepancies among them. There is no doubt that "the way of long life and lasting vision"[268] must have derived from the *Lao Tzu*.

[264] Ch'eng Hao in *I-shu*, 1:6b.

[265] Ts'ai Ch'ing (1453–1508). He served in a number of posts, including that of Surveillance Vice Commissioner of Education in Kiangsi. In 1507 he was appointed Chancellor of the Imperial University in Nanking on the retirement of Chang Mou, but he died before he could assume office.

[266] According to Ts'ai's preface to the *Ssu-shu meng-yin* (A Beginner's Guide to the Four Books), the draft of the initial part of the work was lost for some time. When it was recovered, he found that there were inconsistencies between the earlier and later parts of the work. He wished to revise it so as to eliminate the inconsistencies but had not the time to do so. Therefore the title of the work reflects his humble attitude toward his accomplishment.

[267] In *Ssu-shu meng-yin*, 3:53b–62b. In his discussion of *kuei* and *shen*, Ts'ai analyzes the passage in Chu Hsi's *Chung-yung chang-chü*, commentary on the *Mean*, 16, where Ch'eng I is quoted as having said, "Positive and negative spiritual forces are the operation of heaven and earth *(t'ien ti chih kung-yung)*," and Chang Tsai is quoted as having described them as "the spontaneous activity of yin and yang *(erh-ch'i chih liang-neng)*." See *Ssu-shu chang-chü chi-chu*, (KHCPTS ed.) p. 11; also in *Ssu-shu chi-chu (Shushigaku taikei* ed.), 2:31. Ts'ai points out that Ch'eng I's statement did not make evident that *kuei* and *shen* are associated with the two aspects of *ch'i*, yin and yang. Therefore Chang Tsai's statement was needed to amplify it. Chang Tsai's statement in turn did not make evident that the spontaneous activity of the two aspects of *ch'i* was actually the expansion and contraction of a unitary *ch'i*. Therefore Chu Hsi went on to specify that these statements referred to a unitary *ch'i*. Ts'ai's view is that these three statements must be combined. He says *(Ssu-shu meng-yin*, 3:55a–b), "*Kuei* and *shen* are the operation of heaven and earth and the spontaneous activity of yin and yang. Having expanded to the utmost and produced *shen, [ch'i]* reverts and produces *kuei*. Yin and yang themselves are not *kuei* and *shen*. The fact that yin and yang are capable of contraction and expansion and that they follow a cycle of departure and return—this is *kuei* and *shen*. Thus *kuei* and *shen* are just the active and tranquil phases of the operation of *ch'i*."

[268] Alludes to *Tao-te ching*, 59.

65. In the *Ts'an-t'ung ch'i* (Book of the Kinship of the Three) Wei Po-yang[269] advanced a great many theories about the sixty-four hexagrams. These were clever but lacked the slightest jot of usefulness. Therefore there came about the theory of "a separate transmission outside the [exoteric] teachings."[270] Later on Chang P'ing-shu[271] made it all clear when he said,

> The task is easy, and the drug is near at hand,
> People have to laugh about it once
>   they understand.[272]

If our Master Chu had been fully aware that it was laughable, would he have bothered to devote his attention to it? In fact, Master Chu edited and corrected this text[273] for the same reason that he wrote his commentary on the *Ch'u-tz'u* (Elegies of Ch'u).[274] For his feeling at the time was very deep, and those who belong to our school should be aware of this.[275]

---

[269] A Taoist philosopher and alchemist of the second century. Biographical accounts indicate that he was a native of Wu in modern Kiangsi. However, little reliable information about him is available, and his role in the authorship of the surviving text of the *Ts'an-t'ung ch'i* is debatable.

[270] A Taoist borrowing of the Ch'an notion of "a separate transmission outside the sutras."

[271] A prominent Taoist writer of the Northern Sung period, he was the author of the *Wu-chen p'ien* (Treatise on the Awakening to Truth). Biographical accounts indicate that he died at the age of ninety-nine at some time during the Yüan-feng period (1078–1086).

[272] Chang Po-tuan, *Wu-chen p'ien* (in *Wu-chen p'ien cheng-i, Tao-tsang ching-hua,* Ser. 1, no. 4), B:49. The commentary on this passage by Tung Te-hsien explains that, properly realized, "The task [of cultivation] is very simple and involves nothing abstruse. The drug lies within myself. What need is there to seek it from others? If people can be brought to realize this secret, they will take delight in the fact that the Way is near at hand and will laugh at the idea of seeking it afar."

[273] Chu Hsi seems to have had a high opinion of the *Ts'an-t'ung ch'i,* describing it (in *Chu Tzu yü-lei,* 125:12b) as "superlative," but he believed that the language of the text had become almost unintelligible to readers at a remove of some ten centuries. This prompted him to write his commentary on the text. His redaction of the text and commentary on it, the *[Chou I] Ts'an-t'ung ch'i k'ao-i* (Inquiry into Variants of the *Ts'an-t'ung ch'i*) is found in TT 623 and in *Shou-shan ko ts'ung-shu,* vol. 30, among other editions. See the analysis of the background of the work by Sakai Tadao in *Shushigaku nyūmon* (Introduction to the Chu Hsi School), in *Shushigaku taikei,* 1:415–18.

[274] The *Ch'u-tz'u chi-chu* (Collected Commentaries on the *Ch'u-tz'u*) is found in a number of sources, including *Ku-i ts'ung-shu.* There are also several modern editions, including two published in Peking in 1953 and 1963.

[275] Wm. Theodore deBary has observed that Tai Hsien in his *Chu Tzu shih-chi* provides illuminating background to Chu Hsi's "deep feelings" at the time of publishing his

66. The hidden meaning of the *Ts'an-t'ung ch'i* may be understood from the work of six commentators: P'eng Hsiao,[276] Ch'en Hsien-wei,[277] Ch'u Hua-ku,[278] Yin Chen-jen,[279] Yü Yen,[280] and Ch'en Chih-hsü.[281] Yü's annotation is the best, followed by the commentaries of the two Ch'ens and Yin, whose interpretations are, however, somewhat obscure, probably because they regard this as an esoteric transmission. Ch'u's commentary is extremely simple, but it does contain insights. P'eng's commentary is not especially clear. There are also commentaries by two anonymous authors, one of whom speaks exclusively about inner alchemy,[282] while the other artificially invokes his interpretation of techniques of regulating the fire.[283] These are wide of the mark. Yü [Yen] also wrote the *I-wai pieh-ch'uan* in one *chüan*,[284] which is also excellent. His statements are on the whole lucid and yet reserved, which is why this is superior to other commentaries.

67. In reading the *Ts'an-t'ung ch'i fa-hui* (Elucidation of the *Ts'an-t'ung ch'i*)[285] one comes to the line, "The toad of the moon and the soul of the

commentary on the *Ch'u-tz'u*. See *Kinseki kanseki sōkan, shisō hen*, vol. 22, 4:20b–22a. For Chu Hsi's views on the *Ch'u-tz'u*, see also Laurence A. Schneider, *A Madman of Ch'u* (Berkeley and Los Angeles: University of California Press, 1980), pp. 73–79.

[276] A writer of the T'ang period, he was the author of the *Chou I Ts'an-t'ung ch'i fen-chang chen-i*, 3 ch., in TT 623.

[277] A Sung writer, he was the author of the *Chou I Ts'an-t'ung ch'i chieh*, 3 ch., in TT 628.

[278] Dates unknown. He was the author of the *Chou I Ts'an-t'ung ch'i chu*, 3 ch., in TT 629.

[279] Dates unknown. Also known as Yin Ch'ang-sheng, he was author of the *Chou I Ts'an-t'ung ch'i chu*, 3 ch., in TT 621.

[280] A Sung writer, he was author of the *Chou I Ts'an-t'ung ch'i fa-hui*, 9 ch., in TT 625–27. Also, *Chou I Ts'an-t'ung ch'i shih-i*, in TT 627. See also *Sung Yüan hsüeh-an*, ch. 49.

[281] A Yüan writer, he was author of the *Chou I Ts'an-t'ung ch'i fen-chang chu*, in TT 623. Also, *Chou I Ts'an-t'ung ch'i chu*, in *Tao-tsang chi-yao*, 93.

[282] TT 622. Inner alchemy, the search for the inner elixir, or, as Joseph Needham calls it, physiological alchemy, is the subject of Needham's *Science and Civilisation in China*, V:5.

[283] TT 624. Regulation of the fire or of the furnace was among the Taoist techniques for inducing longevity or promoting material immortality. See Joseph Needham, *Science and Civilisation in China*, V:5:211–12, 214.

[284] TT 629.

[285] See above, n. 280.

hare, the sun and the moon do not shine together."[286] It is only after this that the words "inhalation" and "exhalation" appear.[287] In essence, the mysterious action of the elixir is no more than the phenomenon of respiration. If one does not understand the subtle truth conveyed by these words, he is likely to be distracted by secondary issues.

68. The mysterious essence of the school of immortality may be entirely contained in the *Ts'an-t'ung ch'i*, but one must read the *Wu-chen p'ien* (Treatise on Awakening to Truth)[288] from beginning to end and achieve thorough and complete comprehension before attaining the stage of perfect understanding. The *Wu-chen p'ien* is fundamentally an elucidation of the practices of the immortals. Secondarily, [Chang Po-tuan] devoted his attention to Ch'an. It must have something to it. But if [through the *Ts'an-t'ung ch'i*] one were truly able to attain the stage of perfect understanding, what use would there be [for Ch'an]?

69. Since ancient times there have been few men of intelligence who have not been attracted by theories about divine immortals. In my ignorance I also thought a lot about these things in my early years, and it was only later that I came to see through them. Therefore I have discussed this matter in some detail so that our school might be informed.

If there were, in fact, something in the universe that was undying, it would mean that there would be no creation and transformation. If you truly understand this principle, there will certainly be no need to waste your mental effort [on the question of immortality]. But if your faith is not sufficient, and you are impelled to try your luck against overwhelming

---

[286] From the text of the *Ts'an-t'ung ch'i*.

[287] Yü Yen's commentary on this passage (*Ts'an-t'ung ch'i fa-hui*, p. 152) says: "The toad is the spirit of the moon, and the soul of the hare is the light of the sun. [Where it says,] "The sun and the moon do not shine together," it means that the light of the sun brings about the day, and the light of the moon brings about the night. When the sun comes out, the moon sets, and when the moon comes out, the sun sets, so that the day and the night are illumined by turns. Departure is followed by return and folding by unfolding. How does human respiration differ from this? Doesn't it say in the *Huang-t'ing ching* (Yellow Court Canon), 'The sun comes out and the moon goes in, and thus respiration is maintained'? Inhalation and exhalation are the sun and the moon."

[288] For Chang Po-tuan and the *Wu-chen p'ien* see nn. 271 and 272 above.

odds, who will be to blame when the whole realm is brought down to ruin
with you?[289]

70. Having examined a number of Buddhist texts, I take this opportunity
to discuss their views. The Diamond Sutra (Chin-kang ching) and the Heart
Sutra (Hsin ching) may be considered to epitomize [Buddhist teachings], while
the Sutra of Comprehensive Enlightenment (Yüan-chüeh [ching]) is somewhat
repetitious in words and concepts. Only about twenty or thirty percent of
the Lotus Sutra (Fa-hua [ching]) is important, and the rest is just idle words,
which are mostly absurd and deceptive. Bodhidharma did not set up words
and texts, but emphasized directly pointing to the human mind, perceiving
the nature, and becoming a Buddha. That notwithstanding, the talk that
has gone on subsequently has been interminable.

　　　　I have also looked at the stages the Buddhists adopt. They teach
people that when one first sets the mind on enlightenment, all truths are
delusions. Thus they say, "If one perceives that the various forms (hsiang,
nimitta) are not forms, one perceives the Tathāgata (ju-lai).[290] After one has
become enlightened, there are no delusions which are not also true. Thus
they say, "Ignorance and true suchness (chen-ju, Bhūtatathatā) are not separate realms."[291] Although the adherents of sudden and gradual enlightenment each hold to their own theories, generally speaking, beginning and
end intersect,[292] and truth and delusion are not separated. The evil that
comes of their truth, half-truth, extravagance, depravity, and evasiveness[293]
is such that, were a sage king to appear, he would certainly seize upon the
strategy of Master Han Yü[294] to attack them with fire.[295]

[289]The phrase tsai hsü chi ni alludes to Ode 257. It is also quoted in Mencius,
4A:9:6.

[290]"The one who is thus come," i.e., the Buddha. Alludes to the Diamond Sutra,
T 235, 8:749a.

[291]Sutra of Comprehensive Enlightenment, T 842, 17:914b.

[292]Alludes to the biography of Chia I in Han shu, 48:2230.

[293]Alludes to Mencius, 2A:2:17.

[294]Han Yü (768–824), the great statesman, poet, and leader of the Confucian
assault on Buddhism in the T'ang.

[295]I.e., to burn their books.

71. Master Chu once offered the following answer to a question concerning the basic meaning of the *Diamond Sutra:* "When it speaks of subduing [the mind], it does not refer to a desire to restrain or humble one's own mind; rather it speaks of subduing the minds of all sentient beings in the world and causing them to enter the realm of Nirvana which leaves nothing behind (*wu-yü nieh-p'an, Anupadhiśeṣa*). Whenever they teach the doctrine of 'no mind' (*wu-hsin*), this is what is meant."[296]

I am afraid that he was not correct. The reference here was specifically to "giving rise to the mind of unexcelled, complete enlightenment" (*a-nou to-lou san-miao san-p'u t'i, anuttara samyak-sambodhi*), to which end they seek completely to eliminate all forms (*hsiang, nimitta*) and thus to realize what is called emptiness (*k'ung, śūnyatā*).[297]

72. The section entitled "The Life-span of the Thus Come One" in the *Lotus Sutra*[298] says: "Since my attainment of Buddhahood it has been a very great interval of time. My life-span is incalculable [asaṃkhyeyakalpas], every enduring, never perishing."[299] "[The Thus Come One,] though never extinct, yet speaks of passage into extinction."[300] "By resort to these expedi-

---

[296] *Chu Tzu yü-lei*, 126:17a.

[297] In the passage quoted above, Chu Hsi had expressed the view that the basic idea of the *Diamond Sutra* was contained in the response of the Buddha to a two-fold question of Subhuti: "How should a son or daughter of good family who has set out in the bodhisattva vehicle (literally, giving rise to the mind of unexcelled, complete enlightenment) abide, how control their thoughts?" Chu Hsi said that in response to the question of how to abide, the answer was that the bodhisattva should give rise to a thought that was unsupported by any thing (*fa*) or object of sight (*se*), unsupported by anything (*wu suo chu*). In response to the question of how to subdue the mind (*chiang-fu ch'i hsin*), the answer had been that all beings must be led to the realm of Nirvana that leaves nothing behind (*wu-yü nieh-p'an*). In both cases Chu emphasized the negative force of the word *wu*, concluding (*Chu Tzu yü-lei*, 126:17a) that, "It all comes down the word *wu*." Commenting on this passage, Lo observes that Chu was not correct in this interpretation because the answers of the Buddha had to be understood in relation to the original question concerning unexcelled, complete enlightenment, which is properly associated with emptiness (*k'ung*) rather than with nothingness (*wu*). The text under discussion is from the *Diamond Sutra*, T 235, 8:749a.

[298] T 262, vol. 9, ch. 15, sec. 16.

[299] T 262, 9:42c. Translation by Leon Hurvitz, *Scripture of the Lotus Blossom of the Fine Dharma*, p. 239.

[300] T 262, 9:43a; translation adapted from Hurvitz, *Scripture of the Lotus Blossom*, p. 240.

ent devices [the Thus Come One] teaches and converts sentient beings."[301]
This is the climax of the sutra, for "the mysterious treasury of the Buddhas
and the Tathāgata"[302] is no more than this. And yet they are idle words,
most of which can be discounted.

A gatha in the section entitled "Discrimination of Merits"[303]
says that the five paramitas of charity, discipline, perseverance, assiduity,
and meditation are all meritorious, and goes on to say:

> And if there should be good men and women
> Who, hearing me preach about my life-span,
> Should believe for but a single moment,
> The happiness of these would exceed even that.[304]

In other words, if one has faith in the phrase, "extinct and yet not extinct,"
this in itself is a true and genuine perception. It is prajñā,[305] foremost of
the paramitas, and the merit that attaches to it is inestimable. By comparison, the merit of the other five could be multiplied by a thousand, ten
thousand, or even a million-fold and not come up to it.[306] In reality, the
difference is simply between being enlightened and not yet having attained
enlightenment.

73. The notion of phenomena (shih) and principle (li) as the two "obstructions" is found in the Sutra of Comprehensive Enlightenment,[307] and none of
the errors involved in this view escaped the scrutiny of Master Ch'eng [I].[308]
There is a commentary on this sutra by Tsung-mi,[309] of the Ts'ao-t'ang

---

[301] T 262, 9:42c; Hurvitz, Scripture of the Lotus Blossom, p. 239.

[302] The Lotus Sutra is so designated in its introduction, T 262, 9:1a–b.

[303] T 262, ch. 15, sec. 17.

[304] T 262, 9:45a; Hurvitz, Scripture of the Lotus Blossom, p. 251.

[305] I.e., wisdom.

[306] Lo is here summarizing the idea conveyed in the text which preceded the gatha
just quoted.

[307] T 842, 17:916b–c. See also above, K'un-chih chi, Part II, sec. 59.

[308] I-shu, 18:11a.

[309] Tsung-mi (780–841) was the fifth patriarch of both the Hua-yen (Flower Gar-
land) school and the Ho-tse branch of the Southern school of Ch'an. Tsung-mi's commentary,
entitled Ta-fang-kuang yüan-chueh hsiu-to-lo liao-i ching lüeh-shu is found in T 1795, vol. 39.

[Temple], which I have not yet seen, but I have read both his own preface [to the commentary] and the preface by P'ei Hsiu.[310] Their presentation of Buddhist doctrine is quite clear, but essentially they only discuss the mind, which they assume to be the nature, without ever realizing what the nature really is.

The style of this sutra is smooth and mature, and its coherence is clear. I rather suspect that the translators have adorned it. In general, Buddhist sutras are products of the translators and are not entirely as they were in the original texts. The skill and knowledge [of the translator] determines their superficiality or depth, awkwardness or fluency.

74. The *Mean* quotes the words, "The hawk flies up to heaven; the fish leap in the deep,"[311] and explains the two phrases by saying, "This expresses how [the Way] is seen above and below."[312] There is also a Buddhist saying,

> The absolute greenness of verdant bamboo,
> Just so the Tathāgata.[313]
> A perfect profusion of yellow flowers,
> And nothing but *prajñā*.[314]

There is a definite similarity between the two in terms of ideas, and yet they are not the same. If one is able to discern wherein the difference lies, he will not be subject to delusion.

75. Master Chu discussed Buddhist teachings, and, generally, he said that if one knew them thoroughly, one would be completely free from crime and iniquity. Yet the effect of this teaching in the world has merely been to provide a haven for rebellious ministers and villainous sons.[315] I have not

---

[310]Tsung-mi's preface is found in T 1795, 39:524a–c. P'ei Hsiu's preface is found in T 1795, 39:523b–524a.

[311]*Mean*, 12:3, quoting Ode 239.

[312]*Ibid.*

[313]See above n. 290.

[314]See *Shen-hui yü-lu* (Recorded Conversations of Shen-hui) (in *Shen-hui ho-shang i-chi*, T'ang dynasty MS, ed. by Hu Shih), p. 139. I am indebted to Philip Yampolsky for help in identifying the source of this quotation.

[315]Alludes to *Mencius*, 3B:9:11.

yet been able to find out about the case of Wang Lü-tao,[316] which was cited by him, but I have looked into the case of Hsing Shu,[317] who was clear, discriminating, and talented, and yet was infected with Ch'an. As a result there was nothing that he would not do. What a fearful thing!

[316] Wang An-chung (1076–1134).

[317] A disciple of the Ch'eng brothers, he was considered to have been unduly influenced by Ch'an. For Chu Hsi's judgment of him, see *Chu Tzu yü-lei*, 130:11a–b. See also *I-Lo yüan-yüan lu*, 2:17.

K'un-chih chi, Part III

(Excerpts)

1. Master Chu once said that I-ch'uan's statement, "The nature is the same as principle,"[1] would be "the basis for pronouncements on the nature for countless future generations."[2] When I began my efforts I often endeavored to achieve personal realization of this statement, but for all my striving to achieve realization there were aspects I could penetrate and others I could not. It went on that way for a number of years, and in the end I was unable to return to unity. I suspected that this statement of I-ch'uan's was somehow incomplete and feared that Master Chu's statement too had been exaggerated so that it was difficult to believe unreservedly.

Then I put the matter aside for a time and took up the terms *li* and *ch'i*, examining one against the other and attempting to achieve personal realization. But for all my striving to achieve realization, there were again aspects I could penetrate and others I could not. Again, this continued for several years, and, as before, I could not return to unity.

I became extremely disheartened. I felt that my intelligence was limited, and I began to fear that in the end I would never succeed in my efforts. I was inclined to give up until suddenly I remembered the words, "Although one is dull, he will [through unremitting effort] surely become intelligent."[3] I could no longer give up but went back and applied myself to I-ch'uan's words, going over them again and again without putting them aside.

One day I came to the point of enlightenment through the words, "Principle is one; its particularizations are diverse."[4] I turned to myself and verified it in relation to my own body and mind and then, by

[1] Cheng I's statement in *I-shu* (Written Legacy), 22A:11a.

[2] *Chu Tzu yü-lei* (Classified Conversations of Master Chu Hsi), 93:8b.

[3] *Mean*, 20:21.

[4] *I-ch'uan wen-chi* (Collection of Literary Works by Ch'eng I), 5:12b.

extension, in relation to other people. I verified it in respect to yin and
yang and the five agents and, once again, verified it in connection with
birds and beasts and plants and trees. Finding that it was consistent in every
instance, I began to feel overwhelming self-confidence and knew that the
words of these two gentlemen[5] would certainly not lead me astray.

That I should express it in such terms implies no sense of self-
importance. For I have often noticed that when one finds writers of our
school denying that "the nature is principle," it is simply because the word
principle, being difficult to explain, is often understood as something that
is obstructed by material force. Once having perceived the inconsistency
that such a view entails, they assume that the words of our Confucian predecessors are unworthy of credence. They do not know that when the task
had been brought to completion [through the formulation "principle is one;
its particularizations are diverse"] there was not a single word to be added.[6]

2. There is nowhere that principle (li) is not fixed. Were it not fixed, it
would not be principle.[7] But when the student probes principle to the utmost, it is necessary that he perceive it in a flexible way and not get bogged
down. Many of our Confucian predecessors spoke about "careful observation,"[8] and this is what they meant. If we perceive it in a flexible way,
principle is vital and animated and is always right before us. And yet one
can neither augment nor diminish it by the slightest bit, nor can one raise
or lower it by the slightest fraction. By perceiving principle in this way,
one realizes that there is nowhere that principle is not fixed. But, although
one may perceive that this is definitely so, if the effort of preserving the

---

[5] I.e., Ch'eng I and Chu Hsi.

[6] This passage is no. 37 in K'un-chih chi hsü, ch. 3.

[7] Wing-tsit Chan observes that this statement may be compared to one of Ch'eng
I's which is included in the Chin-ssu lu, 1:13 (Chu Tzu i-shu ed., 1:2b). As translated by
Professor Chan (Reflections on Things at Hand, p. 13), the passage reads: "According to the
principle of the world, a thing will begin again when it ends, and can therefore last forever
without limit. Being long lasting does not mean being in a fixed and definite state. Being fixed
and definite, a thing cannot last long. The way to be constant is to change according to
circumstances. Unless one knows the Way, how can he understand the constant and lasting
Way of the universe and the constant and lasting principle of the world?"

[8] E.g., Ch'eng I in I-shu, 18:15a, and Chu Hsi in Chu Tzu wen-chi (Collection of
Literary Works by Master Chu Hsi), 30:19b and 31:8b.

mind and nourishing the nature is not complete, principle will not be something that one possesses in oneself, and one will not be able to make use of
it. Therefore it is said, "When one's knowledge is sufficient to attain, but
his humanity is not sufficient to enable him to hold, whatever he may have
gained, he will lose again."[9]

3. *Li* is only the *li* of *ch'i*. It must be observed in the phenomenon of revolving and turning of *ch'i*. Departing is followed by returning, and returning is followed by departing: this is the phenomenon of revolving and turning. And in the fact that departure must be followed by return, and return
must be followed by departure, there is that which is so even without our
knowing why it is so. It is as if there were a single entity acting as a regulating power within things and causing them to be as they are.[10] This is
what we designate as *li* and what is is referred to in the statement, "There
is in the changes the Great Ultimate."[11] If one gains a clear understanding
of this phenomenon of revolving and turning, one will find that everything
conforms to it.

    Master Ch'eng said, "Within heaven and earth there is only
the process of action and reaction. What else is there?"[12] Now given the
action of going, there is the reaction of coming, and, given the action of
coming, there is the reaction of going. Action and reaction follow in endless succession, and there is nowhere that principle does not pertain. It is
the same in nature and in man. Because the Way of nature is what is
common to all, action and reaction are constant and unerring. As the human emotions cannot be free of the encumbrance of selfish desires, action
and reaction may be inconstant and liable to error.

    What acts and reacts is *ch'i*, while the fact that a particular

---

[9] Alludes to *Analects*, 15:22;1. This passage is no. 38 in *K'un-chih chi hsü*, ch. 3.

[10] It should be noted that Lo says "*as if there were* a single entity acting as a
regulating power within things and causing them to be as they are." In *K'un-chih chi*, Part I,
sec. 11, he explicitly denies that this is *actually* the case: "The phrase, 'There is in the changes
the Great Ultimate,' leads some to suspect that the transformations of yin and yang have a
single entity that acts as a regulating power among them. This is not the case." Ren Jiyu et
al. in their discussion of Lo's views on the relation of *li* and *ch'i* (in *Chung-kuo che-hsüeh shih*,
3:316) emphasize the importance of this point.

[11] *Book of Changes*, "Appended Remarks" ("Hsi-tz'u"), 7:17a.

[12] Ch'eng I in *I-shu*, 15:7b.

action involves a particular reaction without there being the slightest possibility of error is principle. Action in conformity with its dictates is auspicious; contravention of it is inauspicious. And that "some go beyond it; some do not come up to it."[13] is the reason for remorse and humiliation. Therefore there is nowhere that *li* is not fixed.[14] However, this is mainly to speak of its effects. One must know that, although the mind may be "still and unmoving,"[15] its *ch'i*, being well blended and harmonious, will still go on acting and reacting spontaneously without the least interruption. Thus the so-called "correct principle which is central and straight"[16] does not allow for an instant's deviation. It is what heaven has decreed and also what constitutes the nature of men and things. I have therefore said that *li* must be identified as an aspect of *ch'i*, and yet to identify *ch'i* as *li* would not be correct.[17] This statement warrants no alteration.[18]

4. The principle of the nature is one, but there are four designations that apply to its virtues. In its aspect of integrated wholeness, it is called humanity. In its aspect of clear order, it is called decorum. In its aspect of resolute forbearance, it is called rightness. In its aspect of incisive discrimination, it is called wisdom. The aspects of clarity, resolution, and incisiveness all figure into the integration, and this is why humanity encompasses the four virtues[19] and constitutes the complete substance of the nature. Its resolution is unaltered by its clarity, and its incisiveness is undisturbed by its resolution. There are four terms, but the reality is one. The reason it is so integrated, clear, resolute, and incisive is that it is naturally so of itself, without any artificial interference or design. This is why it is called the principle of the nature and destiny.[20]

---

[13] *Mean*, 4:2.

[14] See above, sec. 2.

[15] *Book of Changes*, "Appended Remarks," 7:14b.

[16] Alludes to a statement by Ch'eng Hao in *I-shu*, 11:11a.

[17] See above, *K'un-chih chi*, Part II, sec. 35.

[18] This passage is no. 40 in *K'un-chih chi hsü*, ch. 3.

[19] The idea of humanity encompassing the four virtues may be traced to Ch'eng I in *I-ch'uan I-chuan* (Ch'eng I's Commentary on the *Book of Changes*), 1:2b.

[20] This passage is no. 48 in *K'un-chih chi hsü*, ch. 3.

Two Letters to Wang Yang-ming

Summer, 1520

Having received your letter[1] the day before yesterday, I had the honor yesterday to receive the two texts that you graciously sent, "The Old Text of the *Great Learning*" ("*Ta-hsüeh* ku-pen") and "Chu Hsi's Final Conclusions Arrived at Late in Life" ("Chu Tzu wan-nien ting-lun"). I am exceedingly grateful to you.

I am indeed unworthy. When I was in Nanking I benefited greatly from your instruction, but I was suffering greatly from illness, and being too reticent to talk, I was unable to pour out my feelings so that our differences might be resolved. This has been a constant source of regret to me.

During the summer of last year a friend showed me the *Instructions for Practical Living (Ch'uan-hsi lu)*,[2] which I promptly read. All that I had heard about was contained in it, along with many other things I had not heard about before. What good fortune it is now to receive and read two more works from you. Yet in that I am not clever, I have repeatedly examined these texts without having been able to grasp their central meaning. Thus the doubts that I had heretofore, and that I once questioned you about in person, albeit inconclusively, have again accumulated and cannot be resolved. In the profound hope that your gracious willingness to instruct me will not be wasted, I dare to set forth one or two points, anticipating that in your great generosity you will make allowances for my indiscretion.

Careful study of [your reasons for wishing to] return to the old text of the *Great Learning* indicates that you consider that when a person

---

[1] Wang Yang-ming's letter is apparently no longer extant. The surviving letter to Lo Ch'in-shun, which appears in Part 2 of the *Ch'uan-hsi lu (Wang Wen-ch'eng kung ch'üan-shu*, 2:58a–64b; Wing-tsit Chan, trans., *Instructions for Practical Living*, secs. 172–77, pp. 157–65) is in response to this letter.

[2] Lo here refers to Part 1 of the *Instructions for Practical Living*, which includes Wang's sayings and conversations from the period up to 1518.

engages in study, he ought to seek only within himself, whereas according to the theory of the investigation of things of the Ch'eng-Chu school, one cannot avoid seeking outside the self. You contend that the intention of the Sage was contrary to this, and so you have omitted Master Chu's division [of the text of the *Great Learning*] into chapters and deleted the amended commentary that he added.[3] You regard this as fragmentation and consider it useless. One might say that you have been courageous in standing up for virtue without yielding.[4]

It is my humble opinion that in the teaching of the Confucian school learning and action should assist each other. There is the clear teaching that one should be broadly versed in learning.[5] When Yen Yüan praised the "skillful leading" of Confucius, he said, "He broadened me with learning."[6] Is learning really internal or external? This is really not difficult to clarify. Is there anything in what Ch'eng and Chu said that conflicts with this?

If one insists that learning does not depend upon seeking outside the self and that only introspection and self-examination should be regarded as fundamental, then why wouldn't the words [of the *Great Learning* concerning] "rectifying the mind" and "making the intentions sincere" be completely sufficient? Why would it be necessary to burden the student at the beginning with the task of "investigating things" (*ko-wu*)? Yet this passage does exist in the text of the classic, and one is bound to respect and believe it. Since you had to find a way to deal with this, you followed the text but interpreted it to mean that *wu* is the "functioning of the intentions" (*i chih yung*) and *ko* is "to rectify." "It is to rectify what is incorrect so as to return to its original correctness."[7] By interpreting the text in this

---

[3] Chu Hsi had divided the text of the *Great Learning* into one chapter of classical text and ten chapters of commentary and, following Ch'eng I, had supplied a chapter of commentary which he believed had been lost from the text in the course of its transmission.

[4] *Analects*, 15:35.

[5] *Analects*, 6:25.

[6] *Analects*, 9:10.

[7] *Ch'uan-hsi lu* (in *Wang Wen-ch'eng kung ch'üan-shu*, 1:41a; Wing-tsit Chan, trans., *Instructions for Practical Living*, sec. 85, (p. 55). Philip J. Ivanhoe proposes that Lo is here quoting from the *Ku-pen Ta-hsüeh*, published in 1518 and now lost. He suggests, very plausibly, that the quotation begins with "*Wu* is the functioning of the intentions" and runs through "return to its original correctness." This may well be correct but, in the absence of the text, cannot be verified. I am indebted to Mr. Ivanhoe for his suggestion.

way,[8] you meant to make it internal rather than external and thus achieve internal consistency. You have also applied this interpretation, saying, for example, that when the intentions function in serving one's parents, then one investigates the matter of serving one's parents so as to return to correctness and become completely identified with the Principle of Nature.[9]

But even before you have gotten to the word "knowledge," your view has become convoluted, distorted, and difficult to understand. Let us investigate on the basis of your interpretation [of the word *ko* as "rectify"]. If at the beginning of the *Great Learning* one could rectify what is incorrect in every event and thing and return to a state of correctness, thus becoming completely identified with the Principle of Nature, then the mind would already be rectified and the intentions would already be made sincere. Wouldn't it be repetitious, redundant, and pointless to continue toward the goal of making the intentions sincere and rectifying the mind?

"Great is *ch'ien*, to which all things owe their beginning."[10] "Fine is *k'un*, to which all things owe their growth."[11] What is there in this body that I possess and in the myriad things as they are that does not derive from *ch'ien* and *k'un*? Their principle is in every case the principle of *ch'ien* and *k'un*. From my standpoint, external things are definitely "things." From the standpoint of principle, I too am a "thing," altogether merged in the unity of all being. Where then is the distinction of internal and external?

What is of value in the investigation of things is precisely one's desire to perceive the unity of principle in all of its diverse particularizations.[12] Only when there is neither subject nor object, neither deficiency nor surplus, and one has truly achieved unity and convergence, does one speak of knowledge being complete. This is also called knowing where to

[8] I.e., *ko* and *wu*, which Lo preferred to understand, as had Chu Hsi, as involving the intellectual endeavor of investigating things.

[9] *Ch'uan-hsi lu*, Part 1, in *Wang Wen-ch'eng kung-ch'üan-shu*, 1:4a–b. Wing-tsit Chan, trans., *Instructions for Practical Living*, sec. 3 (p. 8).

[10] *Book of Changes*, *ch'ien* hexagram, 1:4a.

[11] *Book of Changes*, *k'un* hexagram, 1:13b.

[12] A reference to Ch'eng I's statement in *I-ch'uan wen-chi* (Collection of Literary Works by Ch'eng I), 5:12b.

rest.[13] A great foundation can then be established, and the universal Way can then be practiced.[14] One proceeds from making [the intentions] sincere and [the mind] correct to governing [the state] and establishing peace [in the world] so that one can achieve an all-pervading unity[15] in which nothing is left behind.

But students differ in their natural endowment, and their effort too is incommensurate. Can one make any simple statement that will fully take into account whether they are able to investigate or not, and whether their investigation is shallow or profound, slow or quick? But when it comes to the Confucian teaching of the *Great Learning,* the Way cannot be changed, and the requirement that the student should enter through this Way cannot be repudiated. In departing from this, some are caught up in boastfulness and carried away by ostentation, in which case they drown in the external and are neglectful of the internal. Some detest complexity and delight in shortcuts, in which case they confine themselves to the internal and neglect the external. To drown in the external and neglect the internal is vulgar learning. To be confined to the internal and neglectful of the external is the learning of Ch'an.

Those who have achieved the ultimate attainment in the learning of Ch'an have always thought that they have "clarified the mind and perceived the nature." But they have always admitted a dualism between nature and man, external things and the self. Can they be said to have a true perception? If what they perceived were true, they would "bring to perfection all the diverse beings in the universe,"[16] and would be unable to despise a single hair because everything would be my body. How could they be willing to rebel against their sovereign and fathers, renounce wives and children, and thus descend to the level of birds and beasts? Now you wish to save people from drowning in vulgar learning, but you have not yet curbed the incipient development of Ch'an. This may cause those who are committed to the learning of the sages and worthies to be confused about their course, and I cannot help feeling the utmost concern in this regard.

[13] *Great Learning,* 2.

[14] *Mean,* 1:4.

[15] An allusion to *Analects,* 4:15, where Confucius is recorded to have said, "My doctrine is that of an all-pervading unity."

[16] *Book of Changes,* "Appended Remarks" ("Hsi-tz'u"), 7:19a.

I have also studied in detail the text of "Chu Hsi's Final Conclusions Arrived at Late in Life." You contend that what he perceived up through his middle years was not correct and that only when he reached his later years was he able to achieve enlightenment. From among thirty or more *chüan* of his essays and letters, you have therefore selected these thirty-odd items. In all of them his idea was to stress interiority, and you consider that this was something he understood in his later years after he had been enlightened. Thus you determine these to be his final conclusions. What you have selected is truly excellent, but I don't know which years you have determined to be these so-called "later years."

Wasted by illness and plagued by the summer heat, I have not been at leisure to investigate this in detail, but I did chance to discover that Master Ho Shu-ching[17] died in the year *i-wei* of the Ch'un-hsi period (1175), and at the time Master Chu was just forty-six. Only two years later in the year *ting-yu* (1177) did the *Collected Commentaries on the Analects and Mencius (Lun Meng chi-chu)* and the *Questions and Answers* [on the *Analects and Mencius*] *(Huo-wen)* appear. Now what you have quoted from Master Chu's four letters in reply to Ho you consider to be his "final conclusions arrived at late in life." But when it comes to the *Collected Commentaries* and the *Questions and Answers*, you consider them tentative theories of his middle years. I am afraid that your research was not sufficiently thorough and that your theorizing was unduly arbitrary.

You have also selected a letter in response to Huang Chih-ch'ing.[18] The edition of the Directorate of Education[19] merely says, "This was an error of former days," and does not contain the words *ting-pen*.[20] In

---

[17] Ho Hao (1128–1175).

[18] Huang Kan (1152–1221), Chu Hsi's son-in-law and biographer.

[19] I.e., the edition of the Kuo-tzu chien.

[20] Chu Hsi's Letter in Response to Huang Chih-ch'ing appears in two places in the *Chu Tzu wen-chi* (Collection of Literary Works by Master Chu Hsi), one in (SPPY ed.), 46:30b, and the other in the *Hsü-chi* (Supplementary Collection) 1:3b. In the first instance it appears in the form quoted by Lo, and in the second, in the form quoted by Wang. In the letter Chu Hsi speaks of a change in his method of study in the direction of a more broad-minded *(k'uan-hsin)* and less literalistic approach to the understanding of texts. In the version which appears in *ch.* 46 of the regular collection, Chu describes the more literalistic approach simply as "a mistake of former days," whereas in the version which appears in the supplementary collection, *ch.* 1, the term *ting-pen* is used in connection with the mistake. Professor Wing-tsit Chan explains, "Since Chu Hsi's letter to Huang Kan appears in both the regular

the present edition these two words have been inserted. You must have some other justification for this. Then in your preface you have substituted the word "old" (*chiu*) for the word "final" (*ting*), but you have not made clear whether or not the word *pen* refers to the same thing.[21] There is a letter written by Master Chu in response to Lü Tung-lai[22] in which the phrase *ting-pen* occurs,[23] but this did not refer to the *Collected Commentaries* or the *Questions and Answers*. For all of these reasons I am compelled to be skeptical. And yet these problems perhaps do not deserve to be labored. No doubt given your extraordinary natural endowment you will go on making new discoveries daily.

[You said that] formerly after you "seemed to have rapidly awakened," you found that having "looked for confirmation in the Five Classics[24]

collection, *ch.* 46, and the supplementary collection, *ch.* 1, most scholars accepted, as did Lo Ch'in-shun, the regular collection as the correct version rather than the supplementary collection. So far no one has disagreed with Lo or Ch'en Chien in accepting the regular collection as more authentic than the supplementary collection." See also Professor Chan's discussion in his *Wang Yang-ming Ch'uan-hsi lu hsiang-chu chi-p'ing*, pp. 437–72, esp. pp. 441–45. Quite apart from any possible question involved in the understanding of *ting-pen* as referring to the "final text" of Chu's commentaries or to his "fundamental principles," Lo was correct in his insistence that there was no evidence Chu Hsi ever repented of his essential commitment to an understanding of the *Great Learning* in which "the investigation of things" was prior to "making the intentions sincere."

[21] Wang's Preface to "Chu Hsi's Final Conclusions Arrived at Late in Life," refers to the "old text" (*chiu-pen*), whereas the text Wang quotes of Chu Hsi's letter to Huang Kan contains the term *ting-pen*. Wang's argument in the Preface was that the search through Chu Hsi's works that he had carried out in 1514 had led him finally to understand that "in his later years he [i.e., Chu] clearly realized the mistakes of his earlier doctrines. He regretted them so deeply as to say that he 'cannot be redeemed from the sin of having deceived others as well as himself.' His *Chi-chu* (Collected Commentaries) and *Huo-wen* (Questions and Answers) that have been transmitted from generation to generation represent the tentative conclusions of his middle age. He blamed himself for not having been able to correct the mistakes of the old texts [of his commentaries], much as he had wanted to." Translation adapted from Wing-tsit Chan, trans., *Instructions for Practical Living*, p. 266. Lo suggests that Wang was taking Chu Hsi's remarks out of context and thus misrepresenting his intention.

[22] Lü Tsu-ch'ien (1137–1181), Chu Hsi's friend and the co-compiler of the *Chin-ssu lu* (Reflections on Things at Hand).

[23] *Chu Tzu wen-chi* (Collection of Literary Works by Master Chu Hsi), 34:14b and 18a.

[24] The *Book of History*, the *Book of Odes*, the *Book of Changes*, the *Record of Rites* (*Li chi*, from the tenth century replaced by the *Rites of Chou*), and the *Spring and Autumn Annals*.

and the Four Masters,[25] it was like a torrent bursting the river bank and rushing to the sea."[26] You also found that, "My thoughts turned out to be more refined, clearer, and surer, and there was absolutely no more doubt left in my mind."[27] I certainly believe that these were not empty words. But you also said, "Only in Master Chu's doctrine did I find some disagreement."[28] Does this make sense? For the time being I shall not venture to cite many of his statements, but I have read the *Collected Writings of Chu Hsi (Chu Tzu wen-chi)* in which the thirty-second *chüan* is entirely devoted to letters in reply to Chang Nan-hsien.[29] In the fourth of these letters it says, "I seemed to be getting more refined and clearer about realities. Then as I once more got hold of the books of the sages and worthies as well as the works of scholars of recent times and read and examined them, I found that I was fully in accord with them. Where I had previously had doubts and perplexities, now without any effort at all, I have always naturally found the solutions."[30] There is not a single word [in Master Chu's letter] that is out of keeping with what you said in your preface. In the course of his letters he elaborated on what he had perceived, leaving nothing unclear. Especially in the last letter in the *chüan* he "outlined and summarized"[31] [his experience] in the most complete detail. In my humble opinion this encompasses the totality of the excellent learning handed down by the thousand sages. I do not know why you should have specifically omitted these letters. This could hardly have been accidental, could it?[32]

[25] Refers to the Four Books, *viz.*, the *Analects*, the *Great Learning*, the *Mean*, and the *Mencius*.

[26] Preface to "Chu Hsi's Final Conclusions Arrived at Late in Life" ("Chu Tzu wan-nien ting-lun") in *Wang Wen-ch'eng kung ch'üan-shu*, 7:21a–22b. Wing-tsit Chan, trans., *Instructions for Practical Living*, p. 265.

[27] *Ibid. Wang Wen-ch'eng kung ch'üan-shu*, 7:21b–22a. Wing-tsit Chan, trans., *Instructions for Practical Living*, p. 266.

[28] *Ibid.*

[29] Chang Shih (1133–1180), a leading member of the Hunan school, carried on an important philosophical exchange with Chu Hsi.

[30] "Ta Chang Ching-fu" (Letter in Reply to Chang Ching-fu), in *Chu Tzu wen-chi*, 32:5a.

[31] Quoting Chu Hsi's letter in *Chu Tzu wen-chi*, 32:5b.

[32] Lo may be referring obliquely to the fact that there were entire phrases in Wang's preface which might almost have been drawn from Chu's letters to Chang Shih, including, for

If you agree that these two letters are correct, then it would be impossible for the *Collected Commentaries on the Analects* and *Mencius*, the *Commentaries on the Great Learning* and the *Mean*, and the *Questions and Answers* to be fundamentally different in conception. Although there might be slight discrepancies among them, this should not prevent our pointing out the discrepancies as they occur. But if you think that [the *Collected Commentaries* and the *Questions and Answers*] do not agree [with the two letters], then your "refined and clear" insight must definitely be different from that of Master Chu.

You have selected all of these thirty-odd pieces solely in order to prove your own lofty theory. When you speak of [Master Chu's having] "apprehended before me what our minds have in common,"[33] how do we know that there were not slight differences which, through evil influences somewhere along the line, have turned into the great "disagreement" [that you refer to in your preface]? I am afraid that you should analyze in detail the reasons for this.

Furthermore, among the scholars who have come after Master Chu, you especially promote Wu Ts'ao-lu,[34] considering his views to have been most correct, so that you selected one of his statements and appended it at the end of the thirty-odd pieces [by Master Chu]. I dare say that it would not be easy to decide whether the views held by Ts'ao-lu in his later years were correct or not. For we Confucians speak about "illumination" (*chao-chao*)[35] and the Buddhists also frequently speak about it, and it is in precisely such an instance that "an infinitesimal mistake [at the beginning may lead to an infinite error at the end]." Even if Ts'ao-lu's experience did

example, the phrase, "becoming more refined and clear" (*i ching ming*), which also occurs in Wang's preface. Yet these letters could not have been selected by Wang for inclusion in "Chu Hsi's Final Conclusions Arrived at Late in Life" because they obviously dated from the 1170s when Chu Hsi was in his "middle years."

[33] Wang was using the language of *Mencius*, 7A:7–8, to express his agreement with certain of Chu Hsi's views. *Wang Wen-ch'eng kung ch'üan-shu*, 7:22b. Wing-tsit Chan, trans., *Instructions for Practical Living*, p. 266.

[34] Wu Ch'eng (1249–1333), the prominent Yüan Confucian who began his career with a thorough grounding in the philosophy of the Ch'eng-Chu school, later moving in the direction of Lu Hsiang-shan. He is considered by some scholars to have emerged with his own synthesis of the two.

[35] E.g., Chu Hsi used the term in *Chu Tzu yü-lei*, 5:11b.

coincide with what we call "illumination," how do we know that this was not the result of his forty years of "sedulous study of the meaning of texts,"[36] so that through exertion over a long period of time he suddenly found himself possessed of a "sudden and total realization of the pervading unity" (*huo-jan kuan-t'ung*)?[37]

Even with Master Ming-tao's lofty intelligence and pure character, coupled with the fact that early in life he studied personally with Lien-hsi and thus acquired his penchant for "humming to the breeze and idling with the moon,"[38] he nonetheless had to "go back and seek within the Six Classics, and only then could he apprehend [the Way]."[39] It was only by virtue of the fact that through his natural endowment he was close to having inborn knowledge that he could hear one point and know ten[40] and thus differ from those who exert the utmost effort in sedulous study.

How could [Ts'ao-lu] have gotten the idea that having spent the previous days in "sedulous study of the meaning of texts" was wrong and that "falling into this rut"[41] was a source of regret? Granted that upon catching the fish, one forgets the fish trap, and that upon catching the rabbit, one forgets the snare.[42] But is it reasonable to boast about catching

---

[36] "Tsun te-hsing tao wen-hsüeh chai chi" (On the Studio for Honoring the Virtuous Nature and Carrying on the Pursuit of Learning) in *Wu Wen-cheng chi* (Collected Works of Wu Ch'eng), 40.2b. The entire essay has been translated by David Gedalecia under the title, "In Commemoration of the Studio to Honor the Virtuous Nature and Maintain Constant Inquiry and Study," in *Wu Ch'eng: A Neo-Confucian of the Yüan*, pp. 203–8.

[37] The phrase *huo-jan kuan-t'ung* derives from Chu Hsi's *Commentary on the Words and Phrases of the Great Learning (Ta-hsüeh chang-chü)*, commentary on *ko-wu*. In *Ssu-shu chang-chü chi-chu*, 1:6.

[38] The phrase *yin-feng lung-yüeh* occurs in the biography of Chou Tun-i in the *Sung shih* (History of the Sung Dynasty), 427:4b and is attributed there to Ch'eng Hao.

[39] Quoting Ch'eng I's "Ming-tao hsien-sheng hsing-chuang" (Biographical Account of Master Ch'eng Hao) in *I-ch'uan wen-chi*, 7.6a. I am grateful to Professor Wing-tsit Chan for pointing out this allusion.

[40] Alludes to *Analects* 5:8:2.

[41] "Tsun te-hsing tao wen-hsüeh chai chi," in *Wu Wen-cheng chi*, 40:3a.

[42] Alludes to *Chuang Tzu* (SPPY ed.), 9:6a. As translated by Burton Watson (*The Complete Works of Chuang Tzu*, p. 302): "The fish trap exists because of the fish; once you've gotten the fish you can forget the trap. The rabbit snare exists because of the rabbit; once you've gotten the rabbit, you can forget the snare. Words exist because of meaning; once you've gotten the meaning, you can forget the words. Where can I find a man who has forgotten words so I can have a word with him?"

the fish and the rabbit and then turn around and find fault with the trap and the snare for having gotten in the way? It is only scholars who engage in sedulous study without knowing that they must "go back and set forth in brief what is essential"[43] who must take profound warning from these words.

Now Ts'ao-lu, having already experienced this so-called "illumination," considered "not allowing a moment's interruption" to be "close to the way of honoring [his virtuous nature]."[44] This is correct. But the following passage says, "If there is something I am not yet able to do, I ask other people and then learn it for myself, being resolutely determined to arrive at a solution."[45] Now whether or not he "allowed a moment's interruption" could hardly involve other people. And if he already knew wherein lay the way of honoring [his virtuous nature], then once there was an interruption, he would simply take up and continue from there. Why should he think that he was incapable of doing this and that there might be some way of learning apart from this?

From this it is clear that to perceive the Way is indeed difficult and personally to demonstrate it is more difficult still. Truly the Way is not easy to apprehend, but surely the study of it cannot be neglected. I am afraid that one cannot be satisfied with his own view and immediately regard it as the ultimate standard. I am not one who knows the Way, but I have put forth effort to seek it over the course of many years. In my rapidly declining years I realize that I have accomplished nothing. Still, I desire to discuss learning with the best of this generation. It is all too clear that I do not know my own limits. You have nonetheless always been generous towards me in your friendship, and even though I am slow and obdurate, I am grateful to you, and admire you, and take delight in your instruction.

I have presented my humble and inadequate opinions in full without daring to conceal anything. There are many other things that I would like to have said, but my brush and inkstone have been so long in disuse that I have been unable to manage. Yet the essentials you see here in brief. I humbly pray that when you have some leisure from your official duties, you will try to have a look at this, and if you will be so kind as to

---

[43] Alludes to *Mencius*, 4B:15.

[44] "Tsun te-hsing tao wen-hsüeh chai chi," in *Wu Wen-cheng chi*, 40:3a.

[45] *Ibid.*

give me a word signifying your approval or disapproval, I shall be extremely fortunate.

Winter, 1528

I have heard indirectly of your approach,[1] and I judge that you will be arriving within a few days in my humble city. I deeply desire to be edified by another meeting with you in order to assuage the longing I have felt for many years. But I have been wracked with illness, and it is difficult for me to travel far. So near and yet so far. I am overcome with disappointment and humbly beg you to understand the circumstances.

Last year I was honored by a letter of yours in which you expressed the desire to arrange a meeting between us. Perhaps you would have been willing to assist me and help me so that I might have accompanied you along the great Way. You are most generous and kind, and my gratitude is boundless. But what can be done about someone as obdurate and stubborn as I? The obdurate cannot help complying with convention, while those who are brilliant are always remarkable in being able to comprehend on their own. Thus I am afraid that, even were we to discuss our points of agreement and disagreement, there would be things that could not be resolved in a single meeting.

But while my illness has precluded a meeting, your generous intentions could hardly be unavailing. Therefore I presume to submit for your judgment my humble views as recently set forth in a number of sections.[2] In an additional section on a separate page I have indicated certain doubts which remain undispelled despite repeated examination of your lofty theory. I am well aware that, inasmuch as your essential point has eluded my understanding, my views must inevitably be of only the most trivial

[1] Wang Yang-ming was at this time on his way home from his last campaign in Kwangsi. He was to die a few weeks later on January 10, 1529.

[2] It is not clear exactly what Lo intended to send to Wang. It may have been the whole of the *K'un-chih chi* in two *chüan*, which was published in 1528, or it may only have been selections on topics which had been most directly at issue between the two scholars.

consequence for you. Still I shall devote my poor efforts to this end. For one who is dull may yet be granted one success in a thousand tries, and though at first we are far apart, we may eventually reach agreement. Your lofty intelligence impels me to be hopeful in this regard and humbly to anticipate the great favor of a decision from you.

[You have said that] a thing (*wu*) is "the functioning of the intentions" (*i chih yung*)[3] and that "to investigate" (*ko*) means "to rectify" (*cheng*). That is, it is to rectify what is incorrect so as to return to a state of correctness.[4] This is your interpretation of "the investigation of things." In an earlier letter you graciously bestowed, you said, "To investigate things is to investigate the things of the mind, the things of the intentions, and the things of knowledge. To rectify the mind is to rectify the mind of things. To make the intentions sincere is to make the intentions of things sincere. To extend knowledge is to extend the knowledge of things."[5] Never since

---

[3] The reference to a "thing" as a "function of the intentions" occurs in Wang's letter to Ku Tung-ch'iao (in *Wang Wen-ch'eng kung chüan-shu*, 2:12b–13a), in which Wang quoted Ku as having written: "As to your [Wang's] contention that 'knowledge is the substance of the intentions and things are functions of the intentions,' and that the word *ko* in the phrase *ko-wu* means to rectify, as in the saying, 'It is only the great man who can rectify (*ko*) what is wrong in the ruler's mind,' although your ideas are lofty and stimulating and are distinguished by not conforming to traditional interpretations, I am afraid that they are nevertheless not in accord with truth." Translation adapted from Wing-tsit Chan, trans., *Instructions for Practical Living*, pp. 102–3. Further on in the same letter (*ibid.*, 13b) Wang wrote: "For the intentions to function, there must be a thing in which they are to function, and the thing is an event. When the intentions function in the service of parents, then serving parents is a thing. When the intentions function in governing the people, then governing the people is a thing. When the intentions function in study, then study is a thing. When the intentions function in hearing a law suit, then hearing a law suit is a thing. Whenever the intentions are applied, there cannot be nothing." Translation adapted from Wing-tsit Chan, trans., *Instructions for Practical Living*, p. 104. Professor Chan observes (p. 103, note 27) that the identification of a "thing" as a "function of the intentions," (or, as Professor Chan translates it, a "function of the will") is "possibly a quotation from Wang's *Ku-pen ta-hsüeh p'ang-shih*, which is not included in the *Wang Wen-ch'eng Kung ch'üan-shu*. The original *Ku-pen ta-hsüeh p'ang-shih* has been lost. The present version, included in the *Han-hai* collection, is considered by scholars to be spurious, although the saying itself may well have come from the original."

[4] *Wang Wen-ch'eng kung ch'üan-shu*, 1:41a. Wing-tsit Chan, trans., *Instructions for Practical Living*, sec. 85 (p. 55). See above, Letter of 1520, n. 7 for another view on the source of this quotation.

[5] "Ta Lo Cheng-an shao-tsai shu," (Letter in Reply to Vice-Minister Lo Cheng-an) in *Wang Wen-ch'eng kung ch'üan-shu*, 2:61a. Translation adapted from Wing-tsit Chan, trans., *Instructions for Practical Living*, p. 161.

the *Great Learning* has been in existence has this interpretation been offered. This is an original perception attained through your own brilliance. How could a humble person like myself be able to perceive it? But given the encouragement of your instruction I have redoubled my efforts. Over and over again I have repeatedly examined it, not daring to be remiss.

When you speak of investigating the things of the mind (*hsin chih wu*), the things of the intentions (*i chih wu*), and the things of knowledge (*chih chih wu*), this assumes three "things." But when you speak of rectifying the mind of things, making sincere the intentions of things, and extending the knowledge of things, you assume that there is just one "thing." On the view that these are three things, Master Ch'eng's definition of "the investigation of things" is still intelligible,[6] whereas your definition of "the investigation of things" is not. On the view that there is only one "thing," then what, after all, is this "thing"? If you insist on considering it as a function of the intentions, then no manner of ingenious manipulation will ultimately yield a solution that is intelligible. This is the first of the points concerning which I can only be skeptical.

Furthermore, you have said that, "When the intentions are directed toward serving parents, then serving parents is a 'thing,' and when the intentions are directed toward serving the emperor, then serving the emperor is a 'thing.'" In cases of this kind your explanation may be said to be adequate. But there are other examples, such as the exclamation [of Confucius] on the river bank in the *Analects*,[7] or the hawk flying and the fish leaping in the *Mean*.[8] These are instances of vital pronouncements by the sage and worthy[9] concerning the human situation.[10] A student who has not been able to understand their significance cannot be said to know what it is to learn. Were I to suppose that the meaning is that my intentions are directed to the flowing of the stream, the flying of the hawk, or the leaping

---

[6] Both Ch'eng Hao and Ch'eng I defined the *ko* in *ko-wu* as "to reach" or "to arrive." This was discussed by Wang in his Letter in Reply to Ku Tung-ch'iao ("Ta Ku Tung-ch'iao shu") in *Wang Wen-ch'eng kung ch'üan-shu*, 2:2b–29b. Wing-tsit Chan, trans., *Instructions for Practical Living*, secs. 130–143 (pp. 91–124).

[7] *Analects*, 9:16.

[8] *Mean*, 12:3, quoting Ode 239.

[9] I.e., Confucius and Tzu-ssu.

[10] *I-shu*, 3:1a.

of the fish, how would I "rectify what is incorrect so as to return to correctness"? This is the second point concerning which I can only be skeptical.

Moreover, you said in a letter which had to do with learning[11] that "The innate good knowing (*liang-chih*) of my mind is the same as the Principle of Nature. When the Principle of Nature in the innate good knowing of my mind is extended to all events and things, all events and things will attain their principle. To extend the innate good knowing of my mind is the extension of knowledge, and to enable all things to attain their principle is the investigation of things."[12] If we accept your interpretation, the *Great Learning* should have said "the investigation of things lies in the extension of knowledge," rather than having said "the extension of knowledge lies in the investigation of things." It should have said "when knowledge is complete, then things are investigated," rather than having said "when things are investigated, then knowledge is complete." You had already spoken of "investigating carefully the Principle of Nature which is in the mind and thereby extending the innate good knowing inherent in it."[13] You also said, "It is precisely in extending the innate good knowing of the mind that one investigates carefully the Principle of Nature which is inherent in the mind."[14] Then are the Principle of Nature and innate good knowing one thing? Or are they not? Thus as far as investigating and extending are concerned, which is prior to the other? This is the third point concerning which I can only be skeptical.

> When I first wrote this letter I had intended to reply to an invitation extended by Yang-ming in the past year for me to give a public lecture. Before the letter was sent out, Yang-ming had died. Alas! My humble views are all stated here, and, feeling that our exchange was not a private matter only, I recorded this.

[11] Letter in Reply to Ku Tung-ch'iao. *Wang Wen-ch'eng kung ch'üan-shu*, 2:2b–29b.

[12] *Wang Wen-ch'eng kung ch'üan-shu*, 2:9b. Translation adopted from Wing-tsit Chan, trans., *Instructions for Practical Living*, sec. 135 (p. 99).

[13] *Wang Wen-ch'eng kung ch'üan-shu*, 2:13a. Translation adapted from Wing-tsit Chan, trans., *Instructions for Practical Living*, sec. 137 (p. 103).

[14] *Wang Wen-ch'eng kung ch'üan-shu*, 2:17a. Translation adapted from Wing-tsit Chan, trans., *Instructions for Practical Living*, sec. 139 (p. 108).

Bibliography

Abbreviations

CITCS	Cheng-i-t'ang ch'üan-shu 正誼堂全書
KHCPTS	Kuo-hsüeh chi-pen ts'ung-shu 國學基本叢書
PNP	Po-na pen 百衲本
SKCSCP	Ssu-k'u ch'üan-shu chen-pen 四庫全書珍本
SPPY	Ssu-pu pei-yao 四部備要
SPTK	Ssu-pu ts'ung-k'an 四部叢刊
T	Taishō Shinshū Dai-zōkyō 大正新脩大藏經
TSCC	Ts'ung-shu chi-ch'eng 叢書集成
TT	Tao-tsang 道藏
ZZ	Dai Nihon zoku-zōkyō 大日本續藏經

Works in Chinese and Japanese

A. Early Works (Pre-1900, including modern editions of such works)

Chan Jo-shui 湛若水. *Chan Kan-ch'üan hsien-sheng wen-chi* 湛甘泉先生文集 (Collected Literary Writings of Master Chan Jo-shui). 1580 ed.

—— *Kan-ch'üan hsien-sheng hsü-pien tu-ch'üan* 甘泉先生續編大全 (Complete and Revised Collection of Literary Works by Master Chan Jo-shui). 1593 ed.

Chang Mou 章懋. *Feng-shan Chang hsien-sheng yü-lu* 楓山章先生語錄 (Recorded Conversations of Master Chang Mou), in *Chin-hua ts'ung-shu* 金華叢書.

Chang Po-hsing 張伯行, comp. *Lien-lo feng-ya* 濂洛風雅 (Poems from the Schools of Lien-hsi and Lo-yang). CITCS ed.

Chang Po-tuan 張伯端. *Wu-chen p'ien* 悟眞篇 (Treatise on Awakening to Truth), ed. entitled *Wu-chen p'ien cheng-i* 悟眞篇正義 in *Tao-tsang ching-hua* 道藏精華. Taipei: 1964, ser. 1, no. 4.

Chang Tsai 張載. *Chang Tzu ch'üan-shu* 張子全書 (Complete Works of Master Chang Tsai). SPPY ed.

—— *Cheng-meng* 正蒙 (Correcting Youthful Ignorance), in *Chang Tzu ch'üan-shu*.

Ch'en Chien 陳建. *Hsüeh-p'u t'ung-pien* 學蔀通辨 (General Critique of Obscurations of Learning). CITCS ed.

Ch'en Hao 陳澔. *Li-chi chi-shuo* 禮記集說 (Collected Explanations of the *Book of Rites*).

[Ch'ing] Shu-t'ang ed.

Ch'en Hsien-chang 陳獻章. *Pai-sha tzu ch'üan-chi* 白沙子全集 (Complete Works of Master Ch'en Hsien-chang). Hong Kong: photographic reproduction of the 1771 ed.

Ch'eng Hao 程顥. *Ming-tao wen-chi* 明道文集 (Collection of Literary Works by Ch'eng Hao), in *Erh-Ch'eng ch'üan-shu*.

Ch'eng Hao and Ch'eng I 程頤. *Erh-Ch'eng ch'üan-shu* 二程全書 (Complete Works of the Two Ch'engs). SPPY ed.

—— *I-shu* 遺書 (Written Legacy), in *Erh-Ch'eng ch'üan-shu*.

—— *Ts'ui-yen* 粹言 (Pure Words), in *Erh-Ch'eng ch'üan-shu*.

Ch'eng I. *I-ch'uan I-chuan* 伊川易傳 (Ch'eng I's Commentary on the *Book of Changes*), in *Erh-Ch'eng ch'üan-shu*.

—— *I-ch'uan wen-chi* 伊川文集 (Collection of Literary Works by Ch'eng I), in *Erh-Ch'eng ch'üan-shu*.

Chin-ling hsüan-kuan chih 金陵玄觀志 (Monograph on Taoist Temples of Nanking). Shanghai: 1937 reprint of a late Ming (?) ed.

Chiu T'ang-shu 舊唐書 (Old History of the T'ang Dynasty). PNP.

Ch'iu Chün 丘濬. *Ta-hsüeh yen-i pu* 大學衍義補 (Supplement to the *Great Learning, Elaborated*). SKCSCP, ser. 2.

Chou I cheng-i 周易正義 (Correct Meaning of the *Book of Changes*). SPPY ed.

Chou Tun-i 周敦頤. *Chou Tzu ch'üan-shu* 周子全書, in *Chou Chang ch'üan-shu*.

—— *T'ung-shu* 通書 (Penetrating the *Book of Changes*), in *Chou Chang ch'üan-shu*.

Chou Tun-i and Chang Tsai. *Chou Chang ch'üan-shu* 周張全書 (Complete Works of Chou Tun-i and Chang Tsai). Kyoto: Chūbun shuppan-sha, 1981.

Chu Hsi 朱熹. *Chou I pen-i* 周易本義 (The Essential Meaning of the *Book of Changes*). SKCSCP, ser. 6.

—— *Chou I Ts'an-t'ung ch'i k'ao-i* 周易參同契考異 (Inquiry into Variants of the *Ts'an-t'ung ch'i*), in *Shou-shan ko ts'ung-shu* 守山閣叢書.

—— *Chu Tzu ch'üan-shu* 朱子全書 (Complete Works of Master Chu Hsi). 1714 ed.

—— *Chu Tzu i-shu* 朱子遺書 (Written Legacy of Master Chu Hsi). Taipei: I-wen yin-shu kuan ed.

—— *Chu Tzu wen-chi* 朱子文集 (Collection of Literary Works by Master Chu Hsi). SPPY ed., in this ed. entitled *Chu Tzu ta-ch'üan* 朱子大全 (Great Collection of Literary Works by Master Chu Hsi).

—— *Chu Tzu yü-lei* 朱子語類 (Classified Conversations of Master Chu Hsi). Taipei: Cheng-chung shu-chü, 1970 reprint of the 1473 ed.

—— *Chung-yung chang-chü* 中庸章句 (Commentary on the Words and Phrases of the *Mean*), in *Ssu-shu chang-chü chi-chu*.

—— *Hu Tzu chih-yen i-i* 胡子知言疑義 (Doubts Concerning *Master Hu's Understanding Words*), in *Yüeh-ya-t'ang ts'ung-shu* 粵雅堂叢書, collection 10.

—— *Hui-an hsien-sheng Chu Wen-kung wen-chi* 晦菴先生朱文公文集 (Collection of Literary Works by Chu Hsi). Kyoto: Chūbun shuppan-sha, 1977.

—— *I-Lo yüan-yüan lu* 伊洛淵源錄 (Records of the Origins of the School of the Two Ch'engs). TSCC ed.

—— *Lun-yü chi-chu* 論語集註 (Collected Commentaries on the *Analects*), in *Ssu-shu chang-chü chi-chu*.

—— *Meng Tzu chi-chu* 孟子集註 (Collected Commentaries on the *Mencius*), in *Ssu-shu chang-chü chi-chu*.

—— *Ssu-shu chang-chü chi-chu* 四書章句集注 (Collected Commentaries on the Words and Phrases of the Four Books). KHCPTS.

—— *Ssu-shu chi-chu* 四書集註 (Collected Commentaries on the Four Books), in *Shushigaku taikei* 朱子学大系, Vols. 7–8. Tokyo: Meitoku shuppansha, 1974.

—— *Ta-hsüeh chang-chü* 大學章句 (Commentary on the Words and Phrases of the *Great Learning*), in *Ssu-shu chang-chü chi-chu*.

—— *Ta-hsüeh huo-wen* 大學或問 (Questions and Answers on the *Great Learning*), in *Chu Tzu i-shu*.

Chu Hsi and Lü Tsu-ch'ien 呂祖謙, comps. *Chin-ssu lu* 近思錄 (Reflections on Things at Hand), in *Chu Tzu i-shu*.

Dai Nihon zoku-zōkyō 大日本續藏經. 750 vols. Kyoto: 1905–12.

Fan Chung-yen 范仲淹. *Fan Wen-cheng kung cheng-fu tsou-i* 范文正公政府奏議 (Memorials on Government by Fan Chung-yen), in *Che-shih chü ts'ung-shu* 擇是居叢書.

Han-shu 漢書 (History of the Former Han Dynasty). Peking: Chung-hua shu-chü, 1972.

Hsieh Liang-tso 謝良佐. *Shang-ts'ai hsien-sheng yü-lu* 上蔡先生語錄 (Recorded Conversations of Master Hsieh Liang-tso). CITCS ed.

Hsin T'ang-shu 新唐書 (New History of the T'ang Dynasty). PNP.

Hsüeh Hsüan 薛瑄. *Tu-shu lu* 讀書錄 (Record of My Reading). 1826 ed.

Hu An-kuo 胡安國. *Ch'un-ch'iu Hu-shih chuan* 春秋胡氏傳 (Mr. Hu's Commentary on the *Spring and Autumn Annals*). SPTK ed.

Hu Chü-jen 胡居仁. *Chü-yeh lu* 居業錄 (Record of Occupying One's Sphere of Activity). Ming ed. Naikaku Bunko.

Hu Hung 胡宏. *Hu Tzu chih-yen* 胡子知言 (Master Hu Hung's Understanding Words), in *Yüeh-ya-t'ang ts'ung-shu* 粵雅堂叢書, collection 10.

Huang Tsung-hsi 黃宗羲. *Ming-ju hsüeh-an* 明儒學案 (Philosophical Records of Ming Confucians). SPPY ed.

Huang Tsung-hsi and Ch'üan Tsu-wang 全祖望 *Sung Yüan hsüeh-an* 宋元學案 (Philosophical Records of Sung and Yüan Confucians). SPPY ed.

I-ching 易經 (Book of Changes). *Chou I cheng-i* 周易正義 (SPPY) ed.

Kao P'an-lung 高攀龍. *Kao Tzu i-shu* 高子遺書 (Written Legacy of Master Kao P'an-lung). 1746 ed. Gest Collection, Princeton University Library.

Ku Yen-wu 顧炎武. *Jih-chih lu* 日知錄 (Record of Daily Knowledge). Taipei: Commercial Press, 1964.

Li T'ung 李侗. *Li Yen-p'ing hsien-sheng wen-chi* 李延平先生文集 (Collection of Literary Works by Master Li T'ung). CITCS ed.

Lo Ch'in-shun 羅欽順. *K'un-chih chi* 困知記 (Knowledge Painfully Acquired). 1622 ed. Library of Congress.

—— *Lo Cheng-an hsien-sheng ts'un-kao* 羅整菴先生存稿 (Occasional Papers of Master Lo Ch'in-shun). SKCSCP, ser. 4.

Lu Hsiang-shan 陸象山. *Hsiang-shan ch'üan-chi* 象山全集 (Complete Works of Lu Chiu-yüan). SPPY ed.

Lü Tsu-ch'ien 呂祖謙. *Tseng-hsiu Tung-lai Shu-shuo* 增修東萊書說 (Lü Tsu-ch'ien's Revised and Expanded Explanations of the *Book of History*), in *Chin-hua ts'ung-shu* 金華叢書.

Ming-shih 明史 (History of the Ming Dynasty). Taipei: Kuo-fang yen-chiu yüan, 1962.

Ou-yang Hsiu 歐陽修. *Ou-yang Yung-shu chi* 歐陽永叔集 (Collected Works of Ou-yang Hsiu). Shanghai: KHCPTS ed., 1958.

Shao Yung 邵雍. *Huang-chi ching-shih shu* 皇極經世書 (Supreme Principles Governing the World). SPPY ed.

—— *I-ch'uan chi-jang chi* 伊川擊壤集 (Striking an Earthen Drum in the I River). *Kinsei kanseki sōkan, shisō hen*, Vol. 4. Taipei: Chung-wen ch'u-pan she, 1972. Also in *Chūgoku koten shinsho* 中国古典新書 ed. Tokyo: Meitoku shuppansha, 1979.

—— *Yü-ch'iao wen-tui* 漁樵問對 (Dialogue of the Fisherman and the Woodcutter), in *Shuo-fu* 說郛. Taipei: Hsin-hsing shu-chü reprint, 1971.

Ssu-ma Ch'ien 司馬遷. *Shih-chi* 史記 (Records of the Historian), in *Hsin-chiao Shih-chi san-chia chu* 新校史記三家注. Taipei: Shih-chieh shu-chü, 1973.

Ssu-ma Kuang 司馬光. *Tzu-chih t'ung-chien* 資治通鑑 (A Comprehensive Mirror for Aid in Government), 10 vols. Peking: Ku-chi ch'u-pan-she, 1956.

Sung Lien 宋濂. *Sung Hsüeh-shih ch'üan-chi* 宋學士全集 (Complete Writings of Academician Sung Lien). TSCC ed.

Tai Hsien 戴銑. *Chu Tzu shih-chi* 朱子實紀 (A True Record of Master Chu Hsi). *Kinsei kanseki sōkan, shisō hen*, Vol. 4. Taipei: Chung-wen ch'u-pan she, 1972.

Taishō Shinshū Dai-zōkyō 大正新脩大藏經 (Taishō ed. of the Buddhist Canon). 85 vols. Tokyo: 1914–22.

T'ang hui-yao 唐會要 (Important Documents of the T'ang). KHCPTS.

Tao-te ching 道德經 (Classic of the Way and Its Power). SPPY ed.

Tao-tsang 道藏 (Taoist Canon). 110 vols. Shanghai: Commercial Press, 1924–26.

T'o-t'o 脫脫 et al. *Sung-shih* 宋史. PNP.

Ts'ai Ch'ing 蔡清. *Ssu-shu meng-yin* 四書蒙引 (A Beginner's Guide to the Four Books). SKCSCP, ser. 3.

Tung Chung-shu 董仲舒. *Ch'un-ch'iu fan-lu* 春秋繁露 (Luxuriant Gems of the *Spring and Autumn Annals*). SPTK ed.

Wang T'ing-hsiang 王廷相. *Wang T'ing-hsiang hsüan* 王廷相選 (Selection of Writings by Wang T'ing-hsiang). 1536 ed. C. V. Starr East Asian Library, Columbia University.

Wang Yang-ming 王陽明. *Wang Wen-ch'eng kung ch'üan-shu* 王文成公全書 (Complete Writings of Wang Yang-ming). SPTK ed.

Wu Ch'eng 吳澄. *Wu Wen-cheng chi* 吳文正集 (Collected Works of Wu Ch'eng). SKCSCP, ser. 2.

Wu Yü-pi 吳與弼. *K'ang-chai chi* 康齋集 (Collected Works of Wu Yü-pi). SKCSCP, ser. 4.

Yang Chien 楊簡. *Tz'u-hu i-shu* 慈湖遺書 (Written Legacy of Yang Chien), in *Ssu-ming ts'ung-shu* 四明叢書.

Yang Shih 楊時. *Kuei-shan hsien-sheng chi* 龜山先生集 (Collected Works of Master Yang Shih). SPTK ed.

Yin T'un 尹焞. *Yin Ho-ching chi* 尹和靖集 (Collected Works of Yin T'un). TSCC ed.

Yü Yen 俞琰. *Ts'an-t'ung ch'i fa-hui* 參同契發揮 (An Elucidation of the *Ts'an-t'ung ch'i*), in *Tao-tsang ching-hua* 道藏精華, ser. 1, no. 2.

B. *Modern Works (Post-1900)*

Abe Yoshio 阿部吉雄. "Nissen-Chū sankoku no shin jugaku no hatten o hikaku shite" 日鮮中三国の新儒学の発展を比較して (A Comparative Study of the Development of Neo-Confucianism in Japan, Korea, and China). *Tōkyō Shinagaku hō* 東京支那学報 (June 1966), 12:1–16.

—— "Nissen-Min ni okeru shuriha shukiha no keifu to sono tokushitsu" 日鮮明における主理派主気派の系譜とその特質 (The Genealogy and Special Characteristics of the School of *Li* and the School of *Ch'i* in Japan, Korea, and Ming China). *Chōsen Gakuhō* 朝鮮学報 (1959), vol. 14.

—— *Nihon Shushigaku to Chōsen* 日本朱子学と朝鮮 (The Chu Hsi School in Japan and its Relation to Korea). Tokyo: Tōkyō Daigaku shuppan-kai, 1965.

Akizuki Tanetsugu 秋月胤継. *Gen Min jidai no jukyo* 元明時代の儒教 (Confucianism during the Yüan and Ming Periods). Tokyo: Kōshisha shobō, 1928.

Araki Kengo 荒木見悟. *Mindai shisō kenkyū* 明代思想研究 (Studies in Ming Thought). Tokyo: Sōbunsha, 1972.

Beijing Ta-hsüeh, Che-hsüeh hsi, Chung-kuo che-hsüeh shih chiao-yen shih 北京大學, 哲學系, 中國哲學史教研室 (Beijing University, Department of Philosophy, Research Center on the History of Chinese Philosophy), comp. *Chung-kuo che-hsüeh shih* 中國哲學史 (A History of Chinese Philosophy). 2 vols. Peking: Chung-hua shu-chü, 1980.

Chan Wing-tsit 陳榮捷. *Wang Yang ming Ch'uan-hsi lu hsiang-chu chi-p'ing* 王陽明傳習錄詳註集評 (Full Annotation and Collected Commentaries of Wang Yang ming's *Instructions for Practical Living*). Taipei: Hsüeh-sheng shu chü, 1983.

—— *Wang Yang-ming yü Ch'an* 王陽明與禪 (Wang Yang-ming and Ch'an). Taipei: Hsüeh-sheng shu-chü, 1985.

Chi Wen-fu 嵇文甫. *Wan-Ming ssu-hsiang shih lun* 晚明思想史論 (Studies on the History of Late Ming Thought). Chungking: 1944.

Ch'ien Mu 錢穆. *Chu Tzu hsin hsüeh-an* 朱子新學案 (A New Philosophical Record of Chu Hsi). Taipei: San-min shu-chü, 1971.

—— *Chung-kuo chin san-pai nien hsüeh-shu shih* 中國近三百年學術史 (A History of Chinese Scholarship in the Past Three Hundred Years). Taipei: Commercial Press, 1968 reprint of 1937 ed.

—— *Sung Ming li-hsüeh kai-shu* 宋明理學概述 (A Survey of the Philosophy of *Li* in the Sung and Ming Periods). Taipei: Chung-hua wen-hua ch'u-pan shih-yen wei-yüan hui, 1955.

Hou Wai-lu 侯外廬. *Wang T'ing-hsiang che-hsüeh hsüan-chi* 王廷相哲學選集 (Selections from the Philosophy of Wang T'ing-hsiang). Peking: K'o-hsüeh ch'u-pan she, 1973 reprint of the 1959 ed.

Hou Wai-lu, Chao Chi-pin 趙紀彬, and Tu Kuo-hsiang 杜國庠. *Chung-kuo ssu-hsiang t'ung-*

shih 中國思想通史 (A General History of Chinese Thought). 6 vols. Peking: Jen-min ch'u-pan she, 1957—60.

Hsieh Wu-liang 謝旡量. *Chung-kuo che-hsüeh shih* 中國哲學史 (A History of Chinese Philosophy). Hong Kong: Chung-hua shu-chü, 1915.

Imai Usaburō 今井宇三郎. "Zenshu hon *Denshūroku* kō" 全書本伝習録考 (Study of the *Instructions for Practical Living*). *Shibun* 斯文 (1945), 27 : 7—9.

Jen Yu-wen 簡又文. *Pai-sha tzu yen-chiu* 白沙子研究 (A Study of Ch'en Hsien-chang). Hong Kong: Meng-chih shu-wu, 1970.

Jung Chao-tsu 容肇祖. *Ming-tai ssu-hsiang shih* 明代思想史 (A History of Ming Thought). Taipei: K'ai-ming shu-tien, 1966 reprint of 1941 ed.

Kubota Ryōon 久保田量遠. *Shina Ju Dō Butsu kōshō shi* 支那儒道仏交渉史 (A History of the Interaction between Confucianism, Taoism, and Buddhism in China). Tokyo: Daitō shuppan-sha, 1943.

Kurita Naomi 栗田直躬. "Jōdai Shina no tenseki ni mietaru 'ki' no kannen" 上代シナの典籍に貝えたる「気」の観念 (The Perspective on *Ch'i* in Ancient Chinese Texts), in *Chūgoku jōdai shisō no kenkyū* 中国上代思想の研究 (Studies in Ancient Chinese Thought). Tokyo: Iwanami shoten, 1949.

Kusumoto Masatsugu 楠本正継. *Sō Min jidai jugaku shisō no kenkyū* 宋明時代儒学思想の研究 (Studies on Confucian Thought in the Sung and Ming Periods). Kashiwa shi: Hiroike gakuen, 1962.

Liang Ch'i-ch'ao 梁啟超. *Ch'ing-tai hsüeh-shu kai-lun* 清代學術概論 (Intellectual Trends in the Ch'ing Period). Hong Kong: Chung-hua shu-chü, 1963 reprint of 1924 ed.

Lo Hsiang-lin 羅香林. "Ch'en Pai-sha yu tzu-jan kuei yü tzu-te chih chiao chi ch'i tui Wang Yang-ming chih ying-hsiang" 陳白沙由自然歸於自得之教及其對王陽明之影响 (Ch'en Hsien-chang's Teaching of from *tzu-jan* to *tzu-te* and its Influence on Wang Yang-ming). *Journal of Oriental Studies* (July 1973), 11 (2) : 227—36.

Mano Senryū 問野潜龍. *Mindai bunkashi kenkyū* 明代文化史研究 (Studies on the History of Ming Culture). Kyoto: Dōbō-sha, 1979.

Morohashi Tetsuji 諸橋轍次 and Yasuoka Masahiro 安岡正篤, eds. *Shushigaku taikei* 朱子学大系 (Compendium on the Chu Hsi School). 14 vols. Tokyo: Meitoku shuppan-sha, 1974—1982).

Okada Takehiko 岡田武彦, *Ōyōmei to Minmatsu no jugaku* 王陽明と明末の儒学 (Wang Yang-ming and Late Ming Thought). Tokyo: Meitoku shuppan-sha, 1970.

Onozawa Seiichi 小野沢精一, Fukunaga Mitsuji 福永光司, and Yamanoi Yū 山井湧, eds. *Ki no shisō* 気の思想 (The Philosophy of *Ch'i*). Tokyo: Tōkyō Daigaku shuppan-kai, 1978.

Ren Jiyu 任繼愈, ed. *Chung-kuo che-hsüeh shih* 中國哲學史 (A History of Chinese Philosophy). Vol. 3. Peking: Jen-min ch'u-pan-she, 1979 reprint of 1964 ed.

Shimada Kenji 島田虔次. *Shushigaku to Yōmeigaku* 朱子学と陽明学 (The Chu Hsi School and the Wang Yang-ming School). Tokyo: Iwanami shoten, 1967.

Sun Shu-p'ing 孫叔平. *Chung-kuo che-hsüeh shih kao* 中國哲學史稿 (Essays in the History of Chinese Philosophy). Shanghai: Jen-min ch'u-pan-she, 1981.

T'ang Chün-i 唐君毅. "Chu Lu i-t'ung t'an-yüan" 朱陸異同探源 (A Discussion of the

Sources of Agreement and Disagreement between Chu Hsi and Lu Hsiang-shan). *Hsin-ya hsüeh-pao* 新亞學報 (February 1967), 8:(1):1–100.

—— "Yang-ming hsüeh yü Chu Lu i-t'ung ch'ung-pien" 陽明學與朱陸異同重辨 (The Learning of Wang Yang-ming and the Agreements and Disagreements between Chu Hsi and Lu Hsiang-shan). *Hsin-ya hsüeh-pao* (August 1968), 8(2):53–126.

Tokiwa Daijō 常盤大定. *Shina ni okeru Bukkyō to Jukyō Dōkyō* 支那に於ける仏教と儒教道教 (Buddhism, Confucianism, and Taoism in China). Tokyo: Tōyō bunko, 1930.

Tomoeda Ryūtarō 友枝龍太郎. *Shushi no shisō keisei* 朱子の思想形成 (The Formation of Chu Hsi's Thought). Tokyo: Shunjū-sha, 1969.

Wong Yuk 王煜. *Ju-chia ti chung-ho kuan* 儒家的中和觀 (The Confucian View of Mean, Equilibrium and Harmony). Hong Kong: Lung-men shu-tien, 1967.

Wu K'ang 吳康. *Sung Ming li-hsüeh* 宋明理學 (The Philosophy of *Li* in the Sung and Ming Periods). Taipei: Hua-kuo ch'u-pan-she, 1973 reprint of 1955 ed.

Yamamoto Makoto 山本命. *Min jidai jugaku no rinrigakuteki kenkyū* 明時代儒学の倫理学的研究 (Studies on Ethical Thought in Ming Confucianism). Tokyo: Risō-sha, 1974.

Yamanoi Yū 山井湧. "Min shin jidai ni okeru 'ki' no tetsugaku" 明清時代における「気」の哲学 (The Philosophy of *Ch'i* in the Ming and Ch'ing Periods). *Tetsugaku zasshi* 哲学雑誌 (1951) 66 (711):82–103.

—— *Min Shin shisō shi no kenkyū* 明清思想史の研究 (Studies on the History of Ming and Ch'ing Thought). Tokyo: Tōkyō Daigaku shuppan-kai, 1980.

Yamashita Ryūji 山下龍二. "Ra Kinjun to ki no tetsugaku" 羅欽順と気の哲学 (Lo Ch'in-shun and the Philosophy of *Ch'i*), in *Nagoya Daigaku Bungakubu kenkyū ronshū* 27 名古屋大学文学部研究論集, Tetsugaku 9 (1961).

—— *Yōmeigaku no kenkyū* 陽明学の研究 (Studies on the Wang Yang-ming School). 2 vols. Tokyo: Gendai Jōhō-sha, 1971.

Yasuda Jirō 安田二郎. *Chūgoku kinsei shisō kenkyū* 中国近世思想研究 (Studies in Modern Chinese Thought). Tokyo: Kōbundō shobō, 1948.

Yü Ying-shih 余英時. "Ts'ung Sung Ming ju-hsüeh ti fa-chan lun Ch'ing-tai ssu-hsiang shih" 從宋明儒學的發展論清代思想史 (Ch'ing Thought as Seen through the Development of Sung and Ming Confucianism). *Chung-kuo hsüeh-jen* 中國學人 (September, 1970), 2:19–41.

Zhang Dainian 張岱年. *Chung-kuo wei-wu-chu-i ssu-hsiang chien-shih* 中國唯物主義思想簡史 (A Brief History of Chinese Materialist Thought). Peking: Ch'ing-nien ch'u-pan-she, 1981 reprint of 1957 ed.

Works in Western Languages

Abe Yoshio. "Development of Neo-Confucianism in Japan, Korea, and China: A Comparative Study." *Acta Asiatica* (1970), 19:16–39.

—— "Influence of Lo Ch'in-shun's *K'un-chih chi* in the Early Edo Period and the State of Prac-

tical Learning among the Students of Kinoshita Jun'an and Yamazaki Ansai." Draft paper
   for the June 1974 ACLS conference on Neo-Confucianism and Practical Learning in
   the Ming and Early Tokugawa Periods.

Baynes, Cary F., trans. (from the German version of Richard Wilhelm). *The I-ching or Book of
   Changes*. Princeton: Princeton University Press, Bollingen Series XIX, 1969.

Blackwood, R. T. and A. L. Herman, eds. *Problems in Philosophy: West and East*. Englewood
   Cliffs, N. J.: Prentice Hall, 1975.

Bloom, Irene. "On the 'Abstraction' of Ming Thought: Some Concrete Evidence from the
   Philosophy of Lo Ch'in-shun." In Wm. Theodore de Bary and Irene Bloom, eds., *Principle
   and Practicality*. New York: Columbia University Press, 1979.

Bruce, J. Percy. *Chu Hsi and His Masters*, London: Probsthain, 1923.

Bunge, Mario. *Scientific Materialism*. Dordrecht: D. Reidel, 1981.

Bury, J. B. *The Idea of Progress; An Inquiry into Its Origin and Growth*. London: Macmillan, 1920.

Busch, Heinrich. *The Tung-lin Academy and Its Political and Philosophical Significance*. Ann
   Arbor: University Microfilms, 1954.

Chan Wing-tsit. "Chan Jo-shui's Influence on Wang Yang-ming." *Philosophy East and West*
   (January and April 1973), 23(1–2):9–30.

—— "The Ch'eng-Chu School of the Early Ming." In Wm. Theodore de Bary, ed., *Self and
   Society in Ming Thought*. New York: Columbia University Press, 1970.

—— "Chinese and Western Interpretations of Jen (Humanity)." *Journal of Chinese Philosophy*
   (March 1975), 2(2):107–29.

—— "Chu Hsi's Completion of Neo-Confucianism." In Françoise Aubin, ed., *Études Song –
   Sung Studies in Memoriam Étienne Balazs* (1973), ser. 2, no. 1, pp. 59–90.

—— "The Evolution of the Confucian Concept of Jen." *Philosophy East and West* (1955),
   4:295–319.

—— "The Evolution of the Neo-Confucian Concept Li as Principle." *Ch'ing-hua hsüeh-pao*
   (Tsing Hua Journal of Chinese Studies) (February 1964), NS IV, 2:123–48.

—— "Neo-Confucianism in Chinese Scientific Thought." *Philosophy East and West* (1957), 4:
   309–32.

Chan Wing-tsit, trans. *Instructions for Practical Living and Other Neo-Confucian Writings by
   Wang Yang-ming*. New York: Columbia University Press, 1963.

—— trans. *Reflections on Things at Hand: The Neo-Confucian Anthology by Chu Hsi and Lü
   Tsu-ch'ien*. New York: Columbia University Press, 1967.

—— *A Source Book in Chinese Philosophy*. Princeton: Princeton University Press, 1963.

Chang, Carsun. "Buddhism as a Stimulus to Neo-Confucianism." *Oriens Extremus* (1955),
   2:157–66.

—— *The Development of Neo-Confucian Thought*. 2 vols. New York: Bookman, 1957 and 1962.

Cheng Chung-ying. "Reason, Substance and Human Desires in Seventeenth-Century Neo-
   Confucianism." In Wm. Theodore de Bary, ed., *The Unfolding of Neo-Confucianism*. New
   York: Columbia University Press, 1975.

Cheng Chung-ying, trans. *Tai Chen's Inquiry into Goodness*. Honolulu: East-West Center Press,
   1971.

Ching, Julia. *To Acquire Wisdom: The Way of Wang Yang-ming*. New York: Columbia University Press, 1976.

Ching, Julia, trans. *The Philosophical Letters of Wang Yang-ming*. Columbia: University of South Carolina Press, 1973.

Dardess, John W. *Confucianism and Autocracy*. Berkeley and Los Angeles, University of California Press, 1983.

de Bary, Wm. Theodore. "Individualism and Humanitarianism in Late Ming Thought." In Wm. Theodore de Bary, ed., *Self and Society in Ming Thought*. New York: Columbia University Press, 1970.

—— "Neo-Confucian Cultivation and the Seventeenth-Century 'Enlightenment.'" In Wm. Theodore de Bary, ed., *The Unfolding of Neo-Confucianism*. New York: Columbia University Press, 1975.

—— *Neo-Confucian Orthodoxy and the Learning of the Mind-and-Heart*. New York: Columbia University Press, 1981.

—— "A Reappraisal of Neo-Confucianism." In Arthur F. Wright, ed., *Studies in Chinese Thought*. Chicago: University of Chicago Press, 1953.

de Bary, Wm. Theodore, Wing-tsit Chan, and Burton Watson, eds. *Sources of Chinese Tradition*. New York: Columbia University Press, 1960.

Demiéville, Paul. "La Pénétration du Bouddhisme dans la Tradition Philosophique Chinoise." *Cahiers d'Histoire Mondiale* (1956), 3 : 19–38.

Forke, Alfred. *Geschichte der neuren chinesischen Philosophie*. Hamburg: Friederichsen de Gruyter, 1938.

—— *The World-Conception of the Chinese: Their Astronomical, Cosmological, and Physico-Philosophical Speculations*. London: Arthur Probsthain, 1925.

Freeman, Mansfield, trans. *Preservation of Learning* (by Yen Yüan). Los Angeles: Monumenta Serica Monograph Series, 1972.

Gedalecia, David. *Wu Ch'eng: A Neo-Confucian of the Yüan*. Ann Arbor: University Microfilms, 1971.

Gillispie, Charles Coulston. *The Edge of Objectivity: An Essay in the History of Scientific Ideas*. Princeton: Princeton University Press, 1960.

Goodrich, L. Carrington and Fang Chao-ying, eds. *Dictionary of Ming Biography*. New York: Columbia University Press, 1975.

Graham, A. C. *Two Chinese Philosophers: Ch'eng Ming-tao and Ch'eng Yi-ch'uan*. London: Lund Humphries, 1958.

Grimm, Tilemann. "Ming Education Intendants." In Charles O. Hucker, ed., *Chinese Government in Ming Times*. New York: Columbia University Press, 1969.

Hatton, Russell. "Ch'i's Role Within the Psychology of Chu Hsi." *Journal of Chinese Philosophy* (December 1982), 9(4):441–69.

Henderson, John B. *The Development and Decline of Chinese Cosmology*. New York: Columbia University Press, 1984.

Hocking, William Ernest. "Chu Hsi's Theory of Knowledge." *Harvard Journal of Asiatic Studies* (1936), 1(1):109–27.

Hou Wai-lu. *A Short History of Chinese Philosophy*. Peking: Foreign Languages Press, 1959.

Hsü, Immanuel C. Y., trans. *Intellectual Trends in the Ch'ing Period* (by Liang Ch'i-ch'ao). Cambridge, Mass.: Harvard University Press, 1959.

Hu Shih. "The Scientific Spirit and Method in Chinese Philosophy." In Charles A. Moore, ed., *The Chinese Mind*. Honolulu: University Press of Hawaii, 1967.

Huang, Ray. *Taxation and Governmental Finance in Sixteenth-Century Ming China*. Cambridge: Cambridge University Press, 1974.

Huang Siu-chi. *Lu Hsiang-shan, A Twelfth Century Idealist Philosopher*. New Haven: American Oriental Society, 1944.

Hucker, Charles O. "The Tung-lin Movement of the Late Ming Period." In John K. Fairbank, ed., *Chinese Thought and Institutions*. Chicago: University of Chicago Press, 1957.

Hughes, E. R. "Chinese Epistemological Methods." In Charles A. Moore, ed., *Essays in East-West Philosophy*. Honolulu: University Press of Hawaii, 1951.

Hurvitz, Leon. *The Scripture of the Lotus Blossom of the Fine Dharma*. New York: Columbia University Press, 1976.

Iki Hiroyuki. "Wang Yang-ming's Doctrine of Innate Knowledge of the Good." *Philosophy East and West* (1961), 11:27–77.

Jen Yu-wen. "Ch'en Hsien-chang's Philosophy of the Natural." In Wm. Theodore de Bary, ed., *Self and Society in Ming Thought*. New York: Columbia University Press, 1970.

Jiang, Paul Yun-ming. *The Search for Mind: Ch'en Pai-sha, Philosopher-Poet*. Singapore: Singapore University Press, 1980.

Kasoff, Ira E. *The Thought of Chang Tsai (1020–1077)*. Cambridge: Cambridge University Press, 1984.

Kilminster, Richard. "Theory and Practice in Marx and Marxism." In G. H. R. Parkinson, ed., *Marx and Marxisms*. Royal Institute of Philosophy Lecture Series 14, Supplement to *Philosophy* 1982. Cambridge: Cambridge University Press, 1982.

Lau, D. C., "A Note on Ke wu," in *Bulletin of the School of Oriental and African Studies*, (1967), vol. 30.

Legge, James, trans. *The Ch'un Ts'ew with The Tso Chuen, The Chinese Classics*. Vol. 5. London: Oxford University Press, 1895.

—— *Chung-yung* (The Mean), in *The Chinese Classics*. Vol. 1. Oxford: Clarendon Press, 1893.

—— *Confucian Analects*, in *The Chinese Classics*. Vol. 1. Oxford: Clarendon Press, 1893.

—— *Li Chi: Book of Rites*. 2 vols. New Hyde Park: University Books, 1967.

—— *The She King (Shih ching), The Chinese Classics*. Vol. 4. London: Oxford University Press, 1871.

—— *The Shoo King (Shu-ching), The Chinese Classics*. Vol. 3. London: Oxford University Press, 1865.

—— *The Works of Mencius, The Chinese Classics*. Vol. 2. Oxford: Clarendon Press, 1893.

Levy, Howard S., trans. *Biography of An Lu-shan*. Berkeley and Los Angeles: University of California Press, 1960.

—— *Biography of Huang Ch'ao*. Berkeley and Los Angeles: University of California Press, 1955.

Liebenthal, Walter, trans. "*Yung Chia Cheng-tao-ko* or Yung Chia's Song of Enlightenment." *Monumenta Serica* (1941), 6:1–39.

Luk, Charles. *Ch'an and Zen Teaching*. Third Series. London: Rider, 1962.

Lukes, Steven. "Marxism, Morality and Justice." In G. H. R. Parkinson, ed., *Marx and Marxisms*. Royal Institute of Philosophy Lecture Series 14, Supplement to *Philosophy* 1982. Cambridge: Cambridge University Press, 1982.

McMorran, Ian. "Wang Fu-chih and the Neo-Confucian Tradition." In Wm. Theodore de Bary, ed., *The Unfolding of Neo-Confucianism*. New York: Columbia University Press, 1975.

Meskill, John. "Academies and Politics in the Ming Dynasty." In Charles O. Hucker, ed., *Chinese Government in Ming Times*. New York: Columbia University Press, 1969.

—— *Academies in Ming China, A Historical Essay*. Tucson: University of Arizona Press, 1982.

Miyuki, Mokusen. *An Analysis of Buddhist Influence on the Formation of the Sung Confucian Concept of Li-Ch'i*. Ann Arbor: University Microfilms, 1966.

Needham, Joseph. *The Grand Titration, Science and Society in East and West*. London: Allen and Unwin, 1979.

—— *Science and Civilisation in China*. 7 vols. projected, 6 published to date. Cambridge: Cambridge University Press, 1956–

Nivison, David S. "The Problem of 'Knowledge' and 'Action' in Chinese Thought Since Wang Yang-ming." In Arthur F. Wright, ed., *Studies in Chinese Thought*. Chicago: University of Chicago Press, 1953.

Pulleyblank, Edwin G. *The Background of the Rebellion of An Lu-shan*. London: Oxford University Press, 1955.

Quinton, Anthony. *Francis Bacon*. Oxford: Oxford University Press, 1980.

Randall, John Herman Jr. *How Philosophy Uses Its Past*. New York: Columbia University Press, 1963.

—— *Nature and Historical Experience: Essays in Naturalism and in the Theory of History*. New York: Columbia University Press, 1958.

Sargent, Galen Eugene. *Tchou Hi contre le Bouddhisme*. Paris: Imprimerie Nationale, 1955.

Schafer, Edward H. *Pacing the Void. T'ang Approaches to the Stars*. Berkeley and Los Angeles: University of California Press, 1977.

Shryock, John K. *The Origin and Development of the State Cult of Confucius: An Introductory Study*. New York: Paragon Reprint, 1966.

T'ang Chün-i. "The criticisms of Wang Yang-ming's teachings as raised by his contemporaries." *Philosophy East and West* (January and April 1973), 23(1–2): 163–86.

—— "Chang Tsai's Theory of Mind and Its Metaphysical Basis." *Philosophy East and West* (1956), 6: 113–36.

—— "The Development of the Concept of Moral Mind from Wang Yang-ming to Wang Chi." In Wm. Theodore de Bary, ed., *Self and Society in Ming Thought*. New York: Columbia University Press, 1970.

Taylor, Rodney L. *The Cultivation of Sagehood as a Religious Goal in Neo-Confucianism: A Study of Selected Writings of Kao P'an-lung*. Missoula, Mont.: Scholars Press, 1978.

Tomoeda Ryūtarō. "The Characteristics of Chu Hsi's Thought." *Acta Asiatica* (October 1971), 21: 52–72.

Tu Wei-ming. *Neo-Confucian Thought in Action: Wang Yang-ming's Youth (1472–1509)*. Berkeley and Los Angeles: University of California Press, 1976.

—— "Subjectivity and Ontological Reality: An Interpretation of Wang Yang-ming's Mode of Thinking." *Philosophy East and West* (1973), 23:187–206.

Wang Tch'ang-tche. *La Philosophie morale de Wang Yang-ming*. Shanghai: 1936.

Watson, Burton, trans. *The Complete Works of Chuang Tzu*. New York: Columbia University Press, 1968.

—— *Records of the Grand Historian of China*. 2 vols. New York: Columbia University Press, 1961.

Wilhelm, Helmut. *Change: Eight Lectures on the I Ching*. Trans. from the German by Cary F. Baynes. New York: Pantheon Books, 1960.

—— "On Ming Orthodoxy." *Monumenta Serica* (1970–71), 29:1–26.

Wood, Allen W. *Karl Marx*. London: Routledge and Kegan Paul, 1981.

Wu Lu-ch'iang and Tenney L. Davis, trans. "An Ancient Chinese Treatise on Alchemy entitled *Ts'an T'ung Ch'i*." *Isis* (1932), 18:210–89.

Yü Ying-shih. "Some Preliminary Observations on the Rise of Ch'ing Confucian Intellectualism." Draft paper for the August 1975 Berkeley planning meeting toward an ACLS conference on Early Ch'ing Thought.

Glossary

ai 愛
Andō Seian 安東省庵
An Lu-shan 安祿山
a-nou-to-lo san-miao san-p'u-t'i 阿耨多羅三藐三菩提

Bodhidharma 菩提達摩
Bunroku 文祿

Chan Fou-min 詹阜民
Chan Jo-shui (Yüan-ming, Kan-ch'üan) 湛若水, 元明, 甘泉
Chan Kan-ch'üan, *see* Chan Jo-shui
Chan Kan-ch'üan hsien-sheng wen-chi 湛甘泉先生文集
Chan Wing-tsit 陳榮捷
Chan Yüan-ming, *see* Chan Jo-shui
Ch'an 禪
chang 暲
Chang Ch'in-fu, *see* Chang Shih
Chang Ching-fu, *see* Chang Shih
Chang Chiu-ch'eng (Tzu-shao) 張九成, 子韶
Chang Feng-shan, *see* Chang Mou
Chang Heng-ch'ü, *see* Chang Tsai
Chang Liang (Tzu-fang) 張良, 子房
Chang Mou (Feng-shan) 章懋, 楓山
Chang P'ing-shu, *see* Chang Po-tuan
Chang Po-tuan (P'ing-shu) 張伯端, 平叔
Chang Shih (Nan-hsien, Ching-fu, Ch'in-fu) 張栻, 南軒, 敬夫, 欽夫
Chang Tsai (Heng-ch'ü, Tzu-hou) 張載, 橫渠, 子厚
Chang Ts'ung 張璁
Chang Tzu-shao, *see* Chang Chiu-ch'eng
"Chang Wu-kou *Chung-yung chieh*" 張無垢中庸解
chao-chao 昭昭
Chao T'o 趙佗
Chao Tun 趙盾
Ch'ao Ts'o 晁錯
chen-ju 眞如
Chen Te-hsiu 眞德秀
ch'en (asterism) 辰
Ch'en Chien 陳建

Ch'en Chih-hsü 陳致虛
Ch'en Ching 陳靖
Ch'en Hao 陳澔
Ch'en Hsien-chang (Pai-sha) 陳獻章, 白沙
Ch'en Hsien-wei 陳顯微
Ch'en Pai-sha, *see* Ch'en Hsien-chang
Ch'en Liang 陳亮
"Ch'en-yen shih-shih" 陳言十事
cheng 正
"Cheng-an lü-li chi" 整菴履歷記
Cheng Hsüan 鄭玄
cheng-hsüeh 正學
Cheng-i-t'ang ch'üan-shu 正誼堂全書
Cheng-meng 正蒙
Cheng-tao ko 證道歌
Cheng-te (Ming reign period, 1506–1522) 正德
ch'eng (sincerity) 誠
Ch'eng (Chou king) 成王
Ch'eng-Chu 程朱
Ch'eng Hao (Ming-tao, Po-tzu) 程顥, 明道, 伯子
Ch'eng I (I-ch'uan, Shu-tzu) 程頤, 伊川, 叔子
ch'eng-i 誠意
Ch'eng I-ch'uan, *see* Ch'eng I
Ch'eng Ming-tao, *see* Ch'eng Hao
Ch'eng Po-tzu, *see* Ch'eng Hao
Ch'eng Shu-tzu, *see* Ch'eng I
Ch'eng T'ang (T'ang the Accomplished) 成湯
Che-shih chü ts'ung-shu 擇是居叢書
chi (subtle, activating forces; first beginnings) 機
ch'i (material force) 氣
ch'i (vessel, utensil, concrete thing) 器
ch'i chi li 氣即理
ch'i-chih 氣質
ch'i-chih chih hsing 氣質之性
ch'i-hsüeh 氣學
ch'i-p'in 氣禀
Chia-ching (Ming reign period, 1522–1567) 嘉靖
Chia I 賈誼
Chia-t'ai p'u-teng lu 嘉泰普燈錄
ch'iang-fu ch'i hsin 降伏其心
chiang-hsüeh 講學
Chiang-men 江門
Chien-chai so-chui lu 謇齋瑣綴錄

chien-wen chih shih 見聞之識

ch'ien (hexagram of the *Book of Changes*) 乾

Ch'ien K'ai-shan, *see* K'ai-shan Tao-ch'ien

Ch'ien Te-hung 錢德洪

chih (matter) 質

chih (will) 志

chih (as a grammatical particle; 之 or, as a verb, to arrive at, to go to)

chih-chih 致知

chih chih wu 知之物

chih-ching 至精

chih liang-chih 致良知

chih-pien 至變

chih-shen 至神

"Chih-tang" 至當

Chin-hua ts'ung-shu 金華叢書

Chin-kang ching 金剛經

chin-shih 進士

Chin-ssu lu 近思錄

Ching (Former Han emperor) 景

ching (seriousness, reverence) 敬

ching i chih nei, i i fang wai 敬以直內, 義以方外

ching-shih 經世

ching-tso 靜坐

Ch'ing (dynasty) 清

ch'ing (feelings) 情

ch'ing (well) 井

ch'ing-chung ch'ang-tuan 輕重長短

Ch'ing-hua hsüeh-pao 清華學報

Ch'ing-li (Sung reign period, 1041–1048) 慶歷

Ch'ing Pu 慶布

chiu 舊

chiu-pen 舊本

Chiu T'ang-shu 舊唐書

Ch'iu Chün (Wen-chuang) 丘濬, 文莊

ch'iung-li 窮理

Chou (dynasty) 周

Chou I pen-i 周易本義

Chou I Ts'an-t'ung ch'i chieh 周易參同契解

Chou I Ts'an-tung ch'i chu (texts by Ch'u Hua-ku and Yin Chen-jen) 周易參同契註

Chou I Ts'an-t'ung ch'i chu (text by Ch'en Chih-hsü) 周易參同契注

Chou I Ts'an-t'ung ch'i fa-hui 周易參同契發揮

Chou I Ts'an-t'ung ch'i fen-chang chen-i 周易參同契分章眞義

Chou I Ts'an-t'ung ch'i fen-chang chu 周易參同契分章注

Chou I Ts'an-t'ung ch'i shih-i 周易參同契釋疑
Chou kung (Duke of Chou) 周公
Chou-li 周禮
Chou Tun-i (Lien-hsi, Mao-shu) 周敦頤, 濂溪, 茂叔
Chou Tzu T'ung-shu 周子通書
Chu (son of Yao) 朱
Chu-fang men-jen ts'an-wen yü-lu 諸方門人參問語錄
Chu Hsi (Yüan-hui, Hui-an) 朱熹, 元晦, 晦菴
chu-hsin 誅心
chu-kuan wei-hsin-chu-i 主觀唯心主義
Chu Piao 朱標
Chu Sung 朱松
chu-tsai 主宰
"Chu Tzu wan-nien ting-lun" 朱子晚年定論
ch'u-ch'u yü-mo 出處語默
Ch'u Hua-ku 儲華谷
Ch'u-tz'u 楚辭
Ch'u-tz'u chi-chu 楚辭集註
Chü-shih chi 居士集
Chü-yeh lu 居業錄
chüan 卷
Ch'uan-hsi lu 傳習錄
Ch'uan-hsin fa-yao 傳心法要
Chuang Tzu 莊子
chüeh 覺
Ch'un-ch'iu 春秋
Ch'un-ch'iu fan-lu 春秋繁露
Ch'un-hsi (Sung reign period, 1174–1189) 淳熙
chung 中
Chung-kung (disciple of Confucius) 仲弓
Chung-yung 中庸
Chung-yung chang-chü 中庸章句
Chung-yung meng-yin 中唐蒙引

Dai Kanwa jiten 大漢和辭典

erh-ch'i chih liang-neng 二氣之良能
erh-pen 二本
erh-wu 二五

fa (law, method, thing, *dharma*) 法
Fa-hua ching 法華經
Fa-yen 法言

Fan-ch'uan wen-chi 樊川文集
Fan Chung-yen (Wen-cheng) 范仲淹, 文正
Fan Wen-cheng, *see* Fan Chung-yen
Fang-kuang ta-chuang yen-ching 方廣大莊嚴經
Fen-men chi-chu Tu Kung-pu shih 分門集註杜工部詩
fu (hexagram of the *Book of Changes*) 復
"Fu Chang Tung-po nei-han" 復張東白內翰
Fu-hsi 伏羲
Fu Yü Tzu-chi lun Hsing-shu 復余子積論性書

Han (dynasty) 漢
Han Ch'i (Han Wei Kung) 韓琦, 韓魏公
Han-hai 函海
Han Hsin 韓信
Han-hsüeh 漢學
Hanlin 翰林
Han shu 漢書
Han Wei Kung, *see* Han Ch'i
Han Yü 韓愈
Hayashi Razan 林羅山
ho (identify) 合
ho (harmony) 和
Ho Ching-ming 何景明
Ho Hao (Shu-ching) 何鎬, 叔京
Ho Shu-ching, *see* Ho Hao
Ho-tse 荷澤
Ho-tung 河東
hou 後
Hou Han shu 後漢書
"Hsi-ming" 西銘
Hsi Shu (Yüan-shan, Wen-t'ung) 席書, 元山, 文同
"Hsi-tz'u chuan" 繫辭傳
Hsi Wen-t'ung, *see* Hsi Shu
hsiang 相
hsiang-shang 向上
Hsiang Yü 項羽
Hsiao Hui 蕭惠
Hsieh Hsien-tao, *see* Hsieh Liang-tso
Hsieh Liang-tso (Shang-ts'ai, Hsien-tao) 謝良佐, 上蔡, 顯道
Hsieh Shang-ts'ai, *see* Hsieh Liang-tso
hsien-t'ien hsing 先天性
hsien-t'ien tao-te 先天道德
Hsien-yü ching 賢愚經

hsin 心
Hsin-chiao Shih-chi san-chia chu 新校史記三家注
hsin chih wu 心之物
Hsin-ching 心經
hsin-hsüeh 心學
Hsin-k'e Leng-chia ching hsü 新刻楞伽經序
"Hsin-lun" 新論
Hsin T'ang-shu 新唐書
hsing 性
hsing-hsiang 形象
hsing-ming chih li 性命之理
Hsing-shu (Book on the Nature) 性書
Hsing Shu 邢恕
hsing-t'i 形體
Hsiu-hsing pen-ch'i ching 修行本起經
Hsü Ai 徐愛
Hsü Ch'eng-chih 徐成之
Hsü-chi 續集
Hsü Chih 許止
Hsü Ch'uan-teng lu 續傳燈錄
Hsü ku-tsun-su yü-yao 續古尊宿語要
hsü-ling chih-chüeh 虛靈知覺
Hsüan-tsung (T'ang emperor) 玄宗
Hsüeh Hsüan (Wen-ch'ing) 薛瑄, 文清
Hsüeh-ku lou 學古樓
"Hsüeh-ku lou ko" 學古樓歌
Hsüeh-p'u t'ung-pien 學蔀通辨
hsüeh-shu 學術
Hsüeh Wen-ch'ing, *see* Hsüeh Hsüan
Hu An-kuo (Wen-ting) 胡安國, 文定
Hu Ching-chai, *see* Hu Chü-jen
Hu Chü-jen (Ching-chai) 胡居仁, 敬齋
Hu Hung (Wu-feng) 胡宏, 五峯
Hu Shih 胡適
Hu Tzu Chih-yen i-i 胡子知言疑義
Hu Wen-ting, *see* Hu An-kuo
Hu Wu-feng, *see* Hu Hung
hua 化
Huang Ch'ao 黃巢
Huang-chi ching-shih shu 皇極經世書
Huang Chih-ch'ing, *see* Huang Kan
Huang Kan (Chih-ch'ing, Mien-chai) 黃榦, 直卿, 勉齋
Huang Ming t'ung-chi 皇明通紀

Huang Ming wen-hai 皇明文海
Huang-po Hsi-yün 黃檗希運
Huang-t'ing ching 黃庭經
Huang Tsung-hsi 黃宗羲
Hua-yen 華嚴
hun-jan 渾然
huo-jan kuan-t'ung 豁然貫通
huo sheng erh chih chih; huo hsüeh erh chih chih; huo k'un erh chih chih 或生而知之　或學而
　　知之　或困而知之

i (one, oneness, unity, undivided) 一
i (intentions) 意
i (rightness, righteousness) 義
i (grammatical particle) 以
i chih yung 意之用
I-ching 易經
i ching ming 益精明
I-ching t'u-shih 易經圖釋
I-chuan, see I-ch'uan I-chuan
I-ch'uan hsien-sheng nien-p'u 伊川先生年譜
I-ch'uan I-chuan 伊川易傳
I-ch'uan wen-chi 伊川文集
i-fa 已發
i-hsüeh 異學
i i chih shih, i li chih hsin 以義制事，以禮制心
I-Lo yüan-yüan lu 伊洛淵源錄
Itō Jinsai 伊藤仁齋
Itō Tōgai 伊藤東涯
I-ts'un Hsüeh-feng 義存雪峰
I-wai pieh-ch'uan 易外別傳
i wei (year) 乙未
I-wei t'ung-kua yen 易緯通卦驗
I Yin 伊尹

jen 仁
jen-hsin 仁心
Jen-tsung (Sung emperor) 仁宗
Ju-lai 如來

Kaibara Ekken 貝原益軒
K'ai-shan Tao-ch'ien 開善道謙
"Kai tsang Pai-sha hsien-sheng mu-pei ming" 改葬白沙先生墓碑銘

Kamakura 鎌倉
Kao P'an-lung 高攀龍
Kao P'ien 高駢
Kao Tsu (Han emperor) 高祖
Kao Tzu (Interlocutor of Mencius) 告子
Keichō (Japanese reign period, 1596–1610) 慶長
k'e-kuan wei-hsin-chu-i 客觀唯心主義
Kimon 崎門
Kinoshita Jun'an 木下順庵
ko 格
Kogaku 古學
ko-wu 格物
K'o Han (Kuo-ts'ai) 柯翰, 國材
K'o Kuo-ts'ai, *see* K'o Han
Ku-i ts'ung-shu 古逸叢書
Ku-liang chuan 穀梁傳
Ku-pen Ta-hsüeh p'ang-shih 古本大學旁釋
Ku Tung-ch'iao 顧東橋
Ku Yen-wu 顧炎武
"Kuan-wu yin" 觀物吟
k'uan-hsin 寬心
kuang-ching 光景
k'uang 狂
kuei 鬼
Kuei O 桂萼
kuei yü chih i 歸於至
Kumamoto 熊本
Kun 鯀
k'un (pain, distress, difficulty, effort) 困
k'un (hexagram of the *Book of Changes*) 坤
K'un-chih chi fu-lu 困知記附錄
K'un-chih chi hsü 困知記續
K'un-chih chi hsü-pu 困知記續補
K'un-chih chi wai-pien 困知記外編
kung (impartiality) 公
Kung-po Liao 公伯寮
Kung-tu 公都
Kung-yang chuan 公羊傳
k'ung 空
K'ung Tzu (Confucius) 孔子
K'ung Ying-ta 孔穎達
Kuo-tzu chien 國子監
Kuo Tzu-i 郭子儀

Lao Tzu 老子

Le-t'an Chan T'ang-chun ch'an-shih 泐潭湛堂準禪師

li (principle, noumenal reality) 理

li (ritual, decorum, propriety) 禮

Li chi 禮記

Li-chi chi-shuo 禮記集說

"Li-ch'i" 禮器

li fu yü ch'i i hsing 理附於氣以行

li-hsüeh 理學

li-i fen-shu 理一分殊

Li Kuang-pi 李光弼

Li Kung 李塨

Li Meng-yang 李夢陽

Li Pi 李泌

Li T'ung (Yen-p'ing) 李侗, 延平

Li Yen-p'ing, *see* Li T'ung

Li Yen-p'ing hsien-sheng wen-chi 李延平先生文集

"Li-yün" 禮運

liang-chih 良知

Lien-Lo feng-ya 濂洛風雅

Lin chi (Japanese, Rinzai) 臨濟

Lin-chi I-hsüan 臨濟義玄

Lin Ch'i-hsi, *see* Lin Kuang

Lin Hsi-yüan 林希元

Lin Kuang (Ch'i-hsi) 林光, 緝熙

ling 靈

Liu An-chieh (Yüan-ch'eng) 劉安節, 元承

Liu Chin 劉瑾

Liu Pang 劉邦

Liu Pao-chai, *see* Liu Ting-chih

Liu Shu-wen 劉叔文

Liu Ting-chih (Pao-chai, Ai-chai) 劉定之, 保齋, 呆齋

Liu Yüan-ch'eng, *see* Liu An-chieh

Lo Cheng-an, *see* Lo Ch'in-shun

Lo Ch'in-chung 羅欽忠

Lo Ch'in-shun (Cheng-an, Yün-sheng) 羅欽順, 整菴, 允升

Lo Ch'in-te 羅欽德

Lo Po-wen, *see* Lo Tsung-li

Lo Tsung-li (Tsung-yüeh, Po-wen) 羅宗禮, 宗約, 博文

Lo Ts'ung-yen (Yü-chang) 羅從彥, 豫章

Lo Wen-chuang ho-chi 羅文莊合集

"Lo Wen-chuang kung chuan" 羅文莊公傳

Lo Yü-chang, *see* Lo Ts'ung-yen

Lo Yung-chün 羅用俊
Lou K'o-chen, *see* Lou Liang
Lou Liang (K'o-chen) 婁諒, 克貞
Lu Ch'eng (Yüan-ching) 陸澄, 原靜
Lu Chia 陸賈
Lu Chiu-shao 陸九韶
Lu Chiu-yüan (Hsiang-shan, Tzu-ching) 陸九淵, 象山, 子靜
Lu Hsiang-shan, *see* Lu Chiu-yüan
Lu Tzu-ching, *see* Lu Chiu-yüan
Lu Yin 魯隱
Lu Yüan-ching, *see* Lu Ch'eng
Lü Ta-lin (Yü-shu) 呂大臨, 與叔
Lü Tsu-ch'ien (Tung-lai) 呂祖謙, 東萊
Lü Tung-lai, *see* Lü Tsu-ch'ien
Lü Yü-shu, *see* Lü Ta-lin
Lun Meng chi-chu 論孟集註
Lun Meng huo-wen 論孟或問
Lun-yü 論語

meng (hexagram of the *Book of Changes*) 蒙
Meng Tzu (Mencius) 孟子
Meng Tzu huo-wen 孟子或問
miao-ho 妙合
Ming (dynasty) 明
ming (destiny, endowment, mandate, command, imperative) 命
ming (name, designation) 名
ming-hsin 明心
Ming-yüan lu 鳴冤錄
mo 末
mo chih wei erh wei che 莫之爲而爲者
Muromachi 室町

nei-k'u 內庫
neng-che yang chih i fu 能者養之以福
neng-che yang i chih fu 能者養以之福
ning 凝

"O-fang kung fu" 阿房宮賦
Ōtsuka Taiya 大塚退野
Ou-yang Hsiu (Wen-chung, Yung-shu) 歐陽修, 文忠, 永叔
Ou-yang Wen-chung, *see* Ou-yang Hsiu
Ou-yang Yung-shu chi 歐陽永叔集

Pai-sha tzu ku-shih chiao chieh 白沙子古詩教解
P'ang chü-shih yü-lu 龐居士語錄
P'ei Hsiu 裴休
pen-hsin 本心
pen-hsing 本性
P'eng Hsiao 彭曉
pien-cheng wei-wu-chu-i 辨証唯物主義
Pi-yen lu 碧巖錄
po-hsüeh 博學
"Po-lu-tung fu" 白鹿洞賦
pu-cheng 不正
pu-chung 不中
p'u-su wei-wu-chu-i 樸素唯物主義

Sakai Tadao 酒井忠夫
se 色
Shang (dynasty) 商
Shang-ch'en 商臣
Shang-shu 尚書
Shao Yung (Yao-fu, K'ang-chieh) 邵雍, 堯夫, 康節
shen (spirit, positive spiritual forces) 神
Shen Chou (Shih-t'ien) 沈周, 石田
Shen-hui ho-shang i-chi 神會和尚遺集
Shen-hui yü-lu 神會語錄
Shen-nung 神農
"Shen Shih-t'ien tso Yü-t'ai t'u t'i-shih ch'i shang chien chi tz'u yün i fu" 沈石田作玉臺
    圖題詩其上見寄次韻以復
Shen-yüeh 神樂
shih (event, phenomenal reality) 事
"Shih Chan Yü" 示湛雨
Shih-chi 史記
Shih-ching 詩經
Shih-chiao 詩教
Shou-shan ko ts'ung-shu 守山閣叢書
Shu-ching 書經
Shun 舜
Shuo-fu 說郛
"Shuo-kua" 說卦
Shu-sun T'ung 叔孫通
ssu-hao 四皓
Ssu-hsin Wu-hsin ho-shang 死心悟新和尚
Ssu-ma Ch'ien 司馬遷
ssu-tuan 四端

Su Ch'e 蘇轍
Su Chi-ming, *see* Su Ping
Su Huang-men Lao Tzu chieh 蘇黃門老子解
Su Ping (Chi-ming) 蘇昞, 季明
Su Shih (Tung-p'o) 蘇軾, 東坡
Su-tsung (T'ang emperor) 肅宗
Sui Ho 隨何
Sung (dynasty) 宋
Sung Ch'ien-hsi, *see* Sung Lien
Sung Hsüeh-shih ch'üan-chi pu-i 宋學士全集補遺
Sung Lien (Ch'ien-hsi) 宋濂, 潛溪
Sung shih 宋史

"Ta Chang Ching-fu" 答張敬夫
"Ta Chang nei-han T'ing-hsiang shu-kua erh ch'eng shih ch'eng Hu Hsi-jen t'i hsüeh" 答張
　　內翰廷祥書括而成詩呈胡希仁提學
Ta-chu Hui-hai 大珠慧海
Ta-fang-kuang yüan-chüeh hsiu-to-lo liao-i ching lüeh-shu 大方廣圓覺修多羅了義經略疏
Ta-hsüeh 大學
Ta-hsüeh ku-pen 大學古本
Ta-hsüeh yen-i 大學衍義
Ta-hui Tsung-kao (Miao-hsi) 大慧宗杲, 妙喜
"Ta Ku Tung-ch'iao shu" 答顧東橋書
"Ta Lo Cheng-an shao-tsai shu" 答羅整菴少宰書
"Ta Lu Tzu-ching" 答陸子靜
"Ta Lu Yüan-ching" 答陸元靜
ta-tao 達道
"Ta Yen Shih-heng" 答嚴時亨
"Ta-Yü mo" 大禹謨
Tai Chen 戴震
Tai Hsien 戴銑
t'ai (hexagram of the *Book of Changes*) 泰
t'ai-chi 太極
T'ai-chi-t'u shuo 太極圖說
"T'ai-chi-t'u T'ung-shu tsung-hsü" 太極圖通書總序
T'ai-chia 太甲
t'ai-ho (Great Harmony) 太和
"T'ai-ho" (section of the *Cheng-meng*) 太和
t'ai-hsü 太虛
t'ai-hsüan 太玄
T'ai-tsung (Sung emperor) 太宗
T'ai-tzu t'ai-pao 太子太保
"T'an-kung" 檀弓

T'ang hui-yao 唐會要

tao 道

tao-hsin 道心

tao-hsüeh 道學

"Tao-hsüeh chuan hsü" 道學傳序

Tao-sheng 道生

Tao-te ching 道德經

Tao-tsang ching-hua 道藏精華

Tao-tsang chi-yao 道藏輯要

tao wen-hsüeh 道問學

te (grasp, attain, apprehend) 得

te (virtue, power) 德

Te-shan Hsüan-chien 得山宣鑒

Te tsung (T'ang emperor) 德宗

Ti-wu Ch'i 第五琦

t'i 體

"T'i Li tsun-shih Sung-shu chang-tzu ko" 題李尊師松樹障子歌

Tiao-t'ai 釣臺

"Tien Ch'iu Ko-lao wen" 奠邱閣老文

t'ien 天

T'ien-ch'i (Ming reign period, 1621–1627) 天啓

t'ien-hsing 天性

t'ien-ken 天根

t'ien-li 天理

t'ien-ming 天命

t'ien-ming chih hsing 天命之性

t'ien-tao 天道

t'ien-ti chih hsing 天地之性

t'ien-ti chih kung-yung 天地之功用

ting-pen 定本

ting-yu 丁酉

ting yü i 定于一

Tokugawa 德川

tsai hsü chi ni 載胥及溺

ts'ai 才

Ts'ai Chieh-fu, *see* Ts'ai Ch'ing

Ts'ai Ch'ing (Chieh-fu) 蔡清, 介夫

"Ts'an-liang" 參兩

Ts'an-t'ung ch'i 參同契

Ts'an-t'ung ch'i fa-hui 參同契發揮

Ts'an-t'ung-ch'i k'ao-i 參同契考異

Ts'ao-t'ang 艸堂

Tseng-hsiu Tung-lai Shu-shuo 增修東萊書說

Tseng Tzu 曾子
"Tseng Tzu wen" 曾子問
Tso Ch'iu-ming 左丘明
Tso chuan 左傳
Tso shih 左氏
tso-yu ts'ang 左右藏
ts'o 錯
ts'u 措
Ts'ui Hsien 崔銑
Ts'ui-yen 粹言
tsun te-hsing 尊德性
"Tsun te-hsing tao wen-hsüeh chai chi" 尊德性道問學齋記
ts'un [ch'i] hsin 存其心
Tsung-mi 宗密
Tu Fu 杜甫
Tu Mu (Mu-chih) 杜牧, 牧之
Tu-shu lu 讀書錄
Tung Chung-shu 董仲舒
Tung-lin 東林
Tung Te-hsien 董德憲
t'ung-ch'e san-chi erh wu-chien 通徹三極而無間
T'ung-shu 通書
Tzu-chih t'ung-chien 資治通鑑
Tzu-hsia 子夏
Tzu-kung 子貢
Tzu-lu 子路
Tzu-ssu 子思
tzu-te 自得
"Tz'u-yün Chang Tung-hai" 次韻張東海

Wai-shu 外書
Wang An-chung (Lü-tao) 王安中, 履道
Wang An-shih 王安石
Wang Fu-chih (Ch'uan-shan) 王夫之, 船山
Wang Hou-chih (Shun-po) 王厚之, 順伯
Wang Lü-tao, *see* Wang An-chung
Wang Po-an, *see* Wang Shou-jen
Wang Shou-jen (Yang-ming, Po-an) 王守仁, 陽明, 伯安
Wang Shun-po, *see* Wang Hou-chih
Wang T'ing-hsiang 王廷相
Wang Yang-ming, *see* Wang Shou-jen
wei 爲
Wei Chiao 魏校

wei-fa 未發
wei-fa chih chung 未發之中
wei-hsin-chu-i 唯心主義
Wei Po-yang 魏伯陽
wei-wu-chu-i 唯物主義
Wen (Chou king) 文王
Wen-chuang 文莊
"Wen-yen" 文言
wu (thing) 物
wu (not, nothing, nothingness) 無
Wu (Chou king) 武王
Wu Ch'eng (Ts'ao-lu, Wen-cheng) 吳澄, 草廬, 文正
Wu-chen p'ien 悟眞篇
Wu-chen p'ien cheng-i 悟眞篇正義
wu-chi 無極
wu-chih ti t'ung-i 物質的統一
wu-hsin 無心
Wu K'ang-chai, *see* Wu Yü-pi
Wu-men kuan 無門關
wu suo chu 無所住
Wu Ts'ao-lu, *see* Wu Ch'eng
wu wo chih hsiang-hsing 物我之相形
wu-yü nieh-p'an 無餘涅槃
Wu Yü-pi (K'ang-chai) 吳與弼, 康齋

Yamaga Sokō 山鹿素行
Yamazaki Ansai 山崎闇齋
yang [ch'i] hsing 養其性
Yang Chien (Tz'u-hu) 楊簡, 慈湖
Yang Fang-chen, *see* Yang Lien
Yang Hsiung (Tzu-yün) 揚雄, 子雲
Yang Kuei-shan *see* Yang Shih
Yang Kuei-shan hsien-sheng yü-lu 楊龜山先生語錄
Yang Lien (Fang-chen) 楊廉, 方震
Yang Shih (Kuei-shan) 楊時, 龜山
Yang Tzu-yün, *see* Yang Hsiung
Yang Yen 楊炎
Yao 堯
"Yao-tien" 堯典
Ya-shu 雅述
Yen Hui (Yen Yüan or Yen Tzu, follower of Confucius) 顏回, 顏淵, 顏子
Yen Shih-heng 嚴時亨
Yen Tzu, *see* Yen Hui

Yen Yüan (follower of Confucius), *see* Yen Hui

Yen Yüan (1635–1704) 顏元

Yi T'oegye 李退溪

Yin Ch'ang-sheng 陰長生

Yin Chen-jen 陰眞人

Yin Chih 尹直

yin-feng nung-yüeh 吟風弄月

Yin Ho-ching, *see* Yin T'un

Yin Ho-ching chi 尹和靖集

Yin T'un (Ho-ching) 尹焞, 和靖

yin/yang 陰, 陽

"Ying Chen" 映枕

Yu Tso 游酢

Yü 禹

Yü-ch'iao wen-tui 漁樵問對

"Yü Ho K'o-kung Huang-men" 與賀壳恭黃門

"Yü Hsü Ch'eng-chih" 與徐成之

"Yü Jung I-chih" 與容一之

"Yü Lin Chün-po" 與林郡博

"Yü Lin Shih-chü" 與林時矩

Yü-t'ai chü-shih 玉臺居士

Yü Tzu-chi, *see* Yü Yu

Yü Yen 兪琰

Yü Yu (Tzu-chi) 余祐, 子積

yüan (period of time) 元

Yüan (dynasty) 元

Yüan-chüeh ching 圓覺經

Yüan-feng (Sung reign period, 1078–1085) 元豐

Yüan shih 元史

Yüan-yu (Sung reign period, 1086–1093) 元祐

"Yüeh-chi" 樂記

yung (courage) 勇

yung (function, use) 用

Yün-men Wen-yen 雲門文偃

Yung-chia Hsüan-chüeh 永嘉玄覺

Zen no goroku 禪の語録

Index

NEO-CONFUCIAN STUDIES

MODERN ASIAN LITERATURE SERIES

TRANSLATIONS FROM THE ASIAN CLASSICS

Chuang Tzu: Basic Writings, tr. Burton Watson, paperback ed. only 1964
The Mahābhārata, Chakravarthi V. Narasimhan. Also in paperback ed.
1965
The Manyōshū, Nippon Gakujutsu Shinkōkai edition 1965
Su Tung-p'o: Selections from a Sung Dynasty Poet, tr. Burton Watson. Also
in paperback ed. 1965
Bhartrihari: Poems, tr. Barbara Stoler Miller. Also in paperback ed. 1967
Basic Writings of Mo Tzu, Hsün Tzu, and Han Fei Tzu, tr. Burton Watson.
Also in separate paperback eds. 1967
The Awakening of Faith, Attributed to Aśvaghosha, tr. Yoshito S. Hakeda.
Also in paperback ed. 1967
Reflections on Things at Hand: The Neo-Confucian Anthology, comp. Chu Hsi
and Lü Tsu-ch'ien, tr. Wing-tsit Chan 1967
The Platform Sutra of the Sixth Patriarch, tr. Philip B. Yampolsky. Also in
paperback ed. 1967
Essays in Idleness: The Tsurezuregusa of Kenkō, tr. Donald Keene. Also in
paperback ed. 1967
The Pillow Book of Sei Shōnagon, tr. Ivan Morris, 2 vols. 1967
Two Plays of Ancient India: The Little Clay Cart and the Minister's Seal, tr.
J. A. B. van Buitenen 1968
The Complete Works of Chuang Tzu, tr. Burton Watson 1968
The Romance of the Western Chamber (Hsi Hsiang chi), tr. S. I. Hsiung. Also
in paperback ed. 1968
The Manyōshū, Nippon Gakujutsu Shinkōkai edition. Paperback text
edition. 1969
Records of the Historian: Chapters from the Shih chi of Ssu-ma Ch'ien. Paper-
back text edition, tr. Burton Watson. 1969
Cold Mountain: 100 Poems by the T'ang Poet Han-shan, tr. Burton Watson.
Also in paperback ed. 1970
Twenty Plays of the Nō Theatre, ed. Donald Keene. Also in paperback ed.
1970
Chushingura: The Treasury of Loyal Retainers, tr. Donald Keene. Also in
paperback ed. 1971
The Zen Master Hakuin: Selected Writings, tr. Philip B. Yampolsky 1971
*Chinese Rhyme-Prose: Poems in the Fu Form from the Han and Six Dynasties
Periods*, tr. Burton Watson. Also in paperback ed. 1971
Kūkai: Major Works, tr. Yoshito S. Hakeda. Also in paperback ed. 1972
*The Old Man Who Does as He Pleases: Selections from the Poetry and Prose of
Lu Yu*, tr. Burton Watson 1973
The Lion's Roar of Queen Śrīmālā, tr. Alex & Hideko Wayman 1974

STUDIES IN ASIAN CULTURE

COMPANIONS TO ASIAN STUDIES

INTRODUCTION TO ASIAN CIVILIZATIONS
Wm. Theodore de Bary, Editor